Chicken Soup
for the Soul®

Loving Our Cats

Our 101 BEST STORIES

Chicken Soup for the Soul® Our 101 Best Stories:
Loving Our Cats; Heartwarming and Humorous Stories about Our Feline Family Members and Best Friends by Jack Canfield, Mark Victor Hansen & Amy Newmark

Published by Chicken Soup for the Soul Publishing, LLC www.chickensoup.com

Cover photos courtesy of iStockPhoto.com/Natural_Warp, mashabuba; and Photos.com/Jupiter Images

Cover and Interior Design & Layout by Pneuma Books, LLC
For more info on Pneuma Books, visit www.pneumabooks.com

Distributed to the booktrade by Simon & Schuster. SAN: 200-2442

Publisher's Cataloging-In-Publication Data
(*Prepared by The Donohue Group, Inc.*)

Chicken soup for the soul. Selections.
  Chicken soup for the soul® : loving our cats : heartwarming and humorous stories about our feline family members / [compiled by] Jack Canfield [and] Mark Victor Hansen ; [edited by] Amy Newmark.

    p. ; cm. -- (Our 101 best stories)

  ISBN-13: 978-1-935096-08-5
  ISBN-10: 1-935096-08-7

1. Cats--Literary collections. 2. Cats--Anecdotes. 3. Cat owners--Anecdotes. 4. Human-animal relationships--Anecdotes. I. Canfield, Jack, 1944- II. Hansen, Mark Victor. III. Newmark, Amy. IV. Title.

PS509.C37 C483 2008
810.8/03629752   2008929328

PRINTED IN THE UNITED STATES OF AMERICA
on acid∞free paper
16 15 14 13 12 10 09 08   01 02 03 04 05 06 07 08

Chicken Soup for the Soul®
Loving Our Cats

Our 101 BEST STORIES

Heartwarming and
Humorous Stories about
Our Feline Family Members

Jack Canfield
Mark Victor Hansen
Amy Newmark

Chicken Soup for the Soul Publishing, LLC
Cos Cob, CT

Contents

❹

~Cat-astrophes~

❺

~Cats and Their Pets~

❻

~The Power of the Bond~

❼
~We Love Each Other~

❽
~Faithful Feline Family Members~

❾
~Purr-fect Pets~

⑩

~Great Cat Moments~

⑪

~Hero Cats~

⑫
~Saying Goodbye~

A Special Foreword

by Jack and Mark

For us, 101 has always been a magical number. It was the number of stories in the first *Chicken Soup for the Soul* book, and it is the number of stories and poems we have always aimed for in our books. We love the number 101 because it signifies a beginning, not an end. After 100, we start anew with 101.

We hope that when you finish reading one of our books, it is only a beginning for you too—a new outlook on life, a renewed sense of purpose, a strengthened resolve to deal with an issue that has been bothering you. Perhaps you will pick up the phone and share one of the stories with a friend or a loved one. Perhaps you will turn to your keyboard and express yourself by writing a Chicken Soup story of your own, to share with other readers who are just like you.

This volume contains our 101 best stories and poems about your well loved family members—your cats. We share this with you at a very special time for us, the fifteenth anniversary of our *Chicken Soup for the Soul* series. When we published our first book in 1993, we never dreamed that we had started what has become a publishing phenomenon, one of the best-selling book series in history.

We did not set out to sell more than one hundred million books, or to publish more than 150 titles. We set out to touch the heart of one person at a time, hoping that person would in turn touch another person, and so on down the line. Fifteen years later, we know that it has worked. Your letters and stories have poured in by the hundreds of thousands, affirming our life's work, and inspiring us to continue to make a difference in your lives.

On our fifteenth anniversary, we have new energy, new resolve, and new dreams. We have recommitted to our goal of 101 stories or poems per book, we have refreshed our cover designs and our interior layout, and we have grown the Chicken Soup for the Soul team, with new friends and partners across the country in New England.

For this volume, we have selected our 101 best cat stories for you from our rich 15-year history. These heartwarming stories will make you appreciate more deeply your own cats and see them with a new eye. You will read of cats who healed people or other pets, saved lives, rejuvenated relationships, gave new meaning to lives, and saved family relationships.

We hope that you will enjoy reading these stories as much as we enjoyed selecting them for you, and that you will share them with your families and friends. We have identified the 18 *Chicken Soup for the Soul* books in which the stories originally appeared, in case you would like to explore our other books about pets. We hope you will also enjoy the additional books about dogs, families, faith, and life in general in "Our 101 Best Stories" series.

With our love, our thanks, and our respect,
~*Jack Canfield and Mark Victor Hansen*

Loving Our Cats

Chapter 1

Bringing Out
Our Best Qualities

*There is, indeed, no single quality of the cat that man
could not emulate to his advantage.*
~ Carl Van Vechton

My Life as a Midwife

People who love cats have some of the biggest hearts around.
~Susan Easterly

I used to lead two separate lives. In one, I took advantage of my six-foot frame and three-hundred-plus pounds of brawn to earn an adequate living as a bouncer. I broke up fights, and, occasionally, had to throw a punch or two. In the ten years that I pursued this profession, I had my nose broken no less than six times. My knuckles will never be a normal size again. I had a minor reputation as a very tough guy.

Then there was my other life — my secret life, in which I served as a midwife for pregnant cats. Imagine, if you will, an outsized, middle-aged man coaching tired and cranky female cats through the pain of childbirth. I have always suspected that I do this because I was unable to be present at the births of my stepchildren and my grandchildren, but that's for my therapist and me to find out.

My split life started when my first cat, Bacall, got herself pregnant before I could afford to have her spayed. She was expecting kittens around the time of my birthday. I arranged for my friend (and future wife) Janet to watch Bacall while I spent that weekend at a conference. Like many conferences I have attended, there was much talk late into the night, and, as a result, I had not gotten a lot of sleep. During the eight-hour drive back from the conference, I was getting more and more tired. All I wanted to do was to get home and go to bed. So, of course, about an hour before I got home, Bacall went into labor.

I pause here for character identification. I was an exhausted, surly and totally unpleasant representative of humanity at this point. My first impulse was to go to bed and let Bacall handle the birth by herself. After all, it was a most natural thing, and her motherly instincts would kick in, wouldn't they? Of course they would. But, somehow, I found myself sitting on my bed, my favorite blanket under Bacall, while I rubbed her ears and back during labor. She gave birth to four healthy kittens, two of whom still share my home today. I was so pleased with her that I sat up half the night trying to get her to eat and drink something.

And so my life as an animal rescuer began.

Unfortunately, the kittens kept coming because pregnant strays kept finding their way to our doorstep. There have been seven mothers-to-be in our house since that night, and I have participated in the births of all twenty-six kittens. I am a sucker for the process, even though, these days, I spend most of my time trying to avoid the whole situation — by convincing people to show some responsibility and have their pets fixed before they can produce offspring!

After Bacall's midnight delivery, the next litter born in our house was Baby's. Baby was a stray who came to stay with us on Christmas day in 1996. Her four kittens, born in January 1997, actually arrived while I slept, but I participated in the birth by giving up my thirty-five-dollar white dress shirt as the birthing bed. Baby must have known that I had only worn the shirt once, and that it was in the laundry basket so I could wash it and wear it to work again.

Shan Li was a calico who came to us when a friend of our son's found her wandering the streets. She was dirty, undernourished and traumatized, as well as de-clawed and pregnant! Five weeks after her arrival, she gave birth to five kittens we ended up calling The Pile — four females and one male. We named the single male Watson, and ended up keeping him because he developed an eye infection and needed "special attention." (This is the excuse we almost always use when my wife and I have fallen in love with a kitten and decide that it can't leave.)

Pregnant cats kept showing up in our lives. Once we had two

cats—Tiffany and Lenore—deliver litters within twelve hours of each other! When Tiffany ultimately rejected her litter, Lenore came to the rescue. Lenore was a tiny cat with a constant harassed look upon her face. After giving birth to her own four kittens, she then took in Tiffany's abandoned three and nursed all seven to health with some assistance (and feedings) from us. By the time the kittens were weaned, she was exhausted. Lenore was the only cat I ever thought was glad to be spayed. We were able to find homes for all seven kittens, and for the mothers as well.

We were especially pleased with the home we found for our beleaguered ex-super-mom. Today, Lenore, aka Lenny, is living a quiet, reflective life in a local retirement home for Franciscan nuns. The good sisters offer prayers every day for our efforts; sometimes, I think it is the only reason we are able to keep doing what we do.

I don't work as a bouncer anymore, but I'm still delivering kittens. We took in another cat just a few weeks ago, and—no surprise—she's pregnant. Any day now, probably in the middle of the night (of course), I'll be playing midwife again. I enjoy the experience, but I wish with all my being that I didn't have to do it. It gets tiring looking for homes for healthy cats with nowhere to go. My wife and I always take the kittens to the vet, getting them altered and inoculated with their first shots before we start looking for homes for them—we want to make sure that we don't perpetuate the problem! This process costs us a few hundred dollars each time, and our vet always lectures about being such soft touches. Still, I'm sure that we'll continue to do it in the future. As long as there are pregnant cats who need help, I am willing to play midwife.

~Brian Baker
Chicken Soup for the Cat Lover's Soul

Tiny and the Oak Tree

Tears are the safety valve of the heart when too much pressure is laid on it.
~Albert Smith

H
e was scary-looking. Standing about six-foot, six-inches tall, he had shoulders the width of my dining room table. His hair hung to his shoulders, a full beard obscured half of his face; his massive arms and chest were covered with tattoos. He was wearing greasy blue jeans and a jean jacket with the sleeves cut out. Chains clanked on his motorcycle boots and on the key ring hanging from his wide leather belt. He held out a hand the size of a pie plate, in which lay a tiny, misshapen kitten.

"What's wrong with Tiny, Doc?" he asked in a gruff voice.

My exam revealed a birth defect. Tiny's spine had never grown together, and he was paralyzed in his back legs. No amount of surgery, medicine or prayer was going to fix him. I felt helpless.

The only thing I could tell this big, hairy giant was that his little friend was going to die. I was ashamed of my prejudice but I felt a little nervous anticipating the biker's reaction. Being the bearer of bad news is never pleasant, but with a rough-looking character like the man in front of me, I didn't know what to expect.

I tried to be as tactful as possible, explaining Tiny's problem and what we could expect, which was a slow, lingering death. I braced myself for his response.

But the big fella only looked at me with eyes that I could barely see through the hair on his face and said sadly, "I guess we gotta do him, huh, Doc?"

I agreed that, yes, the best way to help Tiny was to give him the injection that would end his poor, pain-filled life. So with his owner holding Tiny, we ended the little kitten's pain.

When it was over, I was surprised to see this macho guy the size of an oak tree just standing there holding Tiny, with tears running down his beard. He never apologized for crying, but he managed a choked "Thanks, Doc," as he carried his little friend's body home to bury him.

Although ending a patient's life is never pleasant, my staff and I all agreed that we were glad we could stop the sick kitten's pain. Weeks passed, and the incident faded.

Then one day the oak-sized biker appeared in the clinic again. It looked ominously like we were about to repeat the earlier scenario. The huge man was wearing the same clothes and carrying another kitten in his pie-plate hand. But I was enormously relieved upon examining "Tiny Two" to find he was absolutely, perfectly, wonderfully normal and healthy.

I started Tiny Two's vaccinations, tested him for worms and discussed his care, diet and future needs with his deceptively tough-looking owner. By now, it was obvious that Mr. Oak Tree had a heart that matched his size.

I wonder now how many other Hell's Angel types are really closet marshmallows. In fact, whenever I see a pack of scary-looking bikers roaring past me on the road, I crane my neck to see if I can catch a glimpse of some tiny little kitten poking its head up out of a sleek chrome side-car—or maybe even peeking out from inside the front of a black leather jacket.

~Dennis K. McIntosh, D.V.M.
Chicken Soup for the Pet Lover's Soul

A Miracle Called Faith

The morning was no different from any other—except for the persistent cry from a determined little cat. The school principal and I both froze when we saw her—a small, bedraggled, black-striped, gray kitten with a very mangled front leg. Howling plaintively, she didn't scamper away; she just leaned forward, her front leg deformed, muddied and matted with dried blood.

We found a small box, and the principal took the broken kitten to his office. As a second-year teacher, I couldn't leave my class to take her to the vet, so I did what pretty much all kids do when they're in trouble: I called my dad. Even with a very hectic schedule, he made time for things that really mattered, including a stray kitten with injuries. He said he'd pick her up within an hour. During that time, the kitten continued howling: first for milk (which she heartily lapped up), then for attention and, finally, as if she wanted to tell her story. Her yellow eyes were wide, and she wanted to see everything. We decided that she must have been hit by a car to receive such an awful injury, but she didn't seem to be in pain.

Later in the morning, I called my dad again to get an update on the kitten. "She's okay for now, but the prognosis isn't good," he explained. "The vet said that the injury is at least a day or two old, infected, and the nerves in that leg are dead. He said that she should either be put to sleep or have her front leg amputated."

It was shaping up to be one bad day. My students had been particularly horrible to me and to each other. The school is in a low socioeconomic area, and it has produced rough students who seem only to know how to be tough so they don't get hurt. One student in particular, Darren, was a quiet but very angry boy. He refused to complete any of the activities, work with the other students or answer me. Instead, he'd sit at his desk and stare straight ahead. The rest of the class knew better than to provoke Darren. Although he didn't go out and pick fights, he had no qualms about giving a hard wallop to any kid who crossed him. Earlier in the year, he slammed a boy taller than himself into a wall for going through his book bag. Darren was feared by all.

At the end of the school day, I rushed over to the vet's office. He repeated to me the same options that he had outlined to my dad. Questions flooded my mind: How could I even afford such a procedure? A three-legged cat? What kind of life is that for an animal? I'd have to put it on my credit card—along with many other, older charges that amounted to quite a large figure.

"Could I at least say goodbye to her?" I asked.

They brought me to the back, where she was sleeping in her litter pan on the floor of a cold, metal cage.

"Hello," I called to her, carefully opening the wire-mesh door. "Hello, little lady."

She sleepily lifted her head, her yellow eyes mere slits. Her ears drooped lazily, but she let out a little squeak, then yawned. I reached in and gently picked her up, avoiding the hurt leg that was now bandaged all the way to her shoulder. I could feel her little purr-box working away, and I held her close. "Meow, meow, meow," she responded, as if she were informing me of her trip to the vet and how her stay had been up to that point. I started to cry. In my arms rested a little life that was about to end, and all she could do was purr and talk.

"You know, if you think you might want to save this cat, Sergeant has only three legs, too," the vet said, pointing to a white fur ball who was very busily stalking something. "And he's still a very happy cat."

"Really?" I asked, looking closely at the three-legged feline.

"Sure!" he replied, retrieving a very plump and very three-legged Sergeant. "He hurt his leg a few years ago, and his owners brought him here. I amputated the leg, and he's been the office cat ever since.

Why, he isn't slowed down a bit by that missing leg." Sergeant sprang off the examining table onto the floor, swatted at a loose rolling ball of fur, then scurried down the hallway.

No sooner had I decided to have her leg taken off than ideas began to fill my mind—ideas of how to include this little kitten in my classes. The more advanced students could organize bake sales to help pay for the medical expenses. I would assign all my students a research project to learn more about any animal they chose. And the vet agreed to come and talk with them once the kitten had recovered enough to visit the school.

Three days later, I called the vet to check on the kitten's surgery. "The vet's still in with her," his receptionist said. "But don't worry. He's done this before. It just takes a while."

My students were also disappointed that I couldn't update them on her status. Finally, we learned that the kitten had pulled through just fine. It was safe for the students to finally choose a name for her. Every child either suggested a name or voted, except for Darren. He thought the entire event was absolutely stupid and beneath his efforts. The students finally settled on the name Faith.

One month, 120 research projects (ranging from a picture of a duck to elaborately designed displays) and five bake sales later, the day arrived for Faith and the vet to visit the class. The students were wired and restless, but they knew the rules: stay in your seats and speak only when it's your turn, or the visitors go home.

Darren was particularly ugly that morning, slamming his books, mumbling about stupid cats and boring visitors. Such an angry kid! Faith introduced herself with a squeaky howl from inside her carrier. I couldn't believe how well the students behaved. Faith sat bravely in the vet's arms as they gathered around and gently ran their fingers over her soft fur. Darren watched from his seat.

"Does she still hurt?"

"Has she fallen?"

"Can she wash her face?"

"Can she really walk?"

The vet placed her on the ground, and the students jumped back as though she might explode. Even Darren craned his neck so he could see through the students standing in front of him.

"Wow!"

"She hops!"

"She can walk!"

Faith scampered about the classroom, meowing, squeaking and exploring. She loved when someone scratched her back at the base of her tail. Standing a little wobbly on her three legs, she arched her back and stood on her hind toes.

Later, my principal told me that a reporter from the local paper wanted to visit the students who had adopted Faith, the three-legged cat. We were going to be in the paper!

Everyone wanted something to do or to show for the reporter's visit. One group arranged Faith's progress pictures on a poster board; another presented bake-sale signs; I prepared two students as greeters and hosts. Only Darren, the good-ole-grouch, was left out. All he could do was give me a whaddaya-gonna-do-about-it? glare.

I was going to be the one to watch over Faith. Then I had an idea. I announced, "Darren, you will watch over Faith."

His reaction was, "Huh?"

"She needs someone to hold her cage and make sure nothing goes wrong when the reporter tries to pet her."

The reaction from the class was:

"I want to do that!"

"No! Let me!"

"No, me! Darren can show the projects."

"This job is for Darren and Darren alone," I said firmly. "If he doesn't want to do it, then I will. So there will be no fighting about it."

"I'll do it," Darren said, looking back over his shoulder and grinning slyly at his classmates. "I'll watch Faith."

The reporter's visit was a smashing success—Darren carefully opened the carrier door so the reporter could take Faith out, pet her and see her scar, which was nearly covered over by her grown-back fur. Darren watched over Faith and was her strongest protector.

When the reporter left, the students cleaned up and put the room back in order.

"You did a good job," I told Darren, and I meant it.

He nodded, then looked into her carrier. "Can I pick her up?"

Startled by the question, I hesitated at first, which he didn't notice. "Yes," I replied. "You know to be careful."

"Yes, ma'am, I know."

I watched, holding my breath, as he slowly opened the door, extending both arms into the cage, talking in a voice so soft, I could barely hear him. He cradled Faith to his chest, and she purred and purred. Quietly, I backed away. Something was going on here, and I was not going to interrupt it. He sat down and gently placed her on the desk in front of him. She stood on her three legs, meowed, squeaked and purred, but didn't try to leave. The street-hardened Darren softly scratched under her chin, petted her between her ears, on her neck, down her back. He was gentle and focused.

Something changed in Darren that day. Something that had long been dormant came alive and grew each time he saw Faith. Every Friday, when Faith came to visit, Darren was her special guardian. He made sure the classroom door was shut tight and no one was rough with her. But, most of all, he watched her. Something deep within him connected to that once-broken little kitten.

Darren's transformation continued beyond his Fridays with Faith. The tough exterior and the anger were gone, leaving an eager student who raised his hand to answer questions, completed his work and participated in class. He even smiled just a little more.

I believe that finding Faith in the school hall was no accident. Forces greater than we can ever understand worked through that mangled little kitten — forces that gave me hope as a teacher, brought smiles to a classroom of kids and a little peace to an angry and hardened young heart. Faith, a little gray kitten with three good legs, wandered into a school of tough kids and created a miracle.

~Heather L. Sanborn
Chicken Soup for the Cat Lover's Soul

Me and My Mewse

*Cats do care. For example they know instinctively what time
we have to be at work in the morning and they wake us up
twenty minutes before the alarm goes off.*
~Michael Nelson

According to my dictionary, a "muse" is any of the nine Greek goddesses who preside over the arts. This means that, as a writer, I not only get to work in my pajamas, I can also claim my own goddess who will answer my prayers in times of literary distress.

Luckily, there's no need, since I have Necco, a peach-colored tortoiseshell cat to serve as my own personal "mewse."

The cat discovered us at the local animal shelter. We were looking for a quiet, neat pet to complement our boisterous dog, Emma. We found Necco instead.

As soon as we entered the shelter, she called to us in a noisy chirp that made it clear she required immediate attention. The yellow tag on her cage—the symbol showing that this was her last day—backed up her urgent request. When the cage door swung open, she stepped into my arms and settled back with a look that clearly said, "What took you so long?"

Six months old and barely three pounds, Necco wasted no time establishing herself as the one in charge of our lives. The leather chair was her scratching post. The Christmas tree was her playground. And the mantel, neatly decorated with a collection of brass candlesticks of all shapes and sizes, was where she discovered the Feline Law of Gravity: Cats go up; candlesticks come down. The first dainty swipe of a paw resulted in a satisfying crash. So did the second, third and fourth. By the fifth crash, Necco's face bore the cat equivalent of a grin. She had discovered her purpose in life.

It happened that Necco's skills reached their peak just as my life reached a low point. My twenty-year marriage had shuddered to a stop, leaving me with a ten-year-old daughter, Katie, and a large home to support on an advertising copywriter's salary. Although I worked full-time, the pay was modest and I often found myself with more bills than paycheck. I soon realized I would have to work as a freelance writer just to meet expenses.

That meant getting up at 4:00 A.M., writing for two hours, and then getting ready for work. Eight hours later, I would return home, fix dinner, help Katie with homework, clean the house and get ready for another day's work. I fell into bed exhausted at 11:00 P.M. only to crawl out of bed when the alarm sounded at 4:00 A.M. the next day.

The routine lasted exactly two weeks. Despite gallons of coffee, I couldn't seem to produce anything. I was cranky, frustrated, lonely and ready to admit defeat. Writing was hard. Paying bills was even harder. The only answer was to sell the house and get an inexpensive apartment. Unfortunately, that would mean more losses for Katie and me. Especially since no apartment in town allowed pets.

I hated the thought of finding another home for us all, and I especially hated the thought of telling Katie about the changes in store. Depressed, I slept right through the 4:00 A.M. alarm the next day. And the next and the next. Finally, I quit setting it.

That's when Necco did a curious thing. Knowing that a sudden crash would make a human jump, she decided that the perfect time to make that crash was at 4:00 A.M. Her bedroom bombing raid was timed with military precision. First she set off a small round of artillery in the form of two pencils and my eyeglasses. I rolled over and covered my head with the blanket. Then she moved on to an arsenal of notebooks and the alarm clock. Each crash forced me deeper under the covers. Finally, she brought out the big guns. A half-filled glass of water splashed to the ground. A hardbound book crashed beside me. How could I sleep with the world literally crashing down around my ears? My mewse said it was time to get to work.

Wearily, I made my way to the computer. Necco hopped up on the desk, seeming to feel her job wasn't done yet. Sitting on a pile of unfinished story ideas, she watched with apparent satisfaction as I began to type. Whenever the words seemed slow in coming, she helped me along. Gliding across my keyboard with the grace of a goddess, she produced sentences like: "awesdtrfgyhubjikpl[;' dtrfgbhujni guhnj!" My translation? "I woke you up for a reason. Now, write!" I wrote. And wrote some more.

From then on, every day Necco got me up at 4:00 A.M. sharp, when the ideas were freshest and the world slept around us. With her watching over me as I wrote, I didn't feel so alone. My goals didn't seem so impossible. Slowly, over months of early mornings, stories were born, and polished, and sold.

Today the old house still surrounds us. Katie and I are both doing fine. And although both pets are treated like the cherished family members they are, whenever another story is sold, I give thanks to my muse—a little cat with a mischievous grin, who kept me company in my "darkest hours."

~Cindy Podurgal Chambers
Chicken Soup for the Cat and Dog Lover's Soul

The $100,000 Stray Cat

Most cats, when they are Out want to be In, and vice versa,
and often simultaneously.
~Louis J. Camuti

One orphan kitty with golden eyes—it's hard to believe all he has inspired.

I've always loved cats. But until nine years ago, my pet cats suffered a high mortality rate. I decided that my next cat was going to live indoors only. Besides, I love wild birds, and this way I could be sure my cat wouldn't hunt birds or little woodland creatures.

But then came Oliver. My sister works at a veterinarian's office. One day she called up and pleaded with me to come see a six-month-old kitten that had been abandoned there. They were having trouble finding him a home. The other staff found him ordinary. They only kept him because he was a willing blood donor. It broke my sister's heart to see the little kitten offer his paw for the needle and then purr while his blood was being withdrawn.

I went to the office and within thirty seconds had fallen in love. The kitten had short but soft black fur with a white undercoat, a round, pudgy face and luminous golden eyes. He was dignified but affectionate. I instantly thought of the name Oliver, after the Charles Dickens orphan. Home we went—together.

But Oliver didn't want to be an indoors-only cat. He cried at the door, paced around the house, and tried to run outside whenever we opened a door. After much family discussion, we decided to build an outdoor cat run, an enclosed area where Oliver could safely spend time during the day. With the help of my dad, a retired carpenter, we built a thirty-by-fifteen-foot structure that had chicken-wire fencing on its sides and top.

Inside the cat run was a long strip of grass, food, water, litter pan, toys, scratching posts, a planter with catnip, and plenty of perches and high shelves. Oliver adored it. He loved lying in the grass, basking in the sun, chasing bugs and watching birds fly by.

But that wasn't the end of it. Oh, no. The cat run overlooked our vacant, one-acre lot. Wouldn't it be wonderful, I decided, if we could grow a wildlife garden there to attract more creatures for Oliver to watch? So I read books and magazines, visited nurseries and went on garden tours to educate myself. I was a little nervous about tackling such an ambitious project—I'm rather shy, really—but, I reasoned, no one would ever see the garden but us.

I recruited my dad to help. He quickly became so enthusiastic that he began adding his own ideas. His contagious spirit spread to my other family members, and before I knew it, we were all out there clearing the field, preparing the soil, marking out paths and starting to plant. We put in trees, shrubs, perennials, annuals, bulbs—thousands of plants over a two-year period. Dad built arbors, trellises, pergolas, benches, a pond with waterfalls and a bridge. We started collecting all sorts of garden décor—statues, stepping stones, fountains, planters, wind chimes, flags, birdhouses and wind vanes—all with cat designs. A friend even made me wooden signs saying "Meow Meadows," "Cat Country" and "Kitty Grazing Area." Everything was purr-fect!

And even that wasn't the end of it. A friend recommended our garden for Spokane's big annual garden tour. So on a hot August Sunday afternoon, I had five thousand people tour our garden. People went nuts over it! They didn't respond as much to the planting scheme as to the heartfelt emotion that went into it all. For weeks afterward, I was in the newspaper and being interviewed on TV. People called constantly.

Since that day, the Meyer Cat Garden is no longer our "little family secret." Over 10,000 people have visited it—everyone from nursing home residents to a tour group from a national garden convention. During my now well-practiced speech, I emphasize the importance of caring for your pets properly so they don't harm wildlife.

And wildlife we've got. As the garden has grown, it's attracted birds, frogs, squirrels, chipmunks, even raccoons, skunks and deer. I've grown, too. I'm now a master gardener and president of our local garden club, and I'm comfortable with both writing and public speaking. And our whole family has grown: Working on such a tremendous project has drawn us all closer together.

And what about Oliver? He watches it all contentedly through his cat run—his window to the world. Our family joke is that if we added up the cost of all the thousands of plants, cat decorations and hours of labor that went into the Meyer Cat Garden, we have easily spent over $100,000.

That's why we call Oliver our $100,000 stray cat.

But you know what? He was a bargain.

~ViAnn Meyer
Chicken Soup for the Gardener's Soul

Laser, the Therapist

The moment he reached his little paw through the cage bars at the humane society, I was a goner. I wasn't looking for another cat—I already had two—but was just stopping by to give the animals some attention. When the shelter volunteer, apparently knowing a sucker when she saw one, asked if I would like to hold him, there was no longer any doubt. He came home with me that day.

He was a gorgeous cat, a five-month-old blue-point Siamese with eyes like blue laser beams: thus, his name. Right from the beginning, it was obvious that Laser was an exceptional cat. He loved everyone—the other cats, visitors to the house, even the dog who later joined the household.

I first heard about animal-assisted therapy several months after we adopted Laser. While most of what I heard was about dogs, it occurred to me that Laser would be perfect for this type of work. I signed up for the training class, and, after completing the preliminary requirements, Laser and I passed the test to become registered Delta Society Pet Partners.

While he had always been a little lovebug at home, Laser found his true calling when we began to go on visits. Whether it was with sick kids at the children's hospital, seniors with Alzheimer's disease, or teens in a psychiatric unit, Laser always knew just what to do. He curled up on laps or beside bed-bound patients and happily snuggled close. He never tried to get up until I moved him to the next person. People often commented that they'd never seen a cat so calm and friendly. Even people who didn't like cats liked him!

One young man, who had been badly burned in a fire, smiled for the first time since his accident when Laser nestled under his lap blanket. A little boy, tired and lethargic from terminal leukemia, rallied to smile, hug Laser and kiss his head, and then talked endlessly about Laser after the visits. Several geriatric patients with dementia, who were agitated and uncommunicative prior to Laser's appearance, calmed down and became talkative with each other and the staff after a visit from my therapeutic feline partner. It has been our hospice visits, though, that I consider the most challenging and rewarding of all our Pet Partner experiences.

One day, I got a phone call telling me about a hospice patient at a nearby nursing home who had requested a visit by a cat. At the time, only one cat—Laser—actively participated in the local program. Even so, my first inclination was to make some excuse not to do it. I have always had issues with death and dying, and a hard time talking about it to anyone, but I quickly realized how selfish I was being—the poor woman was dying, and all she asked was that I bring my cat to visit. I said yes.

A few days later, we made our first visit. Mrs. P. was ninety-one years old, and although her body was weak, her mind was still very sharp. It was a little awkward at first (what do you say to a perfect stranger who knows she's dying?), but Laser was a great conversation catalyst. He crawled into bed with her and curled up right next to her hip—exactly where her hand could rest on his back. She told me stories about the cat she and her husband had years ago.

"See you next week," she said as we got up to leave.

We visited every Sunday during the three months that followed, and a real friendship developed between us. Mrs. P. would excitedly exclaim, "Laser!" every time we appeared at her door and "See you next week!" every time we left. She had been gradually getting weaker, but, one week when we arrived to see her, I was distressed to see that her condition had deteriorated significantly. Still, she smiled and said, "Laser!" when we walked into the room.

She complained of being cold, even though the room was warm, and when Laser cuddled up close to her, she said, "Oh, he's so warm—it feels so good." We had a nice visit, even though Mrs. P. wasn't feeling very well. Her hand never left Laser's back. As we left, she said her usual, "See you next week," and I hoped that was true.

The next Saturday, a phone call informed me that Mrs. P. was going downhill rapidly, and that she probably wouldn't live more than another few days. I asked if we should still come for our visit, and the nurse told me that she thought that would be wonderful.

When we arrived, it was obvious that Mrs. P. was dying. She was fading in and out of consciousness, but when she noticed that Laser and I were beside her bed, she smiled and whispered, "Laser."

She was having a very hard time breathing, so I told her not to try to talk; we would just sit quietly and keep her company. Laser took his spot on the bed next to her hip, and Mrs. P. rested her hand on his soft back. Neither of them moved from that position for the entire length of our visit. This time, when we got up to leave, Mrs. P. whispered, "Thank you." She knew that there would be no "next week" for us.

A couple of days later, I got the phone call telling me that Mrs. P. had died. I was sad—our weekly visits had been so wonderful—but I was glad that she was no longer in pain. I remembered how I had considered declining to make the hospice visits and was so grateful that I had not.

In our seventh year as a Pet Partner team, Laser and I still make visits to several facilities. Laser, the little cat that nobody wanted, is as beautiful on the inside as he is on the outside, and he continues to brighten the lives of everyone he meets.

~Nancy Kucik
Chicken Soup for the Cat Lover's Soul

7

A Cat, Six Kittens and a Wheelchair

I didn't care for Ike at first. Nobody did. Named after Ike Eisenhower, "Grumpy" suited him better. I suppose I'd be grumpy, too, if I sat in a wheelchair all day long.

As a community nurse on the Alaska Highway in northern British Columbia, I often encountered taciturn patients, but Ike took the cake. It was the dead of winter. Snow swirled around, sneaking into my boots as I lurched through snow drifts toward the dilapidated pewter-gray shack on the outskirts of town. Ice crystals pierced my face like needles in the forty-degree-below-zero cold. The front door hung askew, a result of permafrost heaving the foundation. A large crack split the door frame. Wind whistled eerily through the house. Thick frost covered parts of the living room walls in spite of a pot-bellied stove puffing away in the corner. I could see Ike sitting at the kitchen table, a sour look on his bearded face.

How can anyone live like this? I wondered.

I had to treat him for bedsores on his heels caused when he carelessly threw his legs around like wooden posts.

I looked at the alligator head on the TV.

"Where'd you get that thing?" I shuddered.

"Aah, an Indian friend of mine came with me to Florida last year and we bagged it... not bad, eh?" He grunted, waving me off. Ike was like that, adventurous... unusual... didn't let a little thing like paraplegia stop him.

"Meow."

"Was that a cat?"

"Hmmm." Conversation was difficult with this taciturn man. He wanted his dressing to be done and for me to get out of there—a silent but direct attitude.

"How did you break your back, Ike?"

"Oh, I was building a house for my family up at the 'half way' [a place farther north in the wilderness]... it was supposed to be our dream house... had my boy with me... I was stupid really... sat on a rafter and fell off to the basement... broke my back... Jim took the truck... he was only twelve... and drove it to the neighbors twenty miles away... the closest... hardly a road except a dirt track. They got me out to Edmonton by Air Ambulance but there was no hope... so here I am... wife left me a year later."

Rehabilitation helped him cope as a paraplegic but no one helped him cope with being abandoned by his family. He disliked women, especially pesky snoopy community nurses.

"Meow." A plaintiff cry came from underneath the floorboards.

"Ike, that is a cat under your house—we've got to get her out."

"She's been there a couple days now—drives me nuts... ever since the blizzard blocked her escape hole. She can freeze under there for all I care!"

"You can't just let her freeze to death or starve... that's cruel."

"Why not?... no darn good to anyone... just a pest."

"Well, your dressing can wait. I'll see if I can dig her out."

"Yeah sure, you care more for a cat than for your patients."

The snow, like whipped cream, was piled high on the side of the house. I grabbed a shovel and started throwing the snow aside to reveal a hole to the crawl space. I peeked into the cavernous blackness. I could see green eyes peering out at me, but no way was she going to creep out.

"Well, she'll come out now when I'm gone." I finished his dressing.

"She's scared to death... she'll come out," Ike griped. "Then what?"

"Well, you can feed her for heaven's sake. I'll bring you some cheap cat food tomorrow."

Ike didn't answer but rolled his eyes toward the ceiling.

The next day I placed a huge bag of cheap cat food on the table in front of him.

He said little as I did his foot dressings. When I returned the day after that, during a Chinook warm spell, I found Ike with the back door open. A rusty tin pie plate sat on the back step overloaded with dry cat food. A very pregnant, beautiful, long-haired calico cat sat there munching away, quite content.

"Aha, so your heart isn't so hard after all."

"Well, she'll be having a bunch of kittens soon and what am I going to do with those?" He grinned sheepishly. He tried his best to be gruff but couldn't.

By spring, Ike was the proud father of six kittens and a cat. Wild things they were, bouncing all about. They kept their distance, too, but approached gingerly to grab food from Ike's hands and scramble away.

"They'll only come so far, and they won't come for anyone else," he said proudly.

For the next three months, Ike faithfully fed his menagerie and seemed softer, more pliable, less grumpy.

But all kittens grow up. One day, Ike declared he couldn't possibly keep all seven cats.

"I phoned a farmer friend, and she'll take the kittens if I can catch them. This is all your fault so you have to help me."

He handed me a pillow case in which to place the kittens. I leaped about, slithering on the icy stoop, arms akimbo. Ike laughed uproariously as the kittens scampered about, just out of my reach.

"I ought to get more pay for this," I grumbled.

Eventually with a lot of stealth, I got all kittens into the pillow-case, ready for transfer to the farm.

"What about Kitty?"

"Nah, I'll keep her and get her fixed... she's kinda attached to me by now."

"Sure." Kitty owned the place now.

As for Ike... well, he wasn't so bad after all. In fact I got kinda attached to him, too. Even though his coffee was lousy, I always had a cup with him as we laughed and talked about all kinds of things. As far as I know, Ike is still sleeping with his beloved Kitty. And the community nurse still visits and brings Kitty all kinds of treats. It's part of the job description, after all!

~Arlene Alice Centerwall
Chicken Soup for the Working Woman's Soul

8

For Every Cat, There Is a Reason

These were the worst kinds of calls, the ones I had come to dread. As the animal-control officer of a small city, hearing the police dispatcher say the words "animal" and "car" over the radio in the same sentence was never good news. Sighing, I drove to the address I'd been given. Pulling up to the scene, I saw several people out in front of the apartment building huddled over her. She had been a beautiful cat, gray stripes with white paws. She was already gone, which gave me some relief, as it broke my heart to see them suffer. I wrapped her in a blanket that I kept in the car for this purpose and gently laid her down in the back of the wagon. Grabbing my clipboard to write the report, I walked back to the small crowd that had gathered. The building superintendent had his arms folded across his chest, rocking back and forth, and shifting his weight from one foot to the other. He looked like a man who had many things to do, and taking the time to answer questions for my report wasn't one of them.

"There's no pets allowed in this building... no dogs or cats, so I have no idea why this one was around." He looked pointedly from me to the elderly lady who was standing to the other side of me. Her eyes widened, and she quickly looked down at her feet.

"He's right. No pets in this building," she said in a low voice.

I put the clipboard under my arm and said, "I can write the rest of this myself." I wasn't in the mood to deal with yet another person who just didn't care. The super walked off in the opposite direction, obviously glad that this disruption to his schedule was over. As I walked to the car, pulling my pen out of my pocket, I felt a hand on my shoulder. "Please wait," the voice said, "I want to show you something."

It was the lady who had been standing with the super.

I looked at my watch. I was already twenty minutes late to my next call.

"I had to wait until he was gone," she said. She looked in the direction of the departing super. I was beginning to understand.

I walked with her around the back of the building and into the laundry room. The woman crouched down next to a dryer. "I knew the cat who died. I called her Misty because of her gray color, even though she would never come too close to me. I think she was one of those—I think they're called feral cats. She didn't trust people, but I left her a can of food and fresh water every day."

When she paused, I heard a tiny mewing sound coming from the back of the dryer. Reaching my hand in under the machine, I felt a warm, fuzzy lump of fur. I carefully pulled the lump out to find a tiny gray-and-white, spitting, growling, mewing kitten, no more than a week old. She was looking at me with one eye, the other one not yet opened, as is the way with newborn kittens sometimes. She seemed very frightened, although she was actively trying out all the new sounds she was capable of making.

"I couldn't say anything in front of the super," the lady continued. "I've looked all around the building, and this is the only kitten. I couldn't tell she was expecting. Like I said, I could never get that close." The lady struggled to stand up, gripping the dryer for help. She asked, "What's going to happen to her without her mother?"

I understood her concern. Kittens less than five weeks old need a lot of care. Nursing every few hours round-the-clock is only part of the challenge. The local animal shelter didn't have the manpower necessary to care for a kitten so young, but would take her at six weeks when she could eat solid food—which didn't help right now.

I knew that the best place for this kitten would be with a mother cat who could nurse and clean her. Now, where could I find one who would accept this little orphan as her own? "I'll figure something out," I said, tucking the tiny kitten inside my coat. The day had started out with a tragedy, but I was determined not to let it end with another one.

It was easy enough to find the necessary equipment, tiny bottles and kitten formula, and even easier finding the time to stop and care for her during the day, given the nature of my job. It was a common sight to see me at my desk with a cat or a dog on my lap while I filed reports. In the hectic atmosphere of the police station, no one seemed to care or even notice.

At night, I brought the kitten home with me, setting the alarm every three hours for feedings. Unfortunately, the kitten wanted to be fed every two, and, soon, the lack of sleep began taking its toll. I was also starting to worry that the tiny gray kitten didn't seem as strong or to be growing as fast as I would have liked. I felt very alone—solely responsible for her survival and at a loss as to what to do next. To make matters worse, my landlord approached me as I came home one evening and said he'd reached his limit regarding my pets. The kitten needed a home—and fast.

The next morning, the dispatcher told me to "10–33 the lieutenant." This meant that I had to return to headquarters and speak with Lieutenant Harris. He had been with the department longer than anyone else, and even the mention of his name made you stand up straighter. He commanded respect, and even a little fear. Being summoned to his office was probably something very serious, as he rarely had contact with the civilian employees. I left the kitten in a carrier in my car and went inside to face my fate.

I knocked quietly on his door. "Come in," he barked from behind the door. Slowly, I entered his office and stood in front of his desk. Lieutenant Harris didn't look up. I stood there awkwardly, scanning the numerous framed awards and commendations on the wall. He was writing busily on a legal pad.

"You can sit down now," he said, still not looking up.

I sat. The lieutenant put his pen down, sighed, clasped his hands in front of him and looked up at me for the first time, his eyes flinty.

"So, I understand that you have in your custody a very young kitten. Is this so?"

My heart sunk. Now I was in for it! Flustered, I opened my mouth to tell him that, yes, I did have this tiny kitten with me all the time, but I hadn't let it interfere with my job. That I couldn't bring this kitten to the shelter because she was too young to survive there. That I was worried that she wouldn't make it. That I was exhausted because I hadn't slept more than two hours at a time for a week, and I felt like I was going to cry. I was going to say all of these things, but the only words that came out of my mouth were, "Yes, sir," spoken in a hoarse whisper.

He looked at me sternly, then his face broke into smile, and he said, "Can I see it?"

Surprised relief coursed through me, and, eager to comply, I rushed outside and brought in the carrier, a bottle and some formula. "Close the door," the lieutenant said, gesturing for me to give him the kitten.

"She has some longhaired breed in her," Lieutenant Harris said as he carefully scratched behind her ears. I handed him the bottle, and he started to feed the kitten. He looked happier than I had ever imagined he could look. I told him the story of how I had come to have the kitten.

When I finished, he said, "There's something very special about this little cat, surviving like that when the odds were against her. Yes, there's definitely a special reason for this little girl here. Hey, that might be a good name for her: Reason!" He smiled at me and said, "Now let's put our heads together and figure out how we can help her."

By the end of the day, a plan was in place. It seemed as though everyone stopped what they were doing to consider how they could help. The assistant district attorney spoke to the youth officer, who had a friend who bred Persian cats. The youth officer called her friend and learned that one of the Persians had just had a new litter and was nursing. The breeder said I could come over to her apartment to see if her cat would accept Reason and let her nurse with her own kittens.

When we got there, I put Reason down close to the mother cat and the other kittens. The youth officer and I stood there, waiting to see what would happen. The tiny kitten padded over to the others and nosed her way into the crowd. As I stood there, holding my breath, the mother cat stretched out her paw and drew Reason to her. She started bathing her, licking her all over her head, as if she were saying, "Just where have you been? You're filthy!" The gray-and-white kitten then took her place among the five cream-colored Persian kittens to nurse.

Six weeks later, when she was weaned, Reason was adopted by a young woman who, initially, had come to purchase a Persian kitten, but decided that she wanted Reason instead. Reason would be pampered and loved for the rest of her life.

I think the lieutenant was right. Reason was special—surviving against all odds and inspiring a whole police station to rally around her. Too often, in my line of work, situations like these do not end well. For a period of time, a tiny homeless kitten gave all of us who were touched by her plight the opportunity to make this ending a happy one. Reason gave me a reason to believe in others again, and taught me that sometimes all you really have to do when you need help is to ask.

~Lisa Duffy-Korpics
Chicken Soup for the Cat Lover's Soul

Miss Feather's Lesson

Kindness is the language which the deaf can hear and the blind can see.
~Mark Twain

After school one day, I saw some boys poking a stick into a thorn bush and laughing. My worst fears were realized when I heard a faint "meow" from inside the bush. I ran over and grabbed the stick away from them and peered into the bush. There I saw the most pitiful kitten I'd ever seen. Her color was questionable because of the dirt and blood matted into her coat. The thorns of the bush were pushing into her little body, and she was crying with pain. I had to get her out of there.

Crawling carefully into the bush, I freed her from the entangling thorn branches. My arms got totally covered in scratches—not just from the thorns, but from her claws as well, as the frightened kitten tried to hold on to me.

When I got home, I called out, "Mom! See what followed me home!" My mother was used to me bringing home stray animals. This kitten would be no different—she would have a home if she wanted to stay with us.

After carefully removing thorns, cleaning wounds and bathing this poor creature, I found that I had a beautiful, snow-white, long-haired kitten with sky-blue eyes. Because of her silky coat, I called her "Miss Feather."

The following week, a new family moved into our neighborhood. They had a daughter named Judy Ann. Judy Ann talked "funny" — funny to the kids in our neighborhood, anyway — and they laughed at her. I felt sorry for Judy. I protected her from the kids who were mean to her, and we became friends. Judy Ann adored Miss Feather as much as I did and helped me to take care of her.

One morning at breakfast, Mother said, "Molly, why don't you give Miss Feather to Judy Ann? She has no cats of her own — and you have so many!"

"But, Mom, I found Miss Feather!"

"You just think about it."

That night I lay in bed and thought, and thought and thought. I decided that it would be a good idea to give Miss Feather to Judy Ann. She lived just two doors down, and I could still play with Miss Feather whenever I wanted. Once I had made my decision, I couldn't wait for morning to come so I could tell Judy Ann about it.

Judy Ann was thrilled to tears! We hugged and hugged as I passed the purring kitten to her.

Most pure white cats with blue eyes are deaf, and Miss Feather was no exception. Because little Miss Feather couldn't hear, she required constant and faithful care. Judy Ann was the perfect mistress for her — no one would ever understand Miss Feather's needs as completely as Judy Ann. Do you know why? Because Judy Ann was also deaf.

~Molly Lemmons
Chicken Soup for the Kid's Soul 2

The Shy Girl

To say that I was shy when I was ten is an understatement — I was basically afraid of people. Kids, adults, pretty much everyone made me nervous. I was also what most teachers and parents would call a "good kid." I followed the rules, got good grades in school and rarely questioned authority. But then one day, one single ride on a school bus changed all that.

The school bus that day was crowded, hot, humid and smelly. The windows were all rolled up — bus driver's orders — it was simply raining too hard to have them down. Only a few of my classmates were looking through the windows at the torrents of water filling the street, overflowing the curbs and drains; most of the other kids were engaged in animated conversations, arguments and games. I sat alone as usual, speaking to no one.

I thought that the road outside looked like a flooded stream. I could make out tree limbs, bags, even an umbrella washing down the boulevard. People raced here and there, gripping umbrellas or covering their heads with bunched-up jackets and papers. Over and over, I carefully wiped a small circle through the cloud on my window so that I could see the rushing water outside.

The bus stopped, waiting for an accident to clear. The driver was particularly tense that day and had snapped at several kids who had been messing around, standing up in their seats, yelling, making faces at drivers in passing cars and even one kid who had been licking the window.

As I sat quietly, waiting and watching, I saw a kitty across the street on the other side of the road. Poor cat, I thought. He was all wet and didn't seem to know where to go to get out of the rain. I wanted to go get the kitty, but I knew that the bus driver, Mrs. Foster, would never allow me off the bus. It was against the rules to even stand up, so I knew that I would get in big trouble for trying to rescue a cat across a busy, rainy street. I also thought that if I pointed out the miserable cat, the other kids would probably think that I was weird, even weirder than they already thought I was. I was sure that some of the kids would laugh at the soaked, dripping animal; they would see his misery as their entertainment. I couldn't bear that; I didn't want things to get any worse than they already were.

My window was hazy again, and when I wiped the window clear, I could see that the kitty was now struggling in what seemed to be a surging, grimy river. He was up to his neck in cold water, grasping at the slippery metal bars covering the storm drain in the street. Twigs and other debris rushed past him and down into the black hole. His body had already been sucked into the dark opening of the storm drain, but his little front paws were clinging to the bars. I could see him shaking. He swallowed water and gasped for air as he fought the current with all of his strength. His movements revealed a level of fear that I had never witnessed before. I saw absolute terror in his dark, round eyes.

My heart was racing. Tears were rolling down my cheeks. I felt like I was drowning along with the little kitty. I wanted to rush off the bus without asking permission, and pull the stray cat from the drain, and wrap it up in my warm jacket, safe in my arms. But I also pictured getting into trouble before the cat could be saved, the other kids staring and laughing, and my parents' disappointment in my behavior.

I sat motionless, unable to act. Helpless. The bus began to move forward, the accident traffic finally in motion.

The cat's eyes locked on to mine. He was begging for help. Although the bus was noisy with the clamor of active children, I was sure that I heard his terrified meow. I could see that he was panicking and needed help right away. I glanced around, but no one else seemed to have noticed.

When Mrs. Foster yelled for me to sit down, I was startled. I hadn't even realized that I was standing up. I immediately sat back down. I did not break rules. I cried as the bus lumbered into motion. I prayed that someone else would notice and rescue my courageous friend. As our bus slowly turned the corner away from the flailing cat, I saw a car drive by the storm drain causing a wave to rise up and over the kitty's head. He appeared again coughing and sneezing but this time with some blood trickling from his mouth and nose. One ear was completely folded back, like it was flipped inside out. The weight of hopelessness blanketed down around me. None of the people on the street seemed to notice the tiny orange feline.

Somehow I managed to stand up again, directly disobeying the bus driver.

"Mrs. Foster!" I cried.

Every single person on the bus stopped talking and looked at me. Waiting.

"A cat. There's a cat in the drain," I stammered. "If we don't help him, he'll drown." I held out a shaking hand and pointed.

The bus driver, to my amazement, did not yell at me. Nor did the other kids laugh at me. Instead, Mrs. Foster pulled the bus to the side of the busy road.

"Children," she said sternly. "No one is to leave this bus."

Then the woman rushed out into the traffic and rain. She sloshed across the street to the drain as we all watched in silence. Even the boys looked concerned. No one was laughing. I noticed that I wasn't the only one crying.

With one quick movement, Mrs. Foster grabbed the cat and pulled him into the safety of her arms. She cradled the terrified, clawing creature, removed her own coat to wrap him in it, and then she raced back to the bus. We all cheered until she motioned for us to be quiet.

"We'll have to look for his owners to see if he has a family already," Mrs. Foster said, as she handed me the sopping bundle.

"I know," I stammered.

"I'll help you," the girl sitting in the front seat whispered to me.

"Me too," came another voice, then another and another.

The other kids did help; we put flyers up all over town, one girl's dad put an advertisement in the paper, and we contacted the local animal shelters, veterinarians and pet stores. That means I was forced to talk to a lot of people, both kids and adults. There was no room for shyness and fear. To my surprise, I slowly gained more confidence in myself and made friends with some of the kids who had helped me. We never did find anyone to claim that cat, so he became a cherished member of my family.

Sure, I was still a pretty good kid after that day, but I learned to speak up, to overcome my shyness. I also learned to say a little prayer and then go for it when something really matters.

~Laura Andrade
Chicken Soup for the Girl's Soul

Good Neighbors

The old house behind ours was deserted now. My neighbors, the elderly couple who had lived there for many years, had died within a year of each other. Their children and grandchildren had gathered, grieved and gone.

But looking out my kitchen window one morning, I saw we still had "neighbors." Two white cats had made their way up the back steps of the old house to sit in the sun on the back porch. Their favorite overstuffed chair was gone. Everything was gone. Even from my kitchen window I could see they were pitifully thin. So, I thought, no one is going to claim the cats. They've been left to starve. They'll never leave that old place. They're as shy as their owners were.

I knew they'd never even been inside a house. Even during bitter cold winters, they lived outside. Once, when the female cat had kittens, a dog had killed them. After that the mama cat had her kittens in the attic of the 100-year-old house, entering through a hole in the tin roof. Several times the kittens fell down into the small space between the walls. Once my neighbor told me, "We worked most all afternoon, but we finally got the kittens out. They would have starved to death."

I sighed, looking at the hungry cats sitting on the back porch. A familiar battle began inside me. Part of me wanted desperately to run to the cats. Another part of me wanted to turn away and never look at the starving cats again. It was frustrating to be a forty-year-old mother and still want to pick up stray animals. When I reached twenty-five, then thirty, then surely by thirty-five, I had assumed I would outgrow my obsession with abandoned animals. Now I knew that it was only becoming worse with the years.

Sighing again, I wiped my hands on my apron, grabbed two packages of cat food and headed for the old house. The cats darted beneath the porch as I approached. I crawled part of the way under the house, which sat on concrete blocks, and called, "Here, kitties." I saw four slanted, bright eyes gleaming at me. I could see it would be a long time before I would be able to become friendly with these neighbors.

For several months, I fed the cats this way. One day the mother cat came cautiously toward me and rubbed her face against my hand for a brief moment; then fear sprang into her eyes and she darted away. But after that she met me at the fence at five each day. The other cat would scamper away and hide in the bushes, waiting for me to leave. I decided the white male was probably the female cat's son. I always talked to them as I put out their food, calling them by the names I had given them—Mama and Brother.

One day as Mama rubbed slowly against my leg with her eyes almost shut in contentment, she purred for the first time. My hand didn't reach out, not yet, but my heart did. After that she often rubbed against me and allowed me to stroke her—even before she touched the food. Brother, reluctantly and stiff-necked, allowed me to touch him occasionally; but he always endured my affection, never fully receiving it.

The cats grew fat. One day, I saw Mama kitty on my patio. "Mama kitty," I whispered. She had never come into my yard before. My own cats would never permit that—and yet, here she was. "Good for you, Mama," I said to myself. Suddenly she leaped up into the air, and I thought for a moment that she was choking. Then she seemed to be chasing an object rapidly across the patio. For perhaps the first time in her life, Mama kitty was playing. I watched her toss an acorn into the air and leap after it. My cats came lurking toward the patio door to try to hiss Mama kitty away. She only looked at them and continued playing with the acorn in the sun. Brother sat on the fence, as usual, waiting for supper.

That summer Mama kitty had kittens again—in the attic. She came to my back door to get me. The Realtor had given me the keys to the empty house in case of emergency. I went to the house with the cat and crawled somewhat reluctantly into the dark attic, ignoring the spiders, dust, heat and rattling sounds that I suspected were mice. Finally, I located the three kittens. Brother stood guard over them. I brought the kittens down and fixed a box for them in the empty front bedroom of the old house. Mama kitty wasn't too content with my moving her kittens, but she let them stay—for a while, anyway.

A week later, human neighbors showed up! Unexpectedly, another family moved into the house. Their moving frightened Mama kitty and she returned her kittens to the only safety she knew—the dark, terribly hot attic.

I quickly went over to introduce myself and explained to the family who had moved in about Mama kitty. They gave me permission to go into their attic and rescue the kittens. But I discovered Mama kitty had moved them to another spot. The old attic was a maze of hiding places, and I couldn't find them.

Three times I went back to look, apologizing to the new tenants each time. Three times I was unsuccessful. Back at home, I would look out my window at the tin roof of the house. I could see the heat rising off it. The outside temperature stood in the upper nineties. The kittens couldn't possibly survive.

I couldn't let it go; I felt it was my duty to watch over those cats. One morning as I lay in bed, I prayed, "Lord, I'm asking you to get me those kittens out of that attic. I can't find them. I don't see how you can get them out. But just please do it. If you don't, they're going to die." Silly, maybe, but it didn't feel silly to an animal lover like myself. I hopped from my bed and ran to the back door, half expecting to find the kittens there. They weren't there—no sign of Mama or Brother either. Nevertheless, I expected to get the kittens.

I was worried that I was wearing out my welcome with my new neighbors, but I wanted to go over one last time to look for them. When the wife answered the door to find it was me with the same request yet again, she said, without enthusiasm, that I could go up in the attic. Once I got up there, I heard them meowing!

"I'm coming. I'm coming!" I called out, my heart pounding with joy.

The next moment I couldn't figure out what had happened. I seemed to be falling. Plaster broke loose. I wasn't in the dark, hot attic any more, but dangling into the kitchen. I had forgotten to stay on the rafters and had crashed through the ceiling. I climbed back up onto a rafter, only to fall through again in another place.

Thoroughly shaken, I climbed back down. In the kitchen my neighbor and I looked at the damage. I was horrified, and it was clear that I wasn't making the best impression on this woman. Not knowing what else to do, I grabbed her broom and began sweeping. More plaster fell on us and we coughed in the dust. I apologized over and over, babbling that we would have the ceiling fixed. I assured her I would be back over to talk with her husband. She nodded, silently, with her arms folded, and stared at me with seeming disbelief. I hurried home, humiliated.

That night at supper, when I told my family what had happened, they all stared at me silently, the way my new neighbor had. I was close to tears, partly because of the plight of the kittens and also because of my own stupidity.

The next day I went back to the neighbors' to speak to them about the ceiling. I arrived during a meal. The couple's children were eating with them. They all stared at me as they continued eating. I was introduced as "that woman who goes up in the attic all the time and fell through yesterday." I smiled at them all.

The husband looked up at me, still chewing, and said solemnly, "Get my gun, Ma."

For one horrible moment, my heart froze. Then he broke into a little-boy grin. "Forget it. I'm a carpenter and the ceiling needed repairing, anyway."

I smiled back at him and added, "I came to tell you that I won't be going in your attic any more—ever."

"Okay," he grinned, and I thought I heard his wife sigh.

The next afternoon, our family sat in the living room reading the Sunday paper. Only I wasn't reading, I was praying behind my part of the paper.

"Lord, it seems more hopeless than ever now. But I have no intention of giving up on this request. Give me the kittens, please."

As I prayed, I imagined the kittens in a dark, obscure corner of the attic. I knew almost for certain that Mama kitty had moved them again. Then I imagined a large, gentle hand lifting them up and bringing them down into light and cooler air. I saw it in my mind, over and over, as I prayed. Suddenly, I thought I could actually hear the kittens' tiny, helpless mews.

Silly, I told myself. Your imagination goes wild when you pray.

Jerry put down the sports page; the children looked up from the comics. We all listened quietly, almost without breathing. "Mew, mew, mew." It was real!

The doorbell rang and we all ran for it. I got there first and there stood my neighbor, cobwebs in his hair, dust on his overalls, and the impish little-boy grin on his lean face. We all looked down and there, cradled in his hands, were the kittens.

"Lady, you won't have to look any more for 'em. I found 'em for you."

This time Mama kitty let her brood stay where I put them, in our small storeroom, just off the carport. We found excellent, cat-loving homes for the fat, playful kittens. And I found a permanent solution to the attic/kitten problem. I had Mama kitty spayed.

That was over a year ago. Brother still sits cautiously on my backyard fence, cold and often hungry. I keep trying with him, but he's obviously still skeptical about my neighborly good will.

Not Mama kitty. Now she comes right into the kitchen to eat from my other cats' dishes! She rubs against my leg when I let her in. On cold nights she sleeps curled up in a kitchen chair. And often she sits and watches me type. At first, my cats hissed, growled and fumed. Eventually, they just gave up and accepted Mama kitty.

Now when I look out my window at that old house, I have to smile. It's good to see lights on in the kitchen and children's toys in the yard. The new occupants and I have become pretty close. It's not hard to break the ice — once you've broken the ceiling.

~Marion Bond West
Chicken Soup for the Pet Lover's Soul

Loving Our Cats

Time-Share Cats

It is in the nature of cats to do a certain amount of unescorted roaming.
~Adlai Stevenson

Mayor Morris

The language of friendship is not words but meanings.
~Henry David Thoreau

In his younger days, our cat Morris, now sixteen years old, was the mayor of our neighborhood. A stray I adopted from our local animal shelter when he was about a year old, Morris settled into life as an apartment dweller quite easily, content to give up scavenging for meals and dodging dogs and cars for food from a can and a sunny square of carpet to nap on. Yet as happy as he was to have a home, Morris never completely gave up his love of the outdoors. He would sit for hours by the open bedroom window in our apartment, his nose pressed to the screen, sniffing the air and watching the activity in the park three stories down. At first, I thought he wanted to be out in the fresh air and sunshine, but soon, I realized that it was the hustle and bustle of the outside world that he missed.

When my husband and I moved to our first home — a red-brick row house on a tiny street in Philadelphia — Morris would sit with us on our stoop or lounge in our miniscule front yard greeting the neighbors and holding court. In the spring, he'd sit on our elderly neighbor's stoop, a pace or two from our own door, supervising her attempts to plant flowers in her patch of dirt.

On Halloween, he'd wait at the front door for the trick-or-treaters, his amber eyes glinting in the candlelight from the jack-o'-lanterns. And when our daughter started walking, he'd station himself on the sidewalk in front of the house, keeping a watchful eye on her as she clattered past him, up and down the street, behind her push toys. Morris never seemed to want to venture more than a few feet from his own front door.

A few years later, expecting twins and suddenly needing much more space, we bought a house in a nearby suburb, on a quiet street that wound around in an elongated oval, beginning and ending at the top of the hill. The only traffic was the morning and evening rush of a half-dozen cars taking neighbors to and from work, and the mail and UPS vans making their occasional deliveries.

One midsummer morning, when we had been living there a few months, I walked to the end of our driveway to collect the newspaper, Morris trotting at my heels.

"Is that your cat?" someone called, as I bent to retrieve the papers.

I straightened up. A trim woman in her fifties wearing bright-pink walking shorts and a sleeveless button-down shirt was crossing the lawn toward me. I knew she lived in the house to the right of ours with her husband and a twenty-something-year-old son, but I had not yet met her. I had not met many of our neighbors since I had been closeted in the house for most of the late spring and early summer, first on bed rest, then taking care of my newborns.

"Yes," I said as she stepped onto my driveway. "This is Morris. And I'm Meg. It's nice to finally meet you."

"It's nice to meet you, too," she said, introducing herself and shaking my hand. "And it's nice to know your name," she said, squatting to scratch Morris behind his ears. "My husband will be happy, too," she said, gazing up at me. "Now he'll know what to call him," she said.

My face must have shown my confusion because she laughed.

"My husband and your cat — Morris — have breakfast together on our patio every morning," she explained, standing up. "One morning just after you moved in, my husband went out with his coffee and the newspaper and found Morris sitting in one of the chairs. They had a lovely chat. Now, Morris waits for him on the patio every morning. My husband reads the paper to him, and they discuss world events, don't you Morris?"

Morris had apparently made more friends in the neighborhood than I had in the few months we'd been living there. Every morning he'd meet our neighbor on his back patio for coffee and conversation. Then he'd spend some time playing with the poodles in the house to the left, sitting in the grass at the edge of our driveway just beyond the boundary of their invisible fence, while the dogs ran back and forth, barking and wagging their tails.

When the fall came, he began ambling to the foot of our driveway every afternoon to wait for the school buses to drop the neighborhood kids at the top of the street. He'd greet each kid as they came down the hill past our house, accepting pats and scratches behind his ears. And on Halloween, he took up his place next to the pumpkins and greeted the trick-or-treaters.

Shortly before Thanksgiving every year, our neighbors to the right would travel to Florida, where they spent the winter. Morris took this as a sign to retreat into the house for the winter. In April, when the weather grew warm again, our neighbors would return, and Morris would resume his daily round of social activities. But one spring, our neighbors didn't return. Instead, a for-sale sign appeared in front of the house. Our neighbors had decided to stay in Florida, their son told us when he came by one afternoon to check on the house.

"Oh, by the way," he said, getting into his car, "my dad said to say hi to your cat. He really misses their conversations."

I knew Morris missed those conversations, too. He still waited on the patio every morning for his friend to come out for breakfast.

The house sold quickly, to a Korean family with two teenage daughters and an elderly grandmother. They were friendly neighbors. The girls always stopped to talk to our children when they were playing outside, and the parents would wave and chat for a few minutes whenever we happened to be picking up our newspapers or getting into our cars at the same time. But the elderly grandmother never said a word, ducking her head and looking the other way the few times we'd seen her in the front yard. I'd overheard her granddaughters speaking to her in Korean and suspected that she didn't know any English.

One summer morning, I was watering the plants on our back deck when I heard the soft quavering voice of the elderly grandmother on her patio below. She was speaking quickly and quietly, a steady stream of words in Korean. Occasionally, she'd pause as if asking a question, but I heard no voice answering back. She must be talking to herself, I thought. Quietly, I peered over the deck railing. She was sitting at the wrought-iron table with a cup of tea. Morris, in the chair next to her, was listening intently as she talked to him.

The mayor of the neighborhood had done it again! Morris had a new breakfast companion, and our elderly Korean neighbor had a new friend.

~M. L. Charendoff
Chicken Soup for the Cat Lover's Soul

13

The Cat Who Knew How To Live

If some people didn't tell you,
you'd never know they'd been away on a vacation.
~Kin Hubbard

Cookie was a working cat. He lived in a New York grocery store that he kept mouse-free. Cookie was no slouch, and there wasn't a self-respecting mouse that would dare cross his path.

After patrolling the nooks and crannies of the store at night, he had the run of the neighborhood where he would spend his days wandering. As evening approached, you could almost set your watch by his return to the store. He would arrive promptly five minutes before the store closed.

One cool October evening, Cookie disappeared.

The store's owners and their children searched for him in vain.

The kids were brokenhearted. As autumn turned to winter, the snow began to fall, covering the streets. Everyone worried about Cookie, alone in the freezing weather. "How will he survive?" the kids asked.

Miracle of miracles, the following spring, Cookie magically reappeared, looking healthy and clean. Everyone figured Cookie must have been sowing his wild oats in another neighborhood.

Everything went back to normal at the store. Cookie once more checked all the nooks and crannies of the store to make certain there had been no unwelcome visitors while he was away. He did his job perfectly until autumn, when Cookie once again disappeared!

Once more there was considerable consternation by his owners and their children. How would Cookie weather the winter snows and the freezing cold?

The next spring, just when the baby leaves started to form on the trees, Cookie returned again!

Cookie's owners began asking neighbors for any information as to where he might have been. The kids asked their friends if any of them knew where Cookie went during the freezing winter months.

No one seemed to know.

Finally, one of the children rang the bell of an older couple who lived in a private house near the grocery store.

"You say, a big black cat?" the woman asked. "With white little paws? Oh, yes. My husband and I hated to see him out in the cold. So I gave him a saucer of warm milk. After that he hung around our house almost every day. But we were going to Florida for the winter, as we do every year. I felt so bad about leaving that poor little creature here with no one to take care of him in the freezing weather. So we bought a cat carrier and we've been taking him to Florida with us every year for the past two years. He seems to like it down there. Has loads of friends. But, between you and me, I think he prefers New York in the summer. I think he has a girlfriend up here."

~Arnold Fine
Chicken Soup for the Soul Celebrates Cats

14

A Tale of Two Kitties

They say that cats have nine lives. Well, I don't know about that, but I do know one cat who had two lives. His name was Smokey; at least, that is what I called him. He was a gray-striped tom with a pink nose, four white paws and a silky-furred right ear that folded over at the tip. I found him shivering in our garage as a kitten when I was nine years old and kept him hidden in my bedroom for a week until I was sure that my mom would let me keep him. A stranger might not have thought him much to look at, but, to me, he was the cutest kitten in the world. My mother used to joke about how I was the only girl in Indian Hills, Colorado, who would fall in love with a "dog-eared" cat.

By the time I was eleven, Smokey had pretty much established his own daily routine of returning home in time for dinner, after which he'd curl up on my bed. When I'd slip beneath the covers for the night, he'd move close to my face, nudge his head right under my chin, and, snuggled safe and warm, purr like a small-appliance motor. I never had a bad dream when Smokey slept beside me. He liked my three brothers, but it was obvious that he was a one-kid cat. And I was his girl. Or so I thought.

One night in July, Smokey didn't come home. I was upset, but my mother assured me that it wasn't unusual for a cat to wander off for an adventure now and then. I spent the next few days searching for him, calling his name and expecting to see him any minute, but there was no sign of him. By the end of the week, we were all upset.

My mother agreed that I should go to the general store and put up a missing-cat notice with Smokey's picture. I picked out a photo of him lying sphinx-like across my pillow, his bent ear and white paws clearly visible. As I completed the sign, describing his coloring and distinguishing marks, it was hard to keep from crying. My brother Dave went with me to the store to post the sign. Once it was up, we stood back to see if it was in a good spot. Sure enough, it was—right next to a notice for another missing cat named Ranger. In fact, the only difference between the two cats was their names; their descriptions were identical.

I wrote down the phone number on the other sign and called the moment we got home. The girl who answered said that her missing cat, Ranger, always stayed out at night and came home in the morning, but hadn't shown up in a week. I told her that my cat, Smokey—same coloring, same bent right ear—went out in the morning and came home in the evening, and that he hadn't shown up in a week. It was just too much of a coincidence to be a coincidence. With an unspoken pang of betrayal, we both conceded that her Ranger and my Smokey were one and the same cat—and that he had been living a double life! So much for a one-kid cat. But two-timing tom or not, both of us loved him, and he was still missing.

The girl's name was Evelyn, and we arranged to meet the following day. She was a year older than I, which was probably why we hadn't known each other, even though she lived just a quarter-mile away. She brought over her pictures of Ranger, and I brought out my pictures of Smokey. We spent the afternoon sharing stories about our "dog-eared, one-kid cat," alternately sniffling and laughing at the similarity of his two-household antics. By dinnertime, we'd gone through more than half a box of Kleenex and had become best friends.

Together, Evelyn and I handmade flyers for our missing cat ("answers to the names of Smokey and Ranger"), passed them out all around town, and kept each other from giving up hope by recounting amazing stories of lost animals who'd miraculously found their way home after years. But, by the end of August, even these took on a hollow ring.

Then, a week before school started, we got a phone call that seemed too good to be true. It was from a woman in Golden, about ten miles away, saying she'd seen our flyer in a gas station and believed she had our cat. Her son had found him about a month ago on the side of the road, bloody and near death from an animal attack, and she'd been nursing him back to health. She said that she'd named him Marker because of his bent ear.

My mother drove Evelyn and me to Golden that same afternoon, cautioning us not to get too excited in case the cat wasn't ours. How many dog-eared cats could there be? We wondered, but really didn't want to know. Squeezing each other's hand tightly, we followed the woman into the house where she said Marker was resting. But, the moment we saw him, we had no doubt that Marker wasn't Marker: He was Smokey; he was Ranger. He was ours—and he was alive! His nonstop purring all the way home told us that he was as happy to be found as we were to find him.

Smokey/Ranger continued to live his two lives—dividing his days and nights and love between Evelyn's house and ours—until advancing age and illness got the better of him. When his health worsened, we knew the kindest thing to do was to set him free from his suffering. Evelyn and I were both with him when he died. He seemed to know that we were both there—stroking his white paws, caressing his bent ear—and he drifted from us peacefully, purring to the end.

No, Smokey wasn't the one-kid cat I once thought he was. He was just the best cat that ever was.

P.S. Evelyn, who's remained my best friend for all these years, says the same thing about Ranger.

~June Torrence as told to Hester J. Mundis
Chicken Soup for the Cat Lover's Soul

Double Duty

Our perfect companions never have fewer than four feet.
~Colette

As a member of a "dog family," I had long been conditioned to believe that cats simply didn't possess the ability or desire to be loving companions. This belief was so deeply ingrained that, while I didn't actually dislike cats, I found them, for the most part, uninteresting.

Arriving home from work one afternoon, I discovered a cat at my doorstep. I ignored him, but apparently he was not offended, because he was there again the following day.

"I'll pet you," I told him, "but there's no way you're coming in."

Then one night soon after, as the rain beat down and thunder clapped, I heard a faint meow. I couldn't take it anymore; I became a cat owner.

My new roommate, now named Shotzy, quickly became more than just a stray cat to feed. I liked the way his soft purring greeted me every morning and the way he nudged his head against my leg when I came home each day. His playful antics made me laugh, and soon Shotzy seemed more like a longtime friend than a pet I hadn't really wanted.

Although I suspected Shotzy had been an outdoor cat for a good portion of his life, he seemed perfectly content to stay inside, except for one remarkable exception. As if an alarm had gone off, at about six o'clock every night he'd cry to go out. Then, almost exactly one hour later, he'd be back. He did this for several months before I finally discovered what he had been up to.

One day a neighbor who knew about Shotzy showing up at my doorstep told me she thought the cat might belong to an elderly woman who lived down the street. Worried that I had mistakenly adopted someone's pet, I took Shotzy to the woman's house the next day.

When a white-haired woman opened the door, Shotzy bolted from my arms, ran into the house and made himself at home in a big recliner. The woman just threw her head back and laughed, saying, "Jimmy always did love his chair."

My heart sank—my Shotzy was obviously her Jimmy.

I explained I had taken him in and only discovered the day before that he may have already had a home. Again, the old woman chuckled. She invited me in and explained that the cat did not belong to her.

"But, I thought you called him Jimmy," I questioned.

The woman, who said her name was Mary, explained that Jimmy was her husband's name. He had died about a year before, just a few months after being diagnosed with cancer.

Before Jimmy died, he and Mary would eat dinner at five o'clock every night.

Afterward, they would retire to the living room, Jimmy to his favorite chair, to talk about the day's events. The couple had followed that routine every night for the sixty years they were married. After Jimmy's death, with no other family nearby, Mary said she just felt lost. And more than anything, she missed their nightly after-dinner talks.

Then one night a stray cat meowed demandingly at her screen door. When she cracked open the door to shoo him away, he ran straight to Jimmy's chair and made himself comfortable, as if he had lived there forever.

Mary, who had never had a pet in her life, found herself smiling at the animal. She gave him a little milk and then he cuddled on her lap. She talked to him about her life, but mostly about Jimmy. At about seven o'clock, at which time she normally turned on the TV and made herself some hot tea, the creature slipped off her lap and went to the door. At six o'clock the next evening, the cat was back. Soon, Shotzy and Mary had their own routine.

"Now, I believe in the Good Lord," Mary told me. "I don't know about all that reincarnation stuff, but sometimes it feels just like I'm talking to Jimmy when that little cat is here. I know that sounds strange, and I guess what's important is that the cat is a real comfort to me. But it's interesting to think on, all the same."

So Mary and I continued to share Shotzy. At my house, he revealed to me the many daily joys that come with living with a cat. At Mary's, his presence served to fill the six o'clock hour with happy companionship.

Our marvelous cat seemed to have an uncanny knack for always being in the right place at the right time.

~Lisa Hurt
Chicken Soup for the Cat and Dog Lover's Soul

Chapter
3

Loving Our Cats

Learning to Love
"The Cat"

Beware of people who dislike cats.
~Irish proverb

16

Confessions of a Cat Hater— Who Got Lucky

I remember most clearly watching our daughter carry a young kitten down the path leading to my office. Why, I wondered, would Jenny be bringing a cat to me? She knew quite well that I was not fond of cats. Only recently, we'd had an argument over her decision to bring a cat into the family. I opposed her—and lost. My grandfather disliked cats, my father disliked cats, and, ever the obedient son, I learned at an early age that cats were sinister, evil and altogether disreputable animals. They had no legitimate place in the homes of civilized people, I thought.

My question was quickly answered. Jenny had rescued the cat from a group of stick-wielding young ruffians at a nearby trailer park. At first glance, one might think she'd been too late. The cat looked awful. He was emaciated and had numerous sores on his body, as well as an injured jaw. Obviously, he needed medical attention.

As Jenny held the cat, she reassured him that everything would be all right. And then she said, "Daddy will take you to see Dr. Waggoner."

"Jenny," I said, "you know I don't like cats. Get someone else to take him to the vet."

"I don't have time, Daddy. I'm already late for class." (She was a music student at a local university.) "Oh, Daddy," she continued, almost tearfully, "you don't want him to suffer, do you?"

"Well, no," I replied. (I might not have liked cats, but I wasn't a monster!) "All right," I said reluctantly, "I'll take him to see Dr. Waggoner. But when I bring him back, you will be his caregiver. And when he has recovered, I want you to find a home for him." It was a done deal. Or so I thought.

Dr. Waggoner was acquainted with my feelings about cats—or, more accurately, my lack thereof. After expressing amazement that I had been chosen to bring this unfortunate feline in for his ministrations, he examined the animal, cleaning his wounds and making a few minor adjustments to his injured jaw. Then he gave me some medication for the cat, with instructions to administer it orally two times a day. He said the cat was lucky to be alive, very lucky. "Lucky," I repeated, and the name stuck.

I had never administered medication to a cat before and was surprised by the strength of Lucky's jaws, despite his injury. On my first attempt, he clamped them shut tight, in effect saying, "I ain't taking no medicine for nobody." Fortunately, anticipating this, Dr. Waggoner had shown me how to apply pressure to both sides of the jaw simultaneously, thus forcing the cat's mouth open. As the window of opportunity appeared, I stuck the dropper in the little beast's mouth, squeezed the bulb, and the job was done until the next time.

Day followed day, and I saw very little change in Lucky's attitude. Finally, after ten days, I brought him back to Dr. Waggoner for a follow-up exam. I was dismayed to learn that we needed to continue the treatment for another ten days. This was not what I wanted to hear, but I had gotten the procedure down, and I thought that, just maybe, Lucky's resistance was becoming a little less savage.

Sometime during the second ten-day period, I noticed a few changes. Lucky would occasionally jump up on my computer desk and lie down on the papers that I happened to be working on. Then I noticed that, at feeding time, he would walk around my ankles and purr very softly. One day, he jumped up on the back of my chair, where he curled up and actually went to sleep for a short while.

As the second ten-day period reached its end, I asked Jenny (who seemed to be suspiciously overwhelmed with her work schedule during this time) if she had found a nice home for Lucky. "Not yet," she said. "I'm still looking." Then, casting an eye on Lucky snoozing comfortably on my desk, she said, "It looks to me as though Lucky thinks he has found just the right home."

"Not with me," I said. "You made a promise when I agreed to take him to Dr. Waggoner; now, keep that promise and go find this cat a nice home." But Jenny realized what Lucky had already decided—and I had yet to find out: Those four paws of his were right where they wanted to be.

So, true to the wily personality of the cat, Lucky had worked his way into my life and made himself a very important part of my routine. Evidence of this came as I recognized that I actually had started looking for him at the window and listening for his greeting—a very loud purr as he approached the small office building where I worked and he was determined to live. I even built a small window perch for him (carpeted, no less) and placed a heavy wire screen outside to protect him from the neighborhood dogs. This also made an escape more difficult, if he ever entertained such an idea. These were not steps taken by someone who hated cats. I didn't realize it at the moment, but, soon, it began to sink in.

It sank in for sure (and forever) when I brought him to the vet for the last checkup with my University of Florida colors—orange and blue ribbons—proudly tied to the door of his pet carrier. That's when Dr. Waggoner confessed that Lucky had not strictly needed the second sequence of medication. "Lucky was doing well enough," he explained. "You just needed a little extra time for the bonding process to take hold."

~Marshall Powers as told to Hester Mundis
Chicken Soup for the Cat Lover's Soul

17

Father Meets Cat

My father hated cats. Or so he told us when my sister and I begged for one when we were kids. If we persisted, he catalogued all their bad traits. Cats were lazy. Cats ripped furniture. Cats required too much care. The list went on and on.

After I graduated from the university, I moved to another city. As soon as I unpacked, I headed to the local humane society and adopted a black and brown striped tabby named Tiger. My father harrumphed at the news and predicted a dire end for all my furniture. Tiger must have overheard the conversation because she set out to prove him right.

My father harrumphed even louder the first time he encountered Tiger. The meeting did not go well. As I pointed out to him while I bandaged his hand, drumming one's fingers on the edge of a chair could be seen as a game if you're a cat.

"Only if you're an attack cat," he muttered under his breath. He glared at Tiger who turned her back on him and proceeded to wash her paws.

From that day on, my father and Tiger gave each other a wide berth. My mother, on the other hand, sent Tiger birthday cards and posted pictures of her on their fridge, much to my father's disgust.

I replaced my sofa and got a second cat. A lovely gray and salmon color, she came complete with parasites. Although I officially named her Salmonella, I called her Sammy for short. I waited a month before breaking the news to my father. This time, he snorted in addition to harrumphing.

On his next visit, when he thought I was downstairs, I overheard him talking to Sammy outside my bedroom. "Aren't you a pretty cat. What nice soft fur you have." From the sounds of her purring, I'm fairly sure their encounter involved some serious tummy-rubbing, too.

Over dinner, I asked him what he thought of the newest addition to the family. "She's okay," he said, "for a cat." Then he quickly changed the subject.

A week later, my mother told me my father, whose name was Sam, proudly informed all his friends and relatives I named the "good" cat after him. I didn't have the heart to tell him differently.

During his visits over the next couple of years, Sam and Sammy forged a bond.

Once I thought he was sufficiently softened up, I began a campaign to get my parents their own cat. I mentioned how nice it felt to come home to a warm, furry body that licked your hand in appreciation. I also quoted studies that proved having an animal provided health benefits.

No matter what I said, my father countered with a reason not to get a cat. When my mother weighed in on my side, he gave her a choice: get a cat or continue to travel. With both her daughters and granddaughters living out of town, she conceded defeat. She would have to get her dose of cat-cuddling during her visits to me.

Although my father thought he'd won the war, I knew the battle had just begun.

Five years later, my father was diagnosed with kidney disease and began dialysis. I decided that would be the perfect time to get my parents a cat so they would have something to focus on besides his illness. Since their traveling days were over, he couldn't use that argument anymore. As far as I was concerned, it was a win-win situation. I would win the war, and they would win—a cat.

I visited on Mother's Day and informed them that my mother's gift would be a cat. My mother beamed. My father snorted. I pointed out that the cat was for her, not him, and he could ignore the animal all he wanted. He snorted a second time and marched out of the room.

Two hours and one hundred and ninety dollars later, Puss Puss came home, accompanied by a red nylon carrying case, a litter box, forty pounds of kitty litter, a brush, four different kinds of cat food, three toys and a scratching post. My mother and I set up the litter box, showed Puss Puss where it was, and watched as she explored the basement.

Loud footsteps announced my father's arrival. He stared at the cat for a minute and proclaimed, "The first time she scratches the couch or me, she's out the door." Satisfied he had made his point, he glared at me, turned around and went back upstairs.

Puss Puss, unaware of how tenuous her welcome was, purred her approval of her new home. After playing with her for a while, my mother and I decided to let her investigate by herself, and we went upstairs for coffee. Half an hour later, I headed down to check on her. No cat.

I called her name. I got on my hands and knees and peered under furniture. I rattled a box of food. Still no cat.

I raced upstairs, thinking she might have sneaked up unnoticed. I checked the living room and dining room. Nothing. I went to the second floor and checked my old bedroom and my sister's. Empty.

That only left one room. As I neared my parents' bedroom, I saw my father stretched out in his La-Z-Boy chair—with the cat curled up in his lap. He was so engrossed in petting her that he didn't hear me. I tiptoed away and told my mother that everything was all right. In fact, it was perfect.

For the next three years, Puss Puss was my father's constant companion. Every time I visited, he told me the same thing: "That cat is great company—for your mother."

Like I said, a win-win situation.

~Harriet Cooper
Chicken Soup for the Father & Daughter Soul

A Cat Named Turtle

*There are few things in life more heartwarming
than to be welcomed by a cat.*
~Tay Hohoff

I didn't grow up with cats. Or with dogs. We once harbored the dalmatian of a vacationing aunt and uncle. If all had gone well, we'd have gotten our own dog.

But all did not go well. My brother refused to clean up after the dog, and soon we were permanently critter-free. Not that my mother minded. Having been scratched by a cat when she was little, she feared anything that moved too quickly on too many legs. My father, a city boy, had no experience with animals and less interest in them.

But I married a cat lover. In his meager walk-up flat in New York City, Roy had enjoyed the company of several marvelous felines, one of them a waif from the subway. I listened to his fond recollections in the same way I heard his tales of some other experiences: They were interesting, even compelling, but nothing I thought I'd ever experience myself.

And then we moved to Vermont and found the cats on our land. Or they found us — and it was really their land. They were feral, having lived in the wild for who-knows-how-long. We extended a hand literally and figuratively to newly named Mama Cat, Honey Puss, Herbert and Sylvester, giving them food on the deck, shelter in the carport and veterinary care for the occasional ailment. Now we realized we should have neutered them, too.

We first saw Turtle trotting along behind her mother, in a parade that included several chubby kittens making their way from the blackberry thicket, across the driveway and into the pine trees. She reappeared briefly a year later, unmistakably the same tortoiseshell. The year afterward, she visited often. I named her when I didn't quite like her; she was nervous, pushy, eating Honey Puss's food. Turtle seemed a good name for a tortoiseshell, especially one who didn't yet have my affection.

I was already reading about feral cats. The universal opinion was that unless a feral cat becomes used to people very early in life, taming the cat is virtually impossible. But nobody told Turtle, who grew ever more comfortable with us. She'd fall onto her back with a thud, inviting us to pet her lovely white belly. She'd linger on the deck with our guests, on summer evenings, sampling one lap after another. Then, as soon as everyone had gone, she'd trot off into the darkness.

Could we bring her inside? Roy's on-again-off-again allergy to cats suddenly returned. But she wouldn't want to come inside anyway, I proclaimed.

Or would she? My office, on the second floor, looks out upon our hillside. Many times I'd put down my work to gaze out the window, and I'd see Turtle staring at me, her wide golden eyes and her dear, crooked little face—haphazardly splotched in black and tan—not twenty inches from my own face. Often I heard her talking to me before I saw her.

We were having a new wing constructed, and she found another route to my office one day, staring at me through the side window. Her muddy paw prints on the roofing paper led from my window to the builder's ladder at roof's edge. I was impressed.

She built a nest for herself in the developing new wing, settling into an open carton where the carpenter had tossed his sweaty t-shirt. She was so comfortable here that she barely lifted her head to greet us when we came looking for her. Roy started getting allergy shots.

With the new wing enclosed, Turtle was again outside. But the next time she looked in at my desk, Roy opened the window screen, waited for her to climb in and carried her downstairs. She was purring loudly. She walked through the living room, poking into all the little places: a cupboard, the bottom of a small bookshelf. She seemed oblivious to us, and indeed we were as dumb as chairs. After a few moments, Roy took her outside.

Later that day, she was sitting near him on the deck, when he got up and moved toward the kitchen. She reached the door ahead of him and scrambled inside. She didn't mind being taken out again. I didn't mind either. She might want to be inside (I now conceded the possibility), but did I want her? Wouldn't a feral cat, even a friendly one, shred everything to tatters? Wouldn't she scratch us at the slightest provocation? Wouldn't she yowl all night?

The deciding moment arrived after I'd been away for a few days. Turtle had stayed at the bend in the driveway for most of my absence. But barely fifteen minutes after my return, she was at the kitchen door! When Roy opened the door to bring her some food, she pushed past him into the kitchen and headed straight for me. No curiosity about the house this time. No interest in the food. She jumped into my lap, readjusted her weight and purred—the kind of purring you could hear from twenty feet away. She missed me! She missed me! That was it. I was ready to share my house with her.

Very soon it was also Turtle's house as she figured out the best spot on our bed (between us, lengthwise) and the sunniest corner of our living room. She had a lot to learn. How to sprawl across my in-basket. How to awaken us for her breakfast. How to keep the house free of the tiny mice that sneak inside every autumn, when the cold air ruffles their rodential dispositions. How to launch a steady stream of complaint at the snow. How to stand guard at the bathtub until I could be meowed safely from the water. How to settle her weight on precisely the document I might be reading from, or typing from, or writing on. The litter box? A snap. She managed that in half a day.

I had a lot to learn, too. And to unlearn, from my mother's prejudices. But with Turtle's help, this cat was soon my dear companion, gentle and wise, considerate and affectionate. Roy was delighted to see how I loved her and how she loved us back. She became the subject of several chapters in the book I wrote on feral cats, and I wish she could have understood the gifts and letters she got from adoring readers. Roy however was convinced she understood everything we said, or even thought; he was sure she could read our minds. Once, he was only thinking of her, and was startled to hear her sudden purring from a nearby chair.

She knew plenty, our Turtle. In parts of the British Isles, it is considered a good omen when a tortoiseshell cat comes into the house. The tortoiseshell is considered special. But Turtle was special beyond all other specialness. The sweetest pussycat we've ever known. And the smartest. Never a pest. Never seeking attention when we were heavily preoccupied with work or chores. But there in a flash whenever a lap became available, whenever a head hit a pillow. She was very special. I knew it, Roy knew it, and Turtle knew that we knew it.

She lived with us for ten sweet years, until kidney disease claimed her, and she is buried just up from the bend in the driveway, under a stone that has her coloring. We see the stone from our kitchen.

I bless the day that she decided to chance it with us. She knew so much more than I did, about the important things. She knew enough to make that running leap that day into my house, my lap, my heart.

~Ellen Perry Berkeley
Chicken Soup for the Cat and Dog Lover's Soul

The Ugliest Cat in the World

Beauty is not in the face; beauty is a light in the heart.
~Kahlil Gibran

The first time I ever saw Smoky, she was on fire! My three children and I had arrived at the dump outside our Arizona desert town to burn the weekly trash. As we approached the smoldering pit, we heard the most mournful cries of a cat entombed in the smoking rubble.

Suddenly a large cardboard box, which had been wired shut, burst into flames and exploded. With a long, piercing meow, the animal imprisoned within shot into the air like a flaming rocket and dropped into the ash-filled crater.

"Oh, Mama, do something!" three-year-old Jaymee cried as she and Becky, age six, leaned over the smoking hole.

"It can't possibly still be alive," said Scott, fourteen. But the ashes moved, and a tiny kitten, charred almost beyond recognition, miraculously struggled to the surface and crawled toward us in agony.

"I'll get her!" Scott yelled. As my son stood knee-deep in ashes and wrapped the kitten in my bandanna, I wondered why it didn't cry from the added pain. Later we learned we had heard its last meow only moments before.

Back at our ranch, we were doctoring the kitten when my husband, Bill, came in, weary from a long day of fence-mending.

"Daddy! We found a burned-up kitty," Jaymee announced.

When he saw our patient, that familiar "Oh, no, not again!" look crossed his face. This wasn't the first time we had greeted him with an injured animal. Though Bill always grumbled, he couldn't bear to see any living creature suffer. So he helped by building cages, perches, pens and splints for the skunks, rabbits and birds we brought home. This was different, however. This was a cat. And Bill, very definitely, did not like cats.

What's more, this was no ordinary cat. Where fur had been, blisters and a sticky black gum remained. Her ears were gone. Her tail was cooked to the bone. Gone were the claws that would have snatched some unsuspecting mouse. Gone were the little paw pads that would have left telltale tracks on the hoods of our dusty cars and trucks. Nothing that resembled a cat was left—except for two huge cobalt-blue eyes begging for help.

What could we do?

Suddenly I remembered our aloe vera plant and its supposed healing power on burns. So we peeled the leaves, swathed the kitten in slimy aloe strips and gauze bandages, and placed her in Jaymee's Easter basket. All we could see was her tiny face, like a butterfly waiting to emerge from its silk cocoon.

Her tongue was severely burned, and the inside of her mouth was so blistered that she couldn't lap, so we fed her milk and water with an eyedropper. After a while, she began eating by herself.

We named the kitten Smoky.

Three weeks later, the aloe plant was bare. Now we coated Smoky with a salve that turned her body a curious shade of green. Her tail dropped off. Not a hair remained—but the children and I adored her.

Bill didn't. And Smoky despised him. The reason? He was a pipe smoker armed with matches and butane lighters that flashed and burned. Every time he lit up, Smoky panicked, knocking over his coffee cup and lamps before fleeing into the open air duct in the spare bedroom.

"Can't I have any peace around here?" he'd groan.

In time, Smoky became more tolerant of the pipe and its owner.

She'd lie on the sofa and glare at Bill as he puffed away. One day he looked at me and chuckled, "Damn cat makes me feel guilty."

By the end of her first year, Smoky resembled a well-used welding glove. Scott was famous among his friends for owning the ugliest pet in the country—probably, the world.

Slowly, oddly, Bill became the one Smoky cared for the most. And before long, I noticed a change in him. He rarely smoked in the house now, and one winter night, to my astonishment, I found him sitting in his chair with the leathery little cat curled up on his lap. Before I could comment, he mumbled a curt, "She's probably cold—no fur, you know."

But Smoky, I reminded myself, liked the touch of cold. Didn't she sleep in front of air ducts and on the cold Mexican-tile floor?

Perhaps Bill was starting to like this strange-looking animal just a bit.

Not everyone shared our feelings for Smoky, especially those who had never seen her. Rumors reached a group of self-appointed animal protectors, and one day one of them arrived at our door.

"I've had numerous calls and letters from so many people," the woman said. "They are concerned about a poor little burned-up cat you have in your house. They say," her voice dropped an octave, "she's suffering. Perhaps it should be put out of its misery?"

I was furious. Bill was even more so. "Burned she was," he said, "but suffering? Look for yourself!"

"Here, kitty," I called. No Smoky. "She's probably hiding," I said, but our guest didn't answer. When I turned and looked at her, the woman's skin was gray, her mouth hung open and two fingers pointed.

Magnified tenfold in all her naked splendor, Smoky glowered at our visitor from her hiding place behind our 150-gallon aquarium. Instead of the "poor little burned-up suffering creature" the woman expected to see, tyrannosaurus Smoky leered at her through the green aquatic haze. Her open jaws exposed saber-like fangs that glinted menacingly in the neon light. Moments later the woman hurried out the door—smiling now, a little embarrassed and greatly relieved.

During Smoky's second year, a miraculous thing happened. She began growing fur. Tiny white hairs, softer and finer than the down on a chick, gradually grew over three inches long, transforming our ugly little cat into a wispy puff of smoke.

Bill continued to enjoy her company, though the two made an incongruous pair—the big weather-worn rancher driving around with an unlit pipe clenched between his teeth, accompanied by the tiny white ball of fluff. When he got out of the truck to check the cattle, he left the air conditioner on maximum-cold for her comfort. Her blue eyes watered, the pink nose ran, but she sat there, unblinking, in ecstasy. Other times, he picked her up, and holding her close against his dênim jacket, took her along.

Smoky was three years old on the day she went with Bill to look for a missing calf. Searching for hours, he left the truck door open whenever he got out to look. The pastures were parched and crisp with dried grasses and tumbleweed. A storm loomed on the horizon, and still no calf. Discouraged, without thinking, Bill reached into his pocket for his lighter and spun the wheel. A spark shot to the ground and, in seconds, the field was on fire.

Frantic, Bill didn't think about the cat. Only after the fire was under control, and the calf found, did he return home and remember.

"Smoky!" he cried. "She must have jumped out of the truck! Did she come home?"

No. And we knew she'd never find her way home from two miles away. To make matters worse, it had started to rain—so hard we couldn't go out to look for her.

Bill was distraught, blaming himself. We spent the next day searching, wishing she could meow for help, and knowing she'd be helpless against predators. It was no use.

Two weeks later, Smoky still wasn't home. We were afraid she was dead by now, for the rainy season had begun, and the hawks, wolves and coyotes had families to feed.

Then came the biggest rainstorm our region had experienced in fifty years. By morning, flood waters stretched for miles, marooning wildlife and cattle on scattered islands of higher ground. Frightened rabbits, raccoons, squirrels and desert rats waited for the water to subside, while Bill and Scott waded knee-deep, carrying bawling calves back to their mamas and safety.

The girls and I were watching intently when suddenly Jaymee shouted, "Daddy! There's a poor little rabbit over there. Can you get it?"

Bill waded to the spot where the animal lay, but when he reached out to help the tiny creature, it seemed to shrink back in fear. "I don't believe it," Bill cried. "It's Smoky!" His voice broke. "Little Smoky!"

My eyes ached with tears when that pathetic little cat crawled into the outstretched hands of the man she had grown to love. He pressed her shivering body to his chest, talked to her softly, and gently wiped the mud from her face. All the while her blue eyes fastened on his with unspoken understanding. He was forgiven.

Smoky came home again. The patience she showed as we shampooed her astounded us. We fed her scrambled eggs and ice cream, and to our joy she seemed to get well.

But Smoky had never really been strong. One morning when she was barely four years old, we found her limp in Bill's chair. Her heart had simply stopped.

As I wrapped her tiny body in one of Bill's red neckerchiefs and placed her in a child's shoe box, I thought about the many things our precious Smoky had taught us—things about trust, affection and struggling against the odds when everything says you can't win. She reminded us that it's not what's outside that counts—it's what's inside, deep in our hearts.

~Penny Porter
Chicken Soup for the Unsinkable Soul

Oscar,
the Garbage Can Kitty

People who don't like cats haven't met the right one yet.
~Deborah A. Edwards, D.V.M.

Oscar was named after the Sesame Street character who lives in a garbage can because that is where we first became acquainted. I was working at a pizza delivery chain and had been assigned garbage duty. While tossing bags into a Dumpster, I heard a faint meow. I began digging through the trash, and several layers down I found a cat—bruised and thin. I wasn't sure if the cat had crawled into the Dumpster to scavenge for food or if he had been put there purposely. Our establishment sat directly behind an apartment complex, and unsupervised and abandoned pets were common.

Back on solid ground, it became evident that the cat had an injured leg. He couldn't put any weight on his right hindquarters. The situation created a dilemma for me. Finances were tight, and I was moving back home to my parents' house—with two cats already in tow. Dad barely tolerated the two established felines. His reaction to another injured stray was sure to be less than receptive.

I took the stray to the vet, hoping to patch him up. After shots and X-rays, the vet discovered the cat had a cracked pelvis. I posted notices, hoping someone would claim the cat or adopt him.

Meanwhile, the response at home was swift and firm: No more cats! Dad insisted I take the cat to the Humane Society immediately.

I protested that the cat would be put to sleep. Luckily, my mother intervened. She agreed the injury would make the cat unadoptable, so we would keep him long enough for his hip to heal. Then he would have to go — no arguments.

Oscar must have somehow understood his situation. He seemed to study the other two cats and their interactions with my father. We suspect he bribed Tanner, our golden retriever, with table scraps in exchange for etiquette lessons. When the other cats were aloof, Oscar was attentive. He came when his name was called, and he would roll over on his back to have his belly scratched. As his injury began to heal, he would jump on the ottoman by my father's favorite chair, and, eventually, into his lap. Initially, Dad pushed Oscar away, but persistence paid off. Soon, Oscar and a muttering Dad shared the chair.

At mealtimes, Oscar would come to sit with us. Positioned on the floor by my father's chair, every so often Oscar would reach up with one paw and tap Dad on the knee. At first, this provoked great irritation and colorful expletives expressed in harsh tones. Oscar, however, refused to be put off. Repetitive knee-taps soon led to semi-covert handouts of choice morsels.

Oscar greeted my father at the top of the stairs every morning and waited for him at the door every evening. My father sometimes ignored Oscar, and, at other times, stepped over him, complaining the whole time. Oscar mastered opening doors by sticking his paw underneath the door and rocking it back and forth until it opened. Soon, he was sleeping in the master bedroom at the foot of the bed. My father was completely disgusted, but couldn't stop the cat from sneaking onto the bed while they were sleeping. Eventually, Dad gave up.

Before long, Oscar, aspiring to his own place at the table during meals, began jumping up into my lap. He was allowed to stay as long as his head remained below table level. Of course, an occasional paw would appear as a reminder of his presence.

Three months passed, and the vet pronounced Oscar healthy and healed. I was heartbroken. How could I take this loving soul away from what had become his home, from the people he trusted? Sick at heart, I brought Oscar home and told my parents what should have been good news: Oscar was a healthy cat with a healed hip. "I'll take him to the Humane Society like I promised," I said dully.

As I turned to put Oscar in the carrier for the trip, my father spoke, uttering three magic words: "Not my cat!"

Oscar is home to stay. He now has his own chair at the table and sleeps—where else?—in the master bedroom between my mother and father. He is their official "grand-kitten" and living proof that deep within the most unlikely heart, there is a cat lover in all of us.

~Kathleen Kennedy
Chicken Soup for the Cat Lover's Soul

21

Kitty Magic

Friendship is a sheltering tree.
~Samuel Taylor Coleridge

After a meeting one night, I felt very tired. Eager to get home and get to sleep, I was approaching my car when I heard mew, mew, mew, mew... Looking under my car, I saw a teeny little kitten, shaking and crying, huddled close to the tire.

I have never had a fondness for cats. I'm a dog person, thank you very much. I grew up with dogs all my young life and cats always bugged me. Kind of creeped me out. I especially hated going into houses that had cat boxes. I wondered if the residents just ignored the awful smell. Plus, cats always seemed to be all over everything—not to mention their hair. And I was semiallergic to them. Suffice it to say, I had never in my life gone out of my way for a cat.

But when I knelt down and saw this scared little red tabby mewing like crazy, something inside urged me to reach out to pick her up. She ran away immediately. I thought, Okay, well, I tried, but as I went to get into my car, I heard the kitten mewing again. That pitiful mewing really pulled at my heart, and I found myself crossing the street to try to find her. I found her and she ran. I found her again and she ran again. This went on and on. Yet I just couldn't leave her. Finally, I was able to grab her. When I held her in my arms, she seemed so little and skinny and very sweet. And she stopped mewing!

It was totally out of character, but I took her into my car with me. The kitty freaked out, screeching and running at lightning speed all over the car, until she settled herself right in my lap, of course. I didn't know what I was going to do with her, and yet I felt compelled to bring her home. I drove home, worrying the whole way, because I knew my roommate was deathly allergic to cats.

I got home very late, put the kitten in the front yard and left some milk for her. I was half hoping she would run away by the time morning came. But in the morning she was still there, so I brought her to work with me. Luckily, I have a very sympathetic boss. Especially when it comes to animals. Once we had a hurt sparrow in the office for weeks that he had found and nursed back to health. All day at work, I tried to find someone who would take the kitten, but all the cat lovers were full up.

I still didn't know what to do with the kitty, so I took her on some errands with me when I left work. Again she freaked in the car and this time wedged herself under the seat. My last stop that afternoon was at my parents' house.

Recently my father had been diagnosed with prostate cancer. He had undergone hormone treatment and the doctors now felt they had arrested the cancer. At least for the present. I liked to go there as often as I could.

That afternoon, parked in front of my parents' house, I was trying to coax the kitten out from under the seat when she zoomed out of the car and into the neighbors' bushes. There are a lot of bushes in that neighborhood, and I realized after looking for a while that it was a lost cause. I felt a bit sad but consoled myself that this area had many families with kids. Surely someone would find her and give her a good home, I told myself.

To be honest, I felt somewhat relieved because I didn't know what I would have done with her. I visited with my parents, and as I was leaving, I told them to call me if the kitty came around their place and I would come pick her up. I kidded my father, saying, "Of course, you could keep her if you wanted," to which he replied, "Not on your life!" I supposed that Dad wasn't that interested in having pets, particularly cats.

That night there was a call on my answering machine from my

father. The kitty had actually shown up on their front doorstep! He said he had her in the house and she was okay, but could I come pick her up the next day? My heart sank. What am I going to do with this cat? I thought. I didn't have the heart to take her to the pound, and I was sure that my roommate wasn't feeling up for a hospital trip to treat a cat-induced asthma attack. I couldn't see a solution.

I called my father the next day and told him I would come over and pick up the kitty. To my great surprise, he said not to rush. He had gone out and bought a cat box (oh, no!), cat food and a little dish. I was amazed and thanked him for his generosity. He proceeded to tell me what a character the kitten was and how late the previous night she had been zooming back and forth across the floor. I listened, open-mouthed. The topper came when he said that "Kitty" came up and lay on his chest when he was lying down. I asked, "You let her do that?"

"Oh yes. I pet her and I can feel her motor running," he replied lovingly. "So take your time, dear, finding a home for her. I can keep her until you do."

I was floored. My dad, Seymour, Mister "Keep-Those-Dogs-Outside," had a kitty purring on his chest. In his bed, no less!

As the weeks went on, Dad got weaker. His cancer had reappeared. Yet whenever I called Dad, I heard more and more about how cute Kitty was, how she zoomed around, how loud her motor was, how she followed him everywhere. When I was at the house, my father would call for her, have her come up on his lap, pet her, talk to her and say how much he loved her.

"Dad, aren't you allergic to cats?" I asked once, as he was putting his handkerchief away after one of his infamous loud honks. He just shrugged his shoulders and smiled sheepishly.

As he got sicker, and could barely move without terrible pain, one of his few joys was to have Kitty lay on his chest. He would pet her and say, "Listen, her motor is running. That's a good Kitty, good Kitty." We all watched in awe at Dad's unabashed affection for this little feline.

Kitty worked her magic on both Dad and me. Charming a

reluctant pet owner, the little cat became one of my father's single greatest comforts in his final days. And me? Kitty opened my eyes to the wonder and mystery of how life unfolds. She taught me to listen to my heart, even when my head is saying no. I didn't realize on that unusual night that I was simply a messenger. An unknowing courier delivering a most beautiful and needed friend.

~Lynn A. Kerman
Chicken Soup for the Pet Lover's Soul

Loving Our Cats

Cat-astrophes

*Even if you have just destroyed a Ming Vase, purr.
Usually all will be forgiven.
~Lenny Rubenstein*

22

"Child" Proof

My husband and I had just returned from the grocery store when a blood-curdling feline scream from outside rattled our front door. I was terrified that one of our two inside cats had slipped past us on our way in and now was in trouble.

When I threw open the door, a strange cat—and I'm not using the word strange loosely—casually padded into the foyer. "Hey, you don't belong here," I told the dusty white animal as I reached down for him. Too late. He was on the run now, into the kitchen.

Our two pampered felines studied the interloper, who looked back and forth between them and the tempting bowls of food on the kitchen floor, as if to ask, "Were you going to finish that?"

Before anyone could answer, he buried his head in the nearest food bowl.

"Hey, fur ball, that's enough," I said, putting him and the confiscated cat chow out on the patio. "Nobody gets in the house without a pass from the vet."

Not only was I not in the market for another cat, but, more importantly, for the first time in years, our household was free of feline leukemia—and I wasn't taking any chances. The scruffy-looking cat was patient. He hung around the patio, basking in the sunshine and eating the food I supplied on cue every time he tapped his paw against the window.

We chatted when I brought him his food, or at least, I chatted. He pretty much nodded his head and swished his tail. He was solid white except for a gold tail and one gold ear. I named him Bogus because he didn't look quite real. He looked like two cats put together into one. I should have suspected that naming him was the same as adopting him, but it took another week of searching for his owners before my husband and I took him to the vet for his official checkup.

We started to realize how clever this cat was, and so did the vet, when Bogus nudged a bottle of vaccine off the table. Then he knocked the syringe out of the vet's hand. Finally, the vet declared Bogus healthy except for sunburned ears, which he assured us would heal on their own without the need for a follow-up visit.

Like that first night, as soon as we opened the door and let him into the house, Bogus made himself at home. He would cozy up to our other cats, then steal their favorite sleeping spots. He was always first in line when dinner was served, and he picked the best lap to sit on at any given moment.

All was well except for one bad habit—well, maybe more than one—toilet-tissue demolition. In a matter of minutes, he could shred a double roll of Charmin.

But we're smarter than the cat, my husband and I told ourselves. We hid the paper in a cabinet over the toilet. It took Bogus about ten minutes to find it. Now, we had streams of toilet tissue flowing out of the cabinet, down the wall, over the bathroom floor, across the hallway and onto Bogus's favorite pillow—one he'd stolen from one of the other cats, of course.

That's when I discovered the child-safety aisle at the market. Among the handy supplies designed to protect children from such hazards as might lurk under kitchen sinks or behind electrical outlets, I found the perfect cabinet lock.

"See this?" I waved the package in a very curious cat's face. "This will keep you out of the toilet tissue once and for all." Bogus watched as I struggled to remove the plastic packaging from around the simple gizmo that I was certain would save the Charmin from his obsession.

Twenty minutes later, with the help of heavy-duty shears, I

managed to free the childproof lock from its wrapping. It was a narrow, U-shaped plastic contraption that fit over the cabinet knobs with a sliding lock that tightened it on one side, making it impossible for any child, furry or otherwise, to open the doors. I was impressed. Now, if it just worked as well as its packaging... Bogus blinked his gold eyes at me from the bathroom doorway.

"There you go, big guy," I laughed as I patted his head and rubbed his gold ear. "Let's see you open that cabinet now."

I settled down in my favorite chair and picked up the novel I'd been reading. Bang, bang, bang, came the sound of the cabinet doors as Bogus tested the new lock. I flipped the page and laughed out loud as the banging grew more intense.

Suddenly, the noise stopped. An eerie silence... the soft padding of paws on the hardwood floor of the hallway... the thump as Bogus landed next to me. I looked down at the childproof lock he'd dropped in my lap.

That's when I knew: I could childproof my home, but I couldn't Bogus-proof my heart. And I wouldn't have it any other way.

~Valerie Gawthrop
Chicken Soup for the Cat Lover's Soul

Serendipity

One must love a cat on its own terms.
~Paul Gray

"Thank goodness you answered the phone! I've tried to fax you for three days. This line's been busy, too."

I didn't know what to say. I checked the machine, and, sure enough, it was off. Again.

"Sorry for the inconvenience," I told my very-most-important-client-in-the-world. "I just turned it back on, so please fax the material now. I'll wait." I glanced at the kitten sleeping on "her" chair across the room and added, "I've been having trouble with office gremlins."

The "office gremlin" in question opened blue-jean-colored eyes, yawned, then came fully awake when the fax squawked back to life. "You nearly cost me a client," I muttered.

The kitten hopped off the chair and raced to her toy du jour. But I stood firm, between Seren(dipity) and her target, poised to collect the fax before the Siamese-wannabe could hole-punch the pages with her baby teeth.

"You've been playing the fax buttons again, haven't you?"

"Mew-mewoy."

"No excuses. I don't care if the fax looked at you funny...."

"Meerowing-ing-ing!"

"Seren, fax machines do not talk dirty!"

"Phttt-ptuii. Merro-wumff."

The five-month-old juvenile delinquent grabbed my ankle as if to punctuate her remarks, executed a thirty-second feline headstand while bunny-kicking my calves, then dashed out the door. I could hear her playing trampoline on the bed in the next room as the fax stuttered to a stop.

Weeks before, a friend discovered the dumped kitten napping in an empty flowerpot on her back porch and called me, her pet-writer buddy, for help. I had been pet-less for longer than I cared to admit. E-mail, phone and fax lines kept me connected to my clients, but I figured the kitten would brighten my long, sometimes lonely work-days. So it was Amy-to-the-rescue, and love at first sight.

I convinced my husband that a sweet, lap-cuddling kitten would be no trouble at all. Less than a month later, though, I realized the cat-gods have a wicked sense of humor.

Seren had no off-switch. She wanted a job—and told me so in long, meow-punctuated conversations, in which she always got the last word.

She emptied my sock drawer. She played patty-cake in the toilet. Sparkle balls (first soaked in the water bowl) sabotaged our shoes. Vital Post-it Note messages were stalked, stolen and killed. Coffee cups invited paw-dipping (and shaking) to create feline splatter art on computer monitors, reference books and pristine manuscripts.

But Seren really pushed my buttons—literally—by tap dancing across the fax machine. The ringing was a kitty dare; emerging paper, a cat temptation; the musical push-button tones, glorious fun. I have no idea how many faxes I missed due to a furry butt-perch taking the machine off-line.

Instead of corporeal punishment—which won't work—I practiced tough love, kitten-style, in the form of squirt-gun interruptions.

Seren decided she liked being squirted.

Dang!

She rattled the wooden blinds, pulled books off shelves, and played "gravity experiments" paw-patting breakables off the man-tel—all to invite games of squirt-gun tag.

I figured water on a fax machine probably invalidated the warranty, so I got a cardboard box and jammed it upside down over the top of the fax machine.

Seren vaulted to the box-covered fax. "Mew-mewoy." She thumped a kitty jig, but the shielded buttons remained mute.

"Ha!" I told her. "Foiled at last!"

"Meerowing-ing-ing!"

"Seren, find something else to play with."

"Phttt-ptuii. Merro-wumff."

And she did.

When engrossed in a writing project, I can lose track of time and of my surroundings. I didn't realize Seren had managed a great escape until I heard the repeated thumps behind me, followed by an ominous silence.

I'd hung a delicate crocheted Christmas ornament on the handle of my office door. The ornament lay on the floor. The door stood ajar. The cat was gone.

The ornament caught the kitty's eye for trouble, so she'd tried to paw-catch the new toy du jour. Hooking claws into the toy, she'd pulled the lever-shaped door handle just enough to unlatch the door—and let freedom ring! I could hear her galumphing up and down the staircase.

I hid the ornament. That didn't stop genius-cat. She remembered every single success.

She leaped for the handle again and again. Every second or third attempt, she managed to hook a paw over the handle. But without the added purchase of crocheted material to claw-clutch, Seren's paws slid off the handle before the door could unlatch.

Thud-slide, claw-scrabble. Leap. "Mew-mewoy." Thud-slide, claw-scrabble.

"At last!" I told her. "Gotcha this time."

"Meerowing-ing-ing!"

"Seren, can't you find something productive to do with your energy?"

"Phttt-ptuii. Merro-wumff."

I wondered what sort of curse she'd hurled at me. "Such language — don't make me wash your mouth out with dog biscuits, little missy."

At last, with the fax protected by its cardboard canopy, and the door-handle exploits thwarted, I felt comfortable leaving the kitten safely sequestered in my office while I ran errands. The first time, I was gone maybe twenty minutes. And, when I returned, I congratulated myself that my office looked the same — and Seren, that angelic purr-kitten, must have slept the whole time.

"How's my Seren-kitty?"

"Mew-mewoy. Purrrrrrrrrrrrrrrrr."

"Took a nap? What a good kitty!"

"Meerowing-ing-ing!" She head-butted my cheek.

All was calm.

It was about a week before I noticed anything wrong. The first e-mail message sounded cordial, but others got increasingly testy. I remembered that my very-most-important-client-in-the-world also had complained about the office phone's busy signal and being unable to reach me. I keep a log of all calls made and realized the phone bill didn't match my records. It listed several long-distance charges to unfamiliar numbers. Wouldn't I remember dialing the Yukon territories or Fink, Texas?

Two days later, I caught the office gremlin in action.

The phone was ringing as I walked into the office. I saw Seren race to my desk, hook one paw under the receiver and tip it off the hook.

"Mew-mewoy?"

She paused (or should I say "paw-sed"), then added, "Meerowing-ing-ing! Phttt-ptuii. Merro-wumff."

I hurried to intercept the call, praying it wasn't from my very-most-important-client-in-the-world. Damage-control time. Maybe the client didn't understand cat curses...

"Hello? This is Amy. How may I help you?" But only a dial tone hummed in my ear.

Seren glared at me, and before I could hang up the receiver, she began paw-playing the buttons on the phone. Probably redialing the Sardine House Take-Out in Moose Run, Arkansas.

I looked at the phone bill again, then at my feline Einstein. She grinned, then dashed out the door to find a new pastime.

I couldn't help smiling and consoled myself, "Just the cost of doing business with a furry muse. At least phone calls are tax deductible."

~Amy D. Shojai
Chicken Soup for the Cat Lover's Soul

24

Sister Seraphim's Deal with God

We can do no great things, only small things with great love.
~Mother Teresa

Mother Superior wrung her hands. "Sister Seraphim, you know full good and well that a convent is not a refuge for every stray cat."

"Yes, Mother."

"One mouser per convent is quite enough."

"Yes, Mother." The diminutive Russian Orthodox nun bowed her head, more to conceal a grin than to convey contrition.

At that moment, a voice in the hallway murmured, "Oh! The sweet precious babies. Please Sister Seraphim, the mama must have another saucer of milk."

The diminutive Russian Orthodox nun slipped unnoticed from the room.

Mother Superior shook her finger at empty air. "And just last week we found the kitchen coffer empty because you took the money to purchase two ragged kitties from little boys who were unable to care for them." Mother added, "And Sister, how many times must I remind you, you are not allowed to raid the refrigerator for meat for the cats."

Sister Seraphim returned to the lecture scene. "Yes Mother, but when I was but a child, I made a deal with God."

"Sister Seraphim," Mother said with long-suffering patience, "We do not make deals with God!"

"I do," Sister said serenely. "I vowed early in life to take care of all living creatures who came my way so long as God provided the means."

Mother Superior sighed as she watched the sisters file into Sister Seraphim's room to coo and pet the newest addition to Sister Seraphim's collection of waifs—Grisette and her three newborn white balls of fluff.

For Sister Seraphim, cats had spirits and every one had to have a name. She rescued Shadrach, Meshach and Abednego (named after the men in the Old Testament who survived the fiery furnace) from the burning heat of the summer sun. The duo hiding behind the nunnery received the Biblical names of Luke and Eli. Mary Magdalene was christened after she waited at a well for Sister.

And then there was Pandora, the born troublemaker. Pandora believed in the virtue of awakening Christian nuns at the crack of dawn. At first she tried to pry Sister's eyes open with her paw. Soon the mere presence of Pandora's paw on Sister Seraphim's face was enough to roust the sister from bed. But that wasn't the worst of Pandora, as Sister Seraphim found out one Sunday after services, when Mother Superior called her over.

Mother Superior stood with her arms folded. "That cat is impossible. Come see what she has done to the convent bathroom."

Sister Seraphim's eyes widened with horror at the destruction. The haughty Pandora was sitting on the window sill, licking her dainty paws.

Sister asked sternly, "What have you to say for yourself?" But Pandora's attitude only said, "See how I have excelled at bathroom transgressions. Pulled down all the curtains and towels. Chewed on the toothbrush bristles. Sharpened my claws on the toilet paper and then shredded it into confetti. One good swipe broke all the pretty bottles and knocked over tin cans. Then I mixed up the powder, vitamins, and cough syrup and rolled in the mess."

Mother Superior continued, "Why just this morning after being ousted from the chapel, again, Pandora actually had the impudence to flick her tail at His Most Holy Reverence the Bishop."

Suppressing a giggle, Sister Seraphim admitted, "Yes, Pandora is incorrigible, but if I don't love her, who will?"

Mother Superior looked at her sternly. She was not going to make any concessions. "Other arrangements will have to be made. For all the cats."

Sister Seraphim's round face grew troubled. She knew she had to obey Mother's instructions, but what would happen to her cats?

Over the next few weeks, after much worry and many phone calls and visits to local families, Sister Seraphim managed to find homes for all the cats. She vowed to start fresh with a slate clean of animals and an uncomplicated life. But it wasn't long before a couple of stray cats appeared, obviously in need of her help. Sister Seraphim fed them. What else could she do? And of course it wasn't long before word spread along the feline grapevine, and more unwanted cats sought succor from the angelic sister.

Mother Superior appeared to turn a blind eye at first, but inevitably, the day came when "other arrangements" had to be made.

And so the years passed. As she grew older, Sister Seraphim began to suffer from respiratory problems and arthritis. The time came when her order arranged for her to move to Arizona, hoping that the dry climate might improve her health.

Of course, Sister Seraphim's compassion for homeless cats didn't lessen at all in her new location. Shortly after arriving in Tucson, she decided to take matters into her own hands. The elderly nun persuaded a local real estate agent to donate a house and land. And there she founded the Hermitage, a no-kill cat shelter. At the Hermitage, Sister Seraphim and her cats found a refuge where, for the rest of her days, she no longer had to make "other arrangements."

And when Sister Seraphim finally met God, they had both kept their end of the bargain.

~Jane Eppinga
Chicken Soup for the Cat and Dog Lover's Soul

25

Trash-Pickin' Kitty

When I adopted a kitten from a local animal shelter, I knew I was in for a real test of my patience. I had raised two other cats, big boys now, and felt sure I was ready for the chaos a new kitten would bring back into my life—and my heart. I did all the right things, like buying top-brand expensive cat food, a big soft bed, and all the best cat toys available. But I soon began to notice that this playful and demanding little being named Lucy had her own ideas about what was best for her.

She only wanted table scraps, she would rather sleep on my bed than hers and she scoffed at her store-bought toys, preferring to amuse herself for hours by stealing balls of paper from my office wastepaper basket. As a writer, I often tried to discourage her from bothering me when I was in my office working, but, try as I might, she would sneak in and overturn the trash can, running off with a mouthful of my old notes and tossed-off ideas. I would yell at her, scold her, try to encourage her to play with her "real" toys—the ones that cost me an arm and a leg—but I could not change her. My patience was wearing thin.

Determined to turn her into a good little kitten, I started locking Lucy out of the office when I was working, only to find her sitting outside the door with big, sad eyes when I came out for a breather. Sometimes, she would dart in between my feet and go straight for the trash can before I even knew what was happening. Then I'd raise my voice and lightly tap her rump, causing her to drop the wad of paper in her mouth and slink off into a corner. I hated to scold her, but she had to stop!

The tables were about to be turned.

Not long thereafter, I realized I had accidentally thrown away a great and very timely story idea, along with a magazine editor's name and contact number, given to me by a supportive writer friend. Frantically, I searched through my half-full trash can, only to realize I had emptied it—and the story idea—the day before in time for the trash pickup. Defeated, I struggled to remember what I could of the idea that I had fleshed out, and figured I could always call my friend—until I realized she was in Europe for two weeks on vacation! I doubted she had the magazine editor's name and phone number with her on her travels.

Resigned to the fact that I would lose the lead completely—or get the info I needed only after someone else had probably covered the story—I resolved never to write ideas on scraps of paper again. Instead, I would type and save them on my computer immediately.

I sat there thinking about all the other ideas and notes I had probably tossed out prematurely or accidentally when I heard a sniffing, rooting sound and turned to find Lucy pulling out a wad of paper from my trash can. I went ballistic, chasing her out of the room and up the stairs to her little cozy corner, where I noticed a handful of other balls of paper on the floor. She hid under a chair and watched me as I picked up the scraps, swearing under my breath. But then I stopped dead—as I noticed one particular paper ball with my handwriting on it. As I unfolded it, I shook my head in disbelief! It was my story idea, and the magazine editor's name and number!

I grabbed Lucy out from under the chair and hugged her tight, smooching her and praising her. She looked at me in total shock, then snuggled her little kitten nose into my chest. I hoped that meant she forgave all my impatience and rude behavior. For, in that instant, I knew that a trash-pickin' kitten is the best kitten a writer could ever have.

No more would I try to change her or scold her for being herself.
I love Lucy—just the way she is.

~Marie D. Jones
Chicken Soup for the Cat Lover's Soul

26

One Smart Cat

There is no snooze button on a cat who wants breakfast.
~Author Unknown

Nicole and I sat on the futon watching a TV movie in the house we shared with three other college students. The music's crescendo, the beating drums, the danger lurking behind the corner on the glowing screen gripped us completely. If there was a world outside the television, we did not know it. Then a sound from upstairs momentarily overrode the pounding drums. Thump, ting! In the back of my mind, I wondered, What is that cat doing? I decided to ignore the sound. What harm could a cat do in the space of a few minutes?

Ting, thump. Then came a strange grating noise, slow and deep at first. "What is that?" I asked Nicole.

"Huh? Probably Nermal," she answered, her eyes fixed on the flickering screen. I was about to dismiss the repeated thumping when it stopped, and, as if on cue, the cat appeared. She hung from the metal banister like an adolescent boy struggling to do chin-ups—forearms extended up, body dangling below like a wet towel. Nermal slid down, gaining speed. She reached the end of the banister and went flying—her journey ending when she landed a few feet from where we sat. It was a spectacular entrance, one never performed before or since.

Nermal looked at us, eyes wide. We stared back at her. The room was still; the booming noise from the television had suddenly gone silent. The stillness was broken only when I started to laugh. Nicole joined in. Nermal licked her paw, as though nothing had occurred. She held our attention, and that was all she had wanted to do.

Nermal does not tolerate inattentiveness. A quiet human with eyes drawn elsewhere is a no-fail formula for mischief. She was given to me when she was no bigger than my palm, and, even as a kitten, she was deceptively innocent, with large green eyes and ears that were too big for her small head. In snapshots taken when she was four months old, she appears to be the epitome of sweetness and serenity, with tigerlike stripes adorning her black-velvet body and green eyes glowing like heated emeralds. Little did I know those eyes were not only marking each passing moment and calculating her plans, but also waiting for the next opportunity to pounce on a sleeping face or a moving foot beneath the comforter.

As an adult cat, she has become amazingly creative and persistent at getting what she wants. When I tell my friends and family about her exploits, no one believes me.

One night recently, I discovered yet another of Nermal's uncanny skills, one that I could hardly believe myself. I lay huddled under my duvet, waiting to fall asleep, Nermal curled into a ball at my feet. She fell asleep before I did, and, as I listened to her snore, I sighed. I knew that, by four o'clock, she would be screaming to be let out into the hallway. It's the same routine every night: She awakens at four, stretches, hops off the bed, and begins to scratch and meow impatiently at the door. This continues until, groggy and slow, I finally shuffle across the floor of my room and let her out. Some mornings (especially those that follow late nights), I find it more convenient to ignore the scratching and meowing until it is my time to get up, announced by the blaring noise of the country-music station coming from my small clock radio. She doesn't like the delay, but, as she can't open the door herself, she has to wait.

That night, as the minutes continued to pass without sleep, I knew that I would have to ignore her early call if I was to get enough rest. Finally, I fell asleep.

One moment, I was sleeping. The next, the twangy voice of

Tim McGraw jarred me from my dreams. It was still dark outside, and, confused, I checked the digital display: 4:11 A.M. Why had the alarm gone off? Had there been a power failure? A single triumphant meow came from beside the bed. It was time for the cat to be let out. Puzzled, I got up and opened the door. The cat gleefully bounded out the door, the bell on her collar announcing her joyous exodus. I shook my head. Fluke, I thought. Cats don't use alarm clocks to wake their humans. And I would have left it at that, too. But the next morning, it happened again. And then again. Until finally, three days later, I caught her in action.

It was one of those nights when more thinking about sleep is done than actual sleeping. No amount of pillow fluffing, rolling over or augmenting blanket layers could remedy my sleepless state. Then, as I stared at the shadow-covered ceiling, I spied a stealthy feline figure slip from bed to nightstand. She stepped lightly, paws making a soundless transition from soft mattress to wooden nightstand. First one forepaw, then the other, both of them followed by two hind feet as she silently stepped up onto the alarm clock. The soft pad on the bottom of one paw pressed the sleep button. Country music began to play: Time to get up! She wanted out.

I couldn't believe it! Nermal must have noticed a correlation between my waking and the alarm going off. I couldn't bring myself to get mad at her. I realized that I was actually proud of her intelligence. I mean, how many cats use alarm clocks to wake up their people? Not that four in the morning is appealing, but, nonetheless, she is one smart cat.

Nermal—for better or worse—has become a fixture in my life, an irreplaceable presence who keeps me on my toes. When I return home after a long day, I call out her name at the foot of the stairs; the faint jingle of her bell always answers my appeal. Following the sound into the living room, I find her perched on top of the covered fish tank. "Ik-ik-ik-eow!" she says. "You're home."

I pick up her soft body and carry her to my rocking chair. She first sits, then stretches out, finally curling up into position on my lap, then a deep purr emerges from her depths. I can feel the vibrations filling my legs, persuading me to relax. I take comfort in her company as she takes comfort in mine.

Her eyelids become heavy, yet before she succumbs to slumber, she looks up at me expectantly. I imagine she's asking me, in that way she has, if I am okay. I smile and caress her soft, warm body until she is convinced she can sleep. And, as she gently snores and drifts into the realm of dreams, I feel immensely lucky, despite the fact that, with Nermal at my side, I know tomorrow will be a very early morning.

~Rebecca A. Eckland
Chicken Soup for the Cat Lover's Soul

27

Catch of the Day

This is the story of the night my ten-year-old cat, Rudy, got his head stuck in the garbage disposal. I knew at the time that the experience would be funny if the cat survived, so let me tell you right up front that he's fine.

My husband Rich and I had just returned from a five-day spring break vacation where I had been as sick as—well, as a dog—the whole time. We had arrived home at nine in the evening, later than we had planned because of airline problems. Exhausted and still suffering from illness-related vertigo, I sat down at my desk to prepare for teaching my morning English class.

At around ten o'clock, I heard Rich hollering something undecipherable from the kitchen. As I raced in to see what was wrong, I saw Rich frantically rooting around under the kitchen sink, and Rudy—or, rather, Rudy's headless body—scrambling around in the sink, his claws clicking in panic against the metal. Rich had just ground up the skin of some smoked salmon in the garbage disposal, and, when he left the room, Rudy (whom we always did call a pinhead) had gone in after it.

It is very disturbing to see the headless body of your cat in the sink. This is an animal that I have slept with nightly for ten years, who burrows under the covers and purrs against my side, and who now looked like a desperate, fur-covered turkey carcass set to defrost in the sink, still alive and kicking. It was also disturbing to see Rich, Mr. Calm-in-an-Emergency, at his wit's end, trying to soothe Rudy, trying to undo the garbage disposal, failing at both, and basically freaking out. Adding to the chaos was Rudy's twin brother Lowell, also upset, racing around in circles, jumping onto the kitchen counter and alternately licking Rudy's butt for comfort and biting it out of fear. Clearly, I had to do something.

First, we tried to ease Rudy out of the disposal by lubricating his head and neck. We tried Johnson's baby shampoo and butter-flavored Crisco. Both failed, and a now-greasy Rudy kept struggling. Rich then decided to take apart the garbage disposal, which was a good idea, but he couldn't do it. Turns out, the thing is constructed like a metal onion: You peel off one layer, and another one appears, with Rudy's head still buried deep inside, stuck in a hard-plastic collar. When all our efforts failed, we sought professional help. I called our regular plumber, who actually called me back quickly, even at eleven o'clock at night, and talked Rich through further layers of disposal dismantling, but still we couldn't reach Rudy. I called the 800 number for Insinkerator (no response); a pest-removal service that advertises twenty-four-hour service (no response); an all-night emergency veterinary clinic (which had no experience in this matter, and, therefore, no advice); and, finally, in desperation, 911. I could see that Rudy's paw pads, normally a healthy shade of pink, were turning blue. The fire department, I figured, got cats out of trees; maybe they could get one out of a garbage disposal.

The dispatcher had other ideas and offered to send over two policemen. The cops didn't arrive until close to midnight, but they were able to think rationally, which we were not. They were, of course, quite astonished by the situation: "I've never seen anything like this," Officer Mike kept saying. Officer Tom, who expressed immediate sympathy for our plight—"I've had cats all my life," he said, comfortingly—also had an idea.

Evidently, we needed a certain tool, a tiny, circular, rotating saw, which could cut through the heavy plastic flange encircling Rudy's neck without hurting Rudy. Officer Tom happened to own one. "I live just five minutes from here," he said. "I'll go get it." He soon returned, and the three of them—Rich and the two policemen—got under the sink together to cut through the garbage disposal. They finally managed to get the bottom off the disposal, so we could now see Rudy's face and knew he could breathe, but they couldn't cut the flange without risk of injuring the cat. Stumped.

Officer Tom had another idea. "You know," he said, "I think the reason we can't get him out is the angle of his head and body. If we could just get the sink out and lay it on its side, I'll bet we could slip him out." That sounded like a good idea—at this point, anything would have sounded like a good idea—and as it turned out, Officer Mike ran a plumbing business on weekends, so he knew how to take out the sink! Again, they went to work, three pairs of legs sticking out from under the sink surrounded by an ever-increasing pile of tools and sink parts. About an hour later—voilà!—the sink was lifted gently out of the countertop and laid on its side, but even at this more favorable angle, Rudy stayed stuck.

Officer Tom's radio beeped, calling him away on some kind of real police business. As he was leaving, though, he had another good idea: "You know," he said, "I don't think we can get him out while he's struggling so much. We need to get the cat sedated. If he were limp, we could slide him out." And off he went, regretfully—a cat lover still worried about Rudy.

The remaining three of us decided that getting Rudy sedated was a good idea. Rich and I knew that the overnight emergency veterinary clinic was only a few minutes away, but we didn't know how to get there. "I know where it is!" declared Officer Mike. "Follow me!"

So Mike got into his patrol car, Rich got into the driver's seat of our car, and I got into the back, carrying the kitchen sink, what was left of the garbage disposal, and Rudy. It was now about two in the morning.

We followed Officer Mike for a few blocks when I decided to put my hand into the garbage disposal to pet Rudy's face, hoping I could comfort him. Instead, my sweet, gentle bedfellow chomped down on my finger, hard—really hard—and wouldn't let go. My scream reflex kicked into gear, and I couldn't stop the noise. Rich slammed on the brakes, hollering, "What? What happened? Should I stop?" checking us out in the rearview mirror.

"No," I managed to get out between screams, "just keep driving. Rudy's biting me, but we've got to get to the vet. Just go!"

Rich turned his attention back to the road, where Officer Mike took a turn we hadn't expected, and we followed. After a few minutes Rudy let go, and, as I stopped screaming, I looked up to discover that we were wandering aimlessly through an industrial park, in and out of empty parking lots, past little streets that didn't look at all familiar.

"Where's he taking us?" I asked. "We should have been there ten minutes ago!"

Rich was as mystified as I was, but all we knew to do was follow the police car until, finally, he pulled into a church parking lot, and we pulled up next to him.

As Rich rolled down the window to ask, "Mike, where are we going?" the cop, who was not Mike, rolled down his window and asked, "Why are you following me?"

Once Rich and I recovered from our shock at having tailed the wrong cop car, the policeman led us quickly to the emergency vet, where Officer Mike greeted us by holding open the door, exclaiming, "Where were you guys?"

We brought in the kitchen sink containing Rudy and the garbage disposal containing his head. The clinic staff was ready. They took his temperature (which was ten degrees lower than normal) and checked his oxygen level (which was half of normal), then the vet declared: "This cat is in serious shock. We've got to sedate him and get him out of there immediately." When I asked if it was okay to sedate a cat in shock, the vet said grimly, "We don't have a choice." With that, he injected the cat, Rudy went limp, and the vet squeezed about half a tube of K-Y Jelly onto the cat's neck and pulled him free.

Then the whole team jumped into "code blue" mode. (I know this from watching a lot of *ER*.) They placed Rudy on a cart, where one person hooked up IV fluids, another put little socks on his paws ("You'd be amazed how much heat they lose through their pads," she said), one covered him with hot-water bottles and a blanket, and another took a blowdryer to warm up Rudy's now very gunky head.

The fur on his head had dried in stiff little spikes, making him look rather pathetically punk as he lay there, limp and motionless.

At this point they sent Rich, Officer Mike and me to sit in the waiting room while they tried to bring Rudy back to life. I told Mike that he didn't have to stay, but he just stood there, shaking his head. "I've never seen anything like this," he said again.

At about three, the vet came in to tell us that the prognosis was good for a full recovery. They needed to keep Rudy overnight to rehydrate him and give him something for the brain swelling they assumed he had, but, if all went well, we could take him home the following night. Just in time to hear the good news, Officer Tom rushed in, finished with his real police work and concerned about Rudy.

Rich and I got back home at about three-thirty. "I need a vacation," I said, and called the office to leave a message canceling my early class.

I slept late, then badgered the vet until he said that Rudy could come home later that day. I was unpacking when the phone rang. "Hi, this is Steve from the *Times-Herald*," a voice told me. "Listen, I was just going through the police blotter from last night. Mostly it's the usual stuff—breaking and entering, petty theft—but there's this one item. Um, do you have a cat?"

So I told Steve the whole story, which interested him. A couple of hours later he called back to say that his editor was interested, too. Did I have a picture of Rudy? The next day, Rudy was front page news, under the ridiculous headline, "Catch of the Day Lands Cat in Hot Water."

There were some noteworthy repercussions to the newspaper article. When I arrived at work, I was famous; people had been calling my secretary all morning to inquire about Rudy's health. When I called our regular vet to make a follow-up appointment for Rudy, the receptionist asked, "Is this the famous Rudy's mother?" When I brought my car in for routine maintenance a few days later, Dave, my mechanic, said, "We read about your cat. Is he okay?" When I called a tree surgeon about my dying red oak, he asked if I knew the person on that street whose cat had been in the garbage disposal. And, when I went to get my hair cut, the shampoo person told me the funny story her grandma had read in the paper about a cat who got stuck in the garbage disposal.

I don't know what the moral of this story is, but I do know that this "adventure" cost me $1,100 in emergency vet bills, follow-up vet care, a new sink, new plumbing, new electrical wiring and a new garbage disposal—one with a cover. Plus, the vet can no longer say he's seen everything but the kitchen sink. And Rudy, whom we originally got for free (or so we thought), still sleeps with me—under the covers on cold nights—and, unaccountably, he still sometimes prowls the sink, hoping for fish.

~Patti Schroeder
Chicken Soup for the Cat Lover's Soul

28

In-Flight Movings

I was settled into my seat for the flight to San Francisco, and, like the rest of the passengers on the sparsely populated airliner, I was prepared for a few hours of suspended numbness. With me, I had a list of things to do on this trip, a good book, and my Bengal cat, Callie Mooner, tucked into her carrier underneath the seat in front of me. It was a morning flight, and all the indications were that it would be a quiet, uneventful journey to the Bay Area.

Callie had expended most of her vocal energy in protest during the short taxi ride to the airport; now, she was resting in preparation for a renewed assault at the rental car counter upon our arrival in San Francisco. I assumed that, after takeoff, she would curl up and simply go to sleep as she usually did when I took her along on a flight. She would be lost in slumber for the majority of the flight, only to complain with a raspy meow when awakened after we landed. Callie is not a volunteer on these flying forays, and she generally picks opportune times to remind me of this.

About an hour into the flight, I looked up from my book, startled by a flight attendant's very concerned look.

"I believe that may be your cat up in the front cabin," she said in a confidential tone.

Uh-oh.

I glanced down at my feet to see a very still carrier with a suspiciously open zipper. Obviously, a feline escape had indeed taken place, and that feline did appear to be mine.

I bolted down the aisle. Callie had worked the zipper open just enough to allow her to emerge and explore one of Boeing's finest. Apparently, she had made a determined beeline to the first-class cabin, where she encamped in a window seat and requested a Bloody Mary and a smaller-sized headset. Unfortunately, making her way to the window seat entailed climbing over the passenger in the aisle seat, as well as his open laptop computer. The gentleman's computer screen was filled with all sorts of backslashes, meaningless keystrokes and blank lines, testimony to Callie's poor typing skills and careless grammar. The passengers in first class had only recently been served a morning shrimp cocktail, a part of which Callie had appropriated from her new seatmate, as evidenced by a shrimp tail protruding from her tight little jaws.

Indeed, that was how I found her. As soon as she saw me, her face registered that she knew the jig was up.

"Callie, honey," I said in my best mother-kitty voice, "we don't have enough miles for an upgrade!" With that, I reached across the previously violated laptop computer and scooped up my cat. I apologized profusely to the extremely startled gentleman, whose journey my cat no doubt had enlivened. As I pulled the shrimp out of Callie's mouth, I offered it back to him in a gesture of goodwill. Graciously, he demurred. I inserted the shrimp back into Callie's mouth, and, since it was now "captured," she figured she would simply growl all the way back to our seat.

It was a terribly long, quiet walk—except for the growling—back to seat 34E, as all the other passengers watched our procession—a red-faced human carrying a cat with a shrimp tail sticking out of her mouth—back to our assigned seat.

To prevent a recurrence of such an "event," I've outfitted the cat carrier with multiple Velcro straps securing the zipper tabs. But, just to be on the safe side, I now travel with my own supply of shrimp.

~Lisa-Maria Padilla
Chicken Soup for the Cat Lover's Soul

Loving Our Cats

Chapter 5

Cats and Their Pets

Animals are such agreeable friends — they ask no questions,
they pass no criticisms.
~George Eliot

29

Ariel and Pongo

A riel, my cat, has two good eyes, four working legs and has never thrown herself into the path of a rattlesnake to save my life. There is, in fact, nothing extraordinary about her. Or so I thought.

In a household of ten pets, she has only distinguished herself by her relationship with my blue-and-gold macaw, Pongo. It has always surprised me that my cats, who regularly chase birds outside, have always kept their distance from him. Perhaps it's because macaws are so large and intimidating, but I like to think the cats know that "Mommy's bird" is off-limits.

Ariel, however, has a special fascination with Pongo. She sits at the base of his cage and looks up at him as though he were a god. In a way, he is. Food falls from his perch into Ariel's waiting mouth—cheese, chicken, whatever I feed him. I don't know whether it's the usual bird messiness or if Pongo is actually sharing his meals. Sometimes, Ariel will even stand on her hind legs and reach up into the cage with her paw. Although Pongo screams if any of the other cats do that, he accepts it from Ariel.

Once when I was leaving on a vacation, I arranged for Pongo to spend two weeks at First Flight, a local bird store that accepted boarders. I always used a large cat carrier to transport him outside the house. He'd managed to chew some large holes in it, but it still served its purpose. I put the carrier on the kitchen counter and went into the living room to get Pongo. He walked readily into his carrier (his only pet trick); I latched the door and carried it to the car, placing it on the front passenger seat.

On the half-hour trip to First Flight, Pongo peered around, chewed a little on the plastic and held onto my finger with his claw. No squawks, no complaints.

We entered the bird store, and I put the carrier down on the counter. When I opened the door, Pongo walked out — a little quicker than usual, I noticed.

We settled him in his cage, and I picked up the carrier to leave. It was still heavy. How could that be?

I looked in and saw Ariel peering out at me. She had obviously climbed in before we left the house and traveled the fifteen miles in the carrier with Pongo. Neither had made a sound during the entire journey. Packed in together, neither had bitten or clawed — not a single feather or drop of blood was shed. Who would have believed it? No one in the bird store did.

In a world filled with warring nations, these natural enemies had forged a relationship that defied the odds. If birds and cats can get along, maybe there's hope for the rest of the world.

P.S. When I picked up Pongo two weeks later, he paused and looked into the carrier before he got in. He may be a bird, but he's not a birdbrain.

~Kerri Glynn
Chicken Soup for the Cat Lover's Soul

30

Jake and the Kittens

Kittens can happen to anyone.
~Paul Gallico

From the beginning, Jake made his feelings clear about the subject of cats: they were best served on a plate, with a side order of fries!

Jake was our resident dog, a large dominant male, part Border collie and part Labrador retriever, with a little German shepherd thrown in. Jake was about two years old when he adopted us from the local animal shelter. He came into our lives shortly after I lost my beloved dog Martha to an unexpected illness. One day we went to the shelter searching for a shaggy-haired female (like Martha) to bring into our home. Instead, we found Jake, a shorthaired male, sitting tall, proud and silent in the middle of all that barking. We told the shelter worker that we wanted Jake to come home with us because we could sense he had a lot of magic inside of him. "That's great," she said. "Just don't bring him back when he shows you that magic!"

Jake immediately became a cherished member of our family. He loved watching the birds we attracted to our yard with numerous feeders and birdbaths. He played with the puppy next door and other dogs in the park, but made it extremely clear that cats would never be allowed on his property, chasing any feline that came too close.

One day I found a litter of wild kittens in our woodpile. Although I had been a "dog person" all my life and had never had the privilege of sharing my life with a cat, my heart went out to these little furballs. They were only about four weeks old, and had beautiful gray-striped bodies and large, frightened eyes. Their mother was nowhere in sight. I put them into a box and brought them inside. Jake heard the meowing and immediately began to salivate. And drool. And pant. Every attempt to introduce him to the kitties ended in near disaster. It was clear we couldn't keep the kittens in the house, even long enough to help find them homes. Our veterinarian told us, "Some dogs just won't accept cats under any condition."

A year after the kitty experience, I looked outside onto our deck and saw Jake with his ears up and his head cocked sideways, staring at the ground. There at his feet was a tiny kitten, sitting very still. Using soothing words to try and keep Jake calm, I moved in closer, hoping to prevent the ugly attack I felt sure was coming. The kitten had badly infected eyes, and it probably couldn't see where it was or what was looming over it. But Jake just looked at the little creature, then looked up at me, and then back at the kitten. I heard some meowing, and discovered another kitten under the deck. So I scooped them both up and brought them into the house, depositing them into a box that would be their temporary home. I put the box in the garage and started making calls to all the animal people I knew, telling each the same story — my dog would never allow these cats into our home, and I needed to relocate them right away.

I bought baby bottles and kitten milk, and as I fed my two little bundles of fur, I told them how much I would have loved to welcome them into our family. But it could never be.

The next morning, we found three more kittens lying in a pile outside the door, huddled together for warmth and protection. So I took them in and added them to the box.

My heart was very heavy. Now we had five little kittens, all with infected eyes, who would be sent out into a world already crowded with unwanted little creatures. I spent the day making phone calls, only to be told over and over that no one had room for more critters. I knew I'd run out of options, so with tears in my eyes, I picked up the phone to make the call to the vet that would take the kittens out of my life forever. At that same moment, my eyes fell on Jake, calmly observing everything going on around him. There was no drooling, no panting. He didn't seem upset or anxious. He was definitely interested, but not in a calculating, just-wait-until-I-get-them-on-my-plate kind of way. I felt something was different. Slow down, I thought. Don't react. Just sit for a minute. Be still.

So I became still and I sat. And I heard a voice in my heart telling me what to do. I called our veterinarian and made an appointment to bring the kittens in and get their eyes checked. On the way home from the doctor, I went to a pet store and bought my first litter box. I came home and brought the box of kittens back into the house. Jake was waiting. The time had come, so I carefully put the babies on the floor of the kitchen and held my breath, ready to come to the rescue if necessary.

Jake walked over and sniffed each of the kittens. Then he sat down in the middle of them and looked up at me with a sweet, sappy grin on his face. The kittens swarmed over him, happy to find a big, warm body of fur to curl up next to. That's when Jake opened his heart to the five little kitties and adopted them as his own. I wondered if he remembered a time when he, too, had needed a home. I knelt down to thank him for his love and compassion and tell him how grateful I was he'd come into my life. But it would have to wait until later — Jake and his kittens were fast asleep.

~Christine Davis
Chicken Soup for the Cat and Dog Lover's Soul

Coco's Cat

"**S**he looks bored," pronounced my daughter, home for a short visit from college.

We both studied the longhaired gray cat I'd adopted the previous week from the D.C. Humane Society. Ever since I'd brought her home, Coco, who had been the most vivacious cat at the shelter, had been listless and apathetic. I tried changing her food, gave her vitamins, played with her more in the evenings. Nothing seemed to pique her interest.

"Maybe she needs a pet," smirked my know-it-all daughter.

A few nights later, I was startled awake by a long, mournful wail coming from a dark mound on the sill of my open bedroom window. "Coco, for goodness sake, what is your problem?" I said as I scooped her up and plopped her in her usual nighttime spot at the end of my bed. As soon as I'd turned off the light, she jumped back down and resumed her wailing position. I won that round by depositing her on the other side of a closed bedroom door, but her scratching kept me awake most of the night.

For the next couple of days, Coco spent most of her time on the windowsill, alternately mewling and wailing—all the while, glaring accusingly at me.

"Let her out," advised my daughter, over the phone from her college dorm.

"Are you serious?" I said. Busy Wisconsin Avenue ran right in front of my apartment building. "She wouldn't last long enough for me to double-lock my door."

After a few more days of listening to an emotionally distressed feline—one who was now on a kitty hunger strike—I was ready to take my daughter's advice. But my second-floor apartment was too high for a cat to come and go. I made a reconnaissance trip to the courtyard in back of my apartment building and looked up at my window, barred for inner-city security. Coco stared down at me in silent appeal.

I widened my gaze. An old, wooden ladder was half-hidden behind some shrubs. I leaned it against the building under my window. There was still a five-foot gap, but it was worth a try.

I tried not to think about other city critters that might find the makeshift entrance inviting as I opened the window just enough for Coco to slip under. She had no trouble jumping down to the top of the ladder. As I watched her disappear around the corner of the building, I prayed she'd be able to make the jump back up again—and that she'd be safe.

I know it's irresponsible to let house cats outside, especially in a busy city, but Coco's need to go out was so intense, I couldn't help but believe she knew what she was doing. Even so, I probably glanced out that window every quarter hour for the rest of the afternoon.

Just as I was starting to worry, I heard the rattle of the mini-blind covering the open window. Coco jumped down to the floor, then turned to stare back at the window. Almost immediately, a black-and-white head pushed aside the blind. Coco gave an encouraging meow, and the newcomer jumped down. The cats touched noses as I stared in disbelief.

The visiting cat wasn't very clean—her spots were more gray than white—and she was extremely thin, except for her belly, which showed obvious signs of late-stage pregnancy. I couldn't imagine how Coco had induced her to make that last five-foot jump onto the sill, let alone enter a strange apartment. But there she was, looking around my bedroom while Coco gently licked her neck and back.

"This is not a good idea," I grumbled as I put out a second dish of food and introduced the visitor to the litter box. "Tomorrow, she has to go to the Humane Society. After all, that's the responsible thing to do with stray cats, especially pregnant stray cats." Both cats ignored my comments.

The next morning, I pulled my cat carrier from under my bed and went looking for the stray. She wasn't in any of the rooms of the apartment. Finally, I noticed Coco sneaking into my hall coat closet. When I opened the door, I found the visitor cat stretched out in a box of winter garments nursing four tiny fur balls. Okay, forget the Humane Society. How heartless would I have to be to turn out a new mother and four adorable babies?

Polly, as I now called her, and her babies stayed in the closet for a couple of weeks, until the babies got big enough and brave enough to venture out into the apartment. During that time, it was apparent Polly wasn't exhibiting natural maternal behavior. She didn't even groom herself, let alone her babies. Coco assumed responsibility for cleaning, cuddling and playing with the kittens. Polly merely served as wet nurse, showing no interest in her offspring, as Coco taught them how to wash and defend themselves, and to use the litter box. In fact, Polly showed little interest in anything and spent most of her time staring into space. As soon as the kittens were weaned, I took her to my vet for spaying and shots. In the course of his examination, he discovered Polly was deaf and possibly brain-damaged.

On the other hand, the kittens were as active and curious as kittens everywhere, getting into everything and getting bigger each day. I decided I would keep Polly and started looking for adoptive homes for the kittens. Within a week, I found homes for all four.

The day the last kitten left, Coco retreated under the couch and refused to come out for her evening meal, occasionally emitting soft kitty moans. The next morning, she was still there, and no amount of coaxing could budge her. I thought about taking a sick day from work, but I was afraid that "my cat's depressed because she lost her foster kittens" was not a legitimate excuse for absence. I rushed home after work and, when Coco failed to meet me at the door, looked under the couch. There was only empty space and some shed fur. I made a tour of the apartment and finally found both cats curled up face-to-face in the box of winter clothes in the hall closet, Polly with both paws around Coco's neck. Coco looked up when I opened the door, but Polly just continued licking Coco's face. Both cats were purring loudly.

Coco and Polly still live with me and are never very far away from each other. Coco never eats her food until she's sure Polly is beside her at her own dish, and she faithfully grooms her daily. Polly remains unresponsive to my attention. She seems happiest when cuddled up against Coco.

I guess my daughter was right: Coco did need a pet, someone to take care of. And Polly and her kittens would never have survived for long on their own. How Coco knew this, I'll never know. And, somehow, by some instinct, Polly recognized when Coco was grieving and was able to offer the comfort she needed, comfort that could only come from another cat.

~Sheila Sowder
Chicken Soup for the Cat Lover's Soul

The Cat and the Grizzly

"Another box of kittens dumped over the fence, Dave," one of our volunteers greeted me one summer morning. I groaned inside. As the founder of Wildlife Images Rehabilitation Center, I had more than enough to do to keep up with the wild animals in our care. But somehow, local people who didn't have the heart to take their unwanted kittens to the pound often dumped them over our fence. They knew we'd try to live-trap them, spay or neuter them, and place them through our network of approximately 100 volunteers.

That day's brood contained four kittens. We managed to trap three of them, but somehow one little rascal got away. In twenty-four acres of park, there wasn't much we could do once the kitten disappeared—and many other animals required our attention. It wasn't long before I forgot completely about the lost kitten as I went about my daily routine.

A week or so later, I was spending time with one of my favorite "guests"—a giant grizzly bear named Griz.

This grizzly bear had come to us as an orphaned cub six years ago, after being struck by a train in Montana. He'd been rescued by a Blackfoot Indian, had lain unconscious for six days in a Montana hospital's intensive care unit, and ended up with neurological damage and a blind right eye. As he recovered, it was clear he was too habituated to humans and too mentally impaired to go back to the wild, so he came to live with us as a permanent resident.

Grizzly bears are not generally social creatures. Except for when they mate or raise cubs, they're loners. But this grizzly liked people. I enjoyed spending time with Griz, giving him personal attention on a regular basis. Even this required care, since a 560-pound creature could do a lot of damage to a human unintentionally.

That July afternoon, I approached his cage for our daily visit. He'd just been served his normal meal — a mix of vegetables, fruit, dog kibble, fish and chicken. Griz was lying down with the bucket between his forepaws, eating, when I noticed a little spot of orange coming out of the blackberry brambles inside the grizzly's pen.

It was the missing kitten. Now probably six weeks old, it couldn't have weighed more than ten ounces at most. Normally, I would have been concerned that the poor little thing was going to starve to death. But this kitten had taken a serious wrong turn and might not even last that long.

What should I do? I was afraid that if I ran into the pen to try to rescue it, the kitten would panic and run straight for Griz. So I just stood back and watched, praying that it wouldn't get too close to the huge grizzly.

But it did. The tiny kitten approached the enormous bear and let out a purr and a mew. I winced. With any normal bear, that cat would be dessert.

Griz looked over at him. I cringed as I watched him raise his forepaw toward the cat and braced myself for the fatal blow.

But Griz stuck his paw into his food pail, where he grabbed a piece of chicken out of the bucket and threw it toward the starving kitten.

The little cat pounced on it and carried it quickly into the bushes to eat.

I breathed a sigh of relief. That cat was one lucky animal! He'd approached the one bear of the sixteen we housed that would tolerate him — and the one in a million who'd share lunch.

A couple of weeks later, I saw the cat feeding with Griz again. This time, he rubbed and purred against the bear, and Griz reached down and picked him up by the scruff of his neck. After that, the friendship blossomed. We named the kitten Cat.

These days, Cat eats with Griz all the time. He rubs up against the bear, bats him on the nose, ambushes him, even sleeps with him. And although Griz is a gentle bear, a bear's gentleness is not all that gentle. Once Griz accidentally stepped on Cat. He looked horrified when he realized what he'd done. And sometimes when Griz tries to pick up Cat by the scruff of the cat's neck, he winds up grabbing Cat's whole head. But Cat doesn't seem to mind.

Their love for each other is so pure and simple; it goes beyond size and species. Both animals have managed to successfully survive their rough beginnings. But even more than that, they each seem so happy to have found a friend.

~Dave Siddon
Chicken Soup for the Pet Lover's Soul

Pedro the Fisherman

There is no faith which has never yet been broken,
except that of a truly faithful dog.
~Konrad Lorenz

The most touching dog story I've ever heard was told to me thirty years ago by a neighbor on her return from a Mediterranean cruise.

The setting of the story is a little cove on the east side of the Spanish island of Mallorca. It was there that an Englishman, a professional diver, lived on his yacht with his dog, a springer spaniel. He had tied his yacht to a pier where diving conditions were ideal. Each time the Englishman made a dive, the dog sat anxiously on the pier, awaiting his return. One day the dog became so concerned when the Englishman disappeared into the water that he dove in after him.

Underwater, the dog saw a school of fish swim past. He grabbed a fish and carried it back to the pier. The Englishman, surprised and pleased, praised him. After that, the dog followed the man on his dives. In the course of the shared diving, the dog developed excellent fishing skills, to the man's considerable amusement. The Englishman told the island's residents of his dog's accomplishments, and they came to the pier to watch. Delighted, they began calling the dog Pedro, after Peter, the fisherman.

One day the Englishman became ill, and shortly thereafter, he died. Townspeople tried to adopt Pedro, but the dog would never leave the beach for fear he would miss his master's return. He waited on the beach through hot sun and driving rain. People tried to feed him, but eventually they gave up. He wouldn't accept food from anyone other than his master. Finally, to feed himself, Pedro went back to fishing.

It happened that on this same island there were a number of stray cats. Ravenous, they would gather to watch Pedro dive into the schools of fish, select the fish he wanted and bring it back to eat on the shore. Then the cats would fight over what the dog had left uneaten. The dog must have observed this, for one morning when Pedro had eaten his fill, he dove into the water again and came back up with a large fish, which he placed on the sand before the group of cats. Then he backed off and watched. One black cat, with greater courage than the others, approached the fish, grabbed it and ran. After that, in addition to keeping vigil for his master, the dog also seemed to consider it his duty to feed those less fortunate. For every morning thereafter, Pedro the fisherman shared his catch with the hungry cats of Mallorca.

~Bob Toren
Chicken Soup for the Dog Lover's Soul

Barney

Kindness is the greatest wisdom.
~Author Unknown

Mary Guy figured that becoming a national celebrity was probably about as much as a squirrel could hope to achieve in one lifetime. But Barney is not your average squirrel.

Mary has a bottled water business in Garden City, Kansas. She is also a known animal lover. One day in August of 1994, one of her customers showed her an orphaned baby fox squirrel that he had found. When he asked if she could care for it, she felt she had to at least give it a try.

It so happened that a week earlier, Mary's cat, Corky, had had four kittens. Mary's husband, Charlie, suggested they try adding the squirrel to the litter of kittens—and it worked! Barney (named by a grandson after a particular purple dinosaur) was not only adopted by Corky, he was accepted as a sibling by all four kittens. He became especially close with one feline sister, Celeste.

Some of the Guys' guests thought this cat/squirrel family was so adorable that they contacted the local newspaper about it. The paper ran a story with a photo of the mother cat nursing her four kittens and Barney under the headline: "One of these kittens seems sort of squirrelly."

The unusual story was picked up by the Associated Press and sent to newspapers all over the country. As a result, Mary received calls and letters from all over the country, and even Canada, by people who were impressed with the story and picture. Barney was a celebrity!

Unfortunately, there was a downside to Barney's fame.

The article was seen by employees of the Kansas Department of Wildlife and Parks. A state official contacted the Guys and told them that it is illegal to keep a squirrel as a pet in the state of Kansas. They would have to return Barney to the wild.

Mary was thunderstruck. Not only had she become attached to her unusual pet, she feared for his life if he were turned loose. He had no fear of cats—he'd been raised by one! But squirrels are rodents and cats are natural enemies of rodents. If Barney were turned loose, he'd be lunch for the first stray cat he met. She explained this to the authorities, but to no avail. The law's the law.

"Well, ma'am," suggested one officer, "if you buy a hunting license, you can legally keep him until the end of squirrel season. It runs until December 31."

It was a temporary solution, but Mary hurried out to pay the thirteen dollars for a hunting license.

Mary grieved as the end of the year approached. She had come to truly love the mischievous little guy and was certain that turning him loose was tantamount to a death sentence.

Also, by this time, all of the kittens had been adopted except Celeste; and she and Barney were now best friends. They played together, slept together and chased each other all over the house. If Mary separated them, Celeste wailed miserably. And Barney showed not the slightest interest in life in the great outdoors.

Mary again approached the newspapers. Perhaps the same notoriety that had landed Barney in this mess could lead to a solution.

The story of Barney's plight went out over the Associated Press wires. By early December, Mary was deluged with calls and letters from all over the country offering their prayers and moral support. Some callers who lived in states with differing laws even offered to take in both Barney and Celeste.

The Wildlife and Parks Department also received calls and mail from around the country. Not wanting to look heartless, they suggested that Barney might be released at the Garden City Zoo's park. The Kansas Attorney General called Mary and suggested that she give Barney to a "rehabilitator" who would teach him to survive in the wild before releasing him.

Still, Mary feared for the safety of her beloved pet—and knew he didn't want to leave his happy life any more than she wanted to lose him.

As New Year's Eve approached, the Guys saw one slim chance. The new year would bring a new administration into the Kansas statehouse. Mary arranged for friends who were invited to the new governor's inaugural celebration to take information about Barney with them.

One of the first acts of the Kansas governor's office in 1995 was to issue the Guys a special permit to keep their squirrel.

And so Barney became the first squirrel in history to not only become a national celebrity, but to receive a pardon from the governor.

No, not your average squirrel at all.

~Gregg Bassett
Chicken Soup for the Pet Lover's Soul

Loving Our Cats

Chapter 6

Cats

The Power of the Bond

*When I play with my cat, who knows if I am not
a pastime to her more than she to me?*
~Montaigne

35

The Cloe Cure

It is impossible to keep a straight face in the presence of one or more kittens.
~Cynthia E. Varnado

"Why do I feel this way?" my daughter blurted out one day. "There's nothing really wrong with my life!"

I knew that depression often hounded young people, but it had been hard to accept that my bright, pretty teen was that unhappy. Corrie had been such a contented child. As an infant, a game of peek-a-boo would elicit baby belly-laughs. When she was a toddler, she stopped to hug every elderly lady at the mall. "Hug?" she would frequently ask me throughout the day, her small arms open to receive. As a young child, she was outgoing and friendly, but I began to notice a tendency toward worry, and, as she approached her teens, she became more and more cheerless.

My husband John and I weren't too worried about our daughter. After all, most teenagers occasionally feel morose and hopeless, and we were confident that we could help her through those instances. But, as time went by, Corrie's depression worsened. The day she questioned me about her dark moods, there was a vague suggestion of despair in her voice that started me thinking. My daughter slept whenever there was a lull in the activity of her day, dragged herself to school and back, and rarely smiled. Daily headaches and a poor appetite plagued her as well. In the past, she had always been an above-average student, but now her marks were dropping steadily.

This was not something that a parent could reason away or kiss and "make better," so I took my daughter to the doctor's office. Corrie was diagnosed as suffering from a chemical imbalance, explained as a lack of serotonin, the brain's mood-lifting neurotransmitter. The doctor prescribed an anti-depressant, and I prayed.

Meanwhile, Corrie was approaching her seventeenth birthday. She wasn't excited by the prospect and couldn't even find enough enthusiasm to decide what she wanted us to give her. John and I knew that she had wanted a cat for years, but we had always said that one pet in the house was enough, and we already had Toby. However, the ten-year-old dog was a good-natured mutt, and John and I had hopes that a kitten would lift Corrie's spirits, if only slightly. At her birthday dinner in April, we gave Corrie a card with a picture of a kitten on it, and the "gift" she opened was a cat toy and a ceramic food dish decorated with playful cat-related drawings. I don't think Corrie was quite sure we meant it. She smiled faintly and asked, "You're giving me a cat?"

Even so, Corrie was eager to begin the search for her perfect companion, and she knew exactly what she was looking for. Corrie's Aunt Janet had a tortoiseshell cat, and Corrie had always admired Mieka's black, cream and caramel coloring. Toby had come from the local animal shelter, and I again wanted to give a neglected animal a home, but the kittens at the shelter were still too young to leave their mother, so I took Corrie to a local pet shop. I had no doubt that God had taken a hand in the matter when we got to the store. There in the window, romping and wrestling with her black and gray companions, was Corrie's heart's desire. The seven-week-old kitten was barely a handful of tortie fur, and, as Corrie held the docile little animal against her shoulder and smiled down into the large golden eyes topped by cream-colored "eyebrows," there was no doubt in my mind that this search would be short-lived. Soon, Corrie was seated in the car cradling a cardboard box emitting tiny questioning mews.

On the way home, Corrie began to think about a name for her kitten, but it would be two days before she finally settled on Cloe, which she selected from the same baby-name book from which I had picked her own name. (Corrie opted for the more unusual spelling — rather than the standard: Chloe.) She had rejected her father's suggestion of Marbles as too cutesy, insisting that it had to be a "real" name.

Cloe purred as she walked about exploring her new home, and we took that as an encouraging sign. We would often see her darting out from under a tablecloth, limbs splayed out like a flying squirrel, in preparation for tackling the unsuspecting dog as he napped on the floor nearby. Immediately following such an antic, I would hear my daughter laughing with delight. What a great sound! Someone once said that it's impossible not to smile in the presence of one or more kittens. They were right. Everything about Cloe enchanted Corrie, from the awkward little kitten walk to the way she wiggled her backside just before she pounced on a "victim." It comforted Corrie to have Cloe curl up next to her on the bed at night. One evening, the kitten jumped up on the bed and started purring and mewing until Corrie couldn't resist sitting up in bed to pet her. Before she knew what had happened, Cloe had taken possession of the pillow, and Corrie giggled as she realized that her kitten had tricked her. Cloe was sociable and easygoing, often adopting the dog's habit of following us from room to room or sauntering over to the door to greet whoever had just come in.

God gave John and me the miracle we were seeking in the form of a tiny multicolored ball of fur. Corrie no longer moaned, "I'm so depressed!" Instead, it was a joyful, "Mom, I love this kitty so much!" She slept less during the day, ate better, suffered fewer headaches, and her marks started to improve.

More than a year later, just the mention of her pet's name still puts a contented grin on our daughter's face. Corrie calls Cloe her "fuzzy angel," and it seems an apt description. Angels, after all, come to help heal our spirits, and Cloe has become a significant part of the remedy her young guardian needs. Sometimes, there's no medicine like the unconditional love of a trusting animal—no balm to the soul like the satisfied purr and silky coat of a little tortie cat resting against your shoulder.

~Marlene Alexander
Chicken Soup for the Cat Lover's Soul

36

Lucky to Be Alive

Wherever there is a human being, there is an opportunity for a kindness.
~Seneca

aria, a gentle, soft-spoken woman of seventy, had always managed to view the world with a child's sense of wonder. She greeted the dawn of each new day with the brightness of the sun itself and found joy in the smallest of things: a dove perched on her birdfeeder, the fresh morning dew, the sweet scent of jasmine in her garden.

A widow, Maria lived alone in a run-down neighborhood in Deerfield Beach, Florida. One day while out tending the small garden in front of her modest home, Maria had been injured in a drive-by shooting. The bullet had pierced her skin with a ferocious bite and lodged itself in the old woman's right thigh. Crying out in agony, she had dropped to the sidewalk. When the mailman found her unconscious nearly an hour later, her injured leg had been bleeding profusely. She'd made it to the hospital just in time and later, the doctor had told Maria she was lucky to be alive.

Returning home, Maria didn't feel so lucky. Before the shooting, the elderly woman had always been grateful that she was healthy for her age. Now just getting the daily mail required a Herculean effort. In addition, her medical bills were mounting alarmingly, straining her meager income. And although she had watched the neighborhood deteriorate, somehow things had seemed safe in the daylight—but not anymore. For the first time in her life, Maria felt frightened, alone and vulnerable.

"I feel defeated," she had told her friend Vera. "I'm just an old woman with nothing to do and nowhere to go."

When Vera came to pick up Maria for her checkup at the medical center, she hardly recognized her old friend. Maria's soft brown eyes held a haunting sadness and her face was gaunt and haggard. All the curtains were drawn and her hands shook with fear as she hobbled out onto the front porch, a cane stabilizing her injured leg.

They were a little early for Maria's appointment, so to try to cheer up Maria, Vera took a longer, more scenic route. They were stopped at a red light when Maria suddenly shrieked. "Look at that cat! It's trying to run across the street!"

Vera looked up to see a small black-and-white cat bounding into the middle of traffic. Both women screamed as they saw one car, then another, and finally a third, hit the cat. The cat lay motionless, its small body flung into the grass. Cars slowed, but no one stopped to help.

"We must save that poor creature," said Maria. Vera pulled over, got out of the car and went to the hurt animal. Miraculously, it was still alive, but badly injured.

"Take my jacket and wrap the kitty in it," said Maria. Vera carefully put the cat on the seat between them. It looked up at Maria and gave her a plaintive, barely audible meow.

"Everything will be all right, my little friend," Maria said tearfully.

Finding an animal clinic, they went inside and told the receptionist what had happened.

"I'm sorry," she said, "but we cannot accept stray animals."

It was the same at the next clinic. Finally, at the third clinic, a kind veterinarian, Dr. Susan Shanahan, agreed to help and quickly started working on the cat.

"This little guy is lucky to be alive," she told Maria and Vera. "If you hadn't been there for him, he never would have made it."

The vet took Maria aside. "The cat's injuries are very serious," she said. "He has severe head trauma, crushed paws and a cracked collarbone. He'll need a lot of expensive medical attention. Today's bill alone will cost at least $400."

Maria gasped. But taking her worn cloth wallet from her handbag, she gave the doctor all the money she had after paying her bills—$50.

"It's all I have right now, but I promise I will pay you the rest over time. Please don't put that kitty to sleep," she pleaded. "I'll take him home. We need each other."

Sensing how important this was, Dr. Shanahan kneeled and took Maria's hands in hers. "I could get into trouble with my boss for doing this," she said gently. "You see, I really shouldn't have helped the cat in the first place, but, don't worry... I will personally pay for this."

While the cat was at the clinic, Maria went to check on him every day. She spoke softly to him and gently stroked his chin with her little finger. As the days passed, the cat began to purr and the sparkle returned to Maria's eyes.

The day arrived for the cat to come home. As excited as a little girl on Christmas morning, Maria smiled brightly as she walked into the clinic to pick him up.

"What have you decided to name the cat?" asked Dr. Shanahan.

Cradling the cat in her arms, Maria answered happily, "I'm going to call him Lucky, because together we have found a new life."

~Christine E. Belleris
Chicken Soup for the Pet Lover's Soul

37

To Find a Friend

During the summer of 2003, the Mustafa Hotel in Kabul, Afghanistan, was thronged with journalists, aid workers, American embassy personnel and businessmen. It offered a wide range of amenities—and a place to find peace after a hard day of stark encounters with the grinding desolation of this war-ravaged city.

As a freelance journalist based in Kabul for my second straight year, I felt reduced to a state of profound depression by circumstances both personal and political. I longed for peace. But what I needed most was a very special friend, a sort of cosmic messenger to miraculously appear and reconnect me to all the goodness and beauty of the universe.

I had such a friend in Kabul the year before. Though now safe at home in America, I had rescued the darling little tuxedo kitten, Queen Soraya, from Kabul's devastated streets, saving her from a stark fate. Now, I needed some fellow inhabitant of Earth to do the same for me.

I was heading toward Pashtunistan Square, a once-grand public space in front of the presidential palace, when I saw him. Right in front of me on the broken sidewalk, as if he had appeared out of nowhere, was a tiny, handsome, tiger kitten, calmly surveying the grim scene of beggars, street kids and burqa-shrouded women. Well-groomed, alert and self-possessed, he was the only whole and healthy thing amid the battered vista.

I scooped him up like a parched man reaching for his first sip of water and plopped him into my briefcase among my clippings and notes. He accepted this with perfect equanimity, as if he had been waiting for such a thing to happen. After I zipped him inside, he pushed his pink-and-black nose through the breathing space left open at the end, his darling kitten snout pointing the way back to the hotel.

Once in the garden of the hotel, I proceeded to examine him. The kitten sported intricate black tiger stripes on a field of gray—and his underside was covered with spots. "So you are not only a babur, you are also a palang!" I said to him, using the Dari (an Afghan dialect) words for tiger and leopard. "You must be very hungry. I will fetch you a meal fit for both."

I fed him my own poor fare—a U.S. Army ration Meals Ready to Eat (MRE)—and pondered what name to give this special little boy who had come into my life when he was most needed. I settled on Dost Mohammad Khan, after the nineteenth-century king of Afghanistan who had been overthrown, but had returned to lead his people to independence and justice. Dost also means "friend," and, indeed, I needed one badly. After obtaining permission to keep him with me—he could stay in the hotel garden—my kitten and I began our life together.

Oh, what fun Dost and I had that summer! He was the most agile, bouncing, playful and happy kitten I had ever seen. He brought sunshine back into my life with his antics, his every movement directed at a joyous affirmation of life. No rose garden could hold him, though. He continually and literally pushed boundaries, racing along the adjoining hotel rooms and darting in any doors left open for curious exploration.

Dost became the darling of the hotel, but no one appreciated his presence more than I. Any hour of the day, Dost met me with welcoming meows so sincere and pure, it was obvious he considered me as special as I did him. He'd grab my pant leg, begging to be held, and then would furiously rub his little pink-and-black nose against mine. I began sneaking Dost into my room at night to indulge in late-night play sessions. Then we'd sleep side by side until he awakened me the next morning with a loving rub against my nose, and I'd sneak him back to the garden for his MRE breakfast.

But sunshine again turned to darkness the day Dost went missing from the hotel.

I looked everywhere, I asked everyone, but no one had seen him. The hotel is a closed and secure compound, with only one way in and out. The little darling of the hotel would not have been allowed to make such an exit by those who knew him. What had happened? I lay awake in my room that night unable to sleep—alone once more, and overwhelmed by feelings of solitude and powerlessness.

The next morning, I learned that workmen doing renovations—not part of the close-knit Mustafa family—were annoyed by his kitten antics, and, to get him out of their way, had often tossed Dost onto the first-story roof that flanked the garden. This last time, he'd obviously jumped to the adjacent alley to resume his explorations of the city of his birth. My dear friend was once again forced to survive without the nurturing hand that desperately needed his nurture.

There was only one thing to do: I had to spread the word.

I placed an ad in The Kabul Weekly, a widely read bilingual journal, describing Dost and the circumstances of his disappearance. I included a reward of 2,500 afghanis (about $50) for his return, the equivalent of a month's pay in a city racked by unemployment and desperate poverty.

"I hope it is not a joke," the editor said, very seriously.

"On my honor, it is not," I answered. "We feringhee (foreigners) have very strong feelings about cats."

Knowing that it would not be enough to simply print an advertisement that many would ignore or regard with derision, I resolved to take more aggressive steps in the search. All Kabul had to know about my quest.

I enlarged the advertisement, made hundreds of copies and posted flyers everywhere: in front of embassies and United Nations offices; opposite the central, blue-domed Pul-i-Khisti mosque; across from Kabul's only synagogue and its two Hindu temples; at kebab stalls and teahouses; and along the fabled commercial boulevards of Chicken and Flower Streets. People took time from pressing business to read about the lost cat. Those who could not read—tragically, a majority of the Afghan population—were told of my quest by those who could.

"His name is Dost!" I heard a woman in a fringed sky-blue burqa tell a ragged little boy outside the Mustafa. "He is the kitten of a very great feringhee who loves him very much and will pay much for his return."

The extent of my greatness was certainly exaggerated by the lady, and the reward was only big in Afghan terms, but she was right about the love part.

The tens of thousands of dirty, ragged children who constantly wander the streets seeking money seemed a promising resource to help retrieve my beloved little wanderer. The only issue was one of conscience: Was it right to use the street children of Kabul toward a personal end, and would I be hurting or helping them in any way?

Most of these waifs are not orphans, but have families dependent on them for survival. There are two schools of thought as to how to deal with the street kids. One is that, as long as the situation in Afghanistan remains so grim, the way of compassion lies in giving them a little something to ensure that they and their families will live to see the better day that the international community is striving to bring about. The other is that individual charity actually hurts them by rewarding the choice of a life on the streets, when they would be better off in school. My own position came to be a compromise between the two, which influenced me to enlist their aid in finding Dost.

I explained my mission to a couple of boys I knew and gave them flyers to pass on to their fellow waifs. I repeated this action on street corners around town. On the whole, the kids were energized by the task I had given them, inspired in no small part by the prospect of the life-transforming sum of money. The fun and play were just as important to them, though—looking for a lost cat relieved the daily drudgery of begging or selling wares, and reintroduced a childlike element back into lives devoid of such innocent endeavors. I took solace in this, and joy in the new sense of wonder I had given them.

My quest to find my friend thus became a citywide phenomenon, the talk of teahouses and kebab stalls, the subject of concerned, quizzical, as well as condescending comments. Yet, after two weeks of heroic striving, there was still no sign of Dost, and I began to feel that I would never see my precious kitten again. How could my campaign that had become the talk of Kabul have failed to yield even a single sighting of my little friend? As I listlessly sipped green tea in my room at the Mustafa, there was a knock at the door, and I opened it to find one of the hotel boys standing there with a Cheshire cat grin on his face.

"Mr. Vanni, there is a little girl downstairs who is asking for you," he beamed. "I think she has some good news for you."

I raced down two flights of stairs into the lobby, where I beheld a sight that I will remember and treasure for the rest of my life.

There in the entrance, bathed in the particular crystalline light of a Kabul afternoon, stood a tiny schoolgirl wearing the universal Afghan girls' school uniform of black trousers, black jacket and white headscarf. She gently rocked something wrapped in a blue shawl, cradling it in her arms like a new mother. Her light-brown oval face seemed perfect in its innocent beauty, save for a scar on one cheek, which was completely obscured by her radiant smile. As she held out the bundle toward me, a little feline head popped up.

"Do-o-o-o-ost!" giggled the girl.

There he was, magnificent in his tiger-leopard uniqueness, once again singing that joyous meow of recognition that had come to be the sweetest music in the world to me. A few moments of passionate nose rubbing and a quick glance at those special markings dispelled all doubts. Dost was back. I had found my little friend.

"Where did you find him?" I handed the girl her richly deserved reward, which I imagined would help her buy schoolbooks and provide for her family.

She spoke no English, so one of the guards interpreted.

"She found him where she lives, in Khair Khana," he said. "She was on her way to school, and he was just there on the sidewalk, watching everyone pass."

"Khair Khana!" I exclaimed as I held Dost up in front of my face. "That's all the way over on the western part of town, miles away! Dost, how did you get all the way over there?" I laughed with that special relief that follows an averted disaster.

A vigorous and self-affirming meow was the only description he offered of what must have been an epic two-week odyssey of dodging cars, avoiding dogs, negotiating rubble and scrounging for food. After profusely thanking the blushing child and giving her some candy as an extra mark of my gratitude, I triumphantly bore Dost up to my room.

There was no question of his returning to live in the rose garden after such a close call and long agony. I resolved that he would stay safe in my room until I took him back with me to America. I wanted to give him a new life and fill his world with sunshine, as he had done for me here in this beautiful, yet heartbreaking place called Kabul.

~Vanni Cappelli
Chicken Soup for the Cat and Dog Lover's Soul

[*Editor's Note*: This award-winning story first appeared, in a different form, in CAT FANCY magazine.]

38

Under His Spell

Dogs have owners, cats have staff.
~Author Unknown

I can feel him watching me
Through golden eyes, unblinking,
And I can't help but wonder
Just what it is he's thinking.

I know his habits, I know his ways
But his moods are hard to tell
The only thing I know for sure is
He knows I'm under his spell.

For eating he's claimed my nicest dish
To nap, my favorite chair
And anytime I want to sit,
He's comfortably resting there.

For play, he's got expensive toys
To chase and romp and caper
But still he's only happy with
A balled-up piece of paper!

He's always begging for attention
To be scratched beneath his chin

And when my writing takes me away from him
He steals my writing pen!

Despite our unique relationship
People ask, "Just who owns who?"
It's really nice to have someone
To look forward to come home to.

And so, I stay enchanted with
This crazy pet of mine
For nothing keeps you spellbound
Like a furry, finicky feline!

~Tami Sandlin
Chicken Soup for the Soul Celebrates Cats

The Uncles

I get by with a little help from my friends.
~John Lennon

Many years ago, we had a cat named Curly. The one thing that people remembered about him was his gorgeous, long black-and-white fur. As a kitten, he was just one big ball of fluff, accented by long curly hairs sticking out of his ears—hence the name.

And, of course, if you'd been around our house long enough, you'd know he was the "top cat" of our group of felines. Self-appointed, of course. This meant that he would have preferred his brother Grayspot to set off for parts unknown and never return. Ditto for Yellowcat, an old stray who was always hanging around. Along with this status went a responsibility that Curly took very seriously: care and concern for all the younger cats.

It all started when Mama Cat, an attractive young stray, decided that the space under our storage shed was the perfect place for her soon-due family. Our other cats accepted her as warmly as if they'd known her all their lives. Soon, she introduced her three new kittens to us: Ginger, a friendly, inquisitive, ginger-colored longhair; Blue Eyes, a beautiful tawny shorthair with big blue eyes; and Stripes, their dark, drab littermate.

All of them loved to play with their "uncles," Grayspot and Curly—especially Curly, who delighted in their merry antics. Unfortunately, they imitated their overly wary mother and refused to have anything to do with us humans. All five felines—kittens and uncles alike—slept together in the cozy nest under the shed, at least until the day the uncles remembered they couldn't stand to be near each other. After that you never saw the kittens with more than one uncle at a time.

Then, one day when the kittens were about four months old, Stripes suddenly became very ill. After two days of constant diarrhea and vomiting, he was so dehydrated that I thought he was already dead. All the other cats were concerned—Curly most of all. What Stripes needed, of course, was a vet's care, but his mother refused to let me near him. Without fluids, little Stripes was a goner. When he collapsed in the backyard a long way from the water dish, there seemed to be no hope.

While I was inside finding a suitable bag for the inevitable burial, I glanced out the window to see something startling. Curly was headed across the backyard toward the water dish. So was Grayspot. But these sworn enemies were walking very slowly—side by side!

Then I saw the reason. Supported between the two of them was poor little Stripes! Inch by inch, Curly and Grayspot moved forward, carrying the sick little kitten with them—all the way to the water dish. And they continued to hold him upright while he drank the life-giving liquid.

After that, Curly never left Stripes's side until the kitten was completely well. Unfortunately, that meant he also caught whatever it was that had made his little friend so ill. He recovered, but his strength never returned.

That year, our rain came early and in torrents. With the kittens rapidly growing, there was now room for only one adult in their safe, dry nest. Curly insisted that Grayspot sleep there with the little ones; Curly stayed just outside, in the driving rain, and refused to let me budge him. Already weakened in his chest area, he quickly succumbed to pneumonia and died.

I don't know how Curly convinced Grayspot to help Stripes that day—perhaps Grayspot volunteered. Curly's beautiful coat was memorable, but his amazing compassion, self-sacrifice and unconditional love are what I remember most about him—and which still fill my heart.

~Bonnie Compton Hanson
Chicken Soup for the Cat Lover's Soul

The Cat and the Christmas Star

I would maintain that thanks are the highest form of thought;
and that gratitude is happiness doubled by wonder.
~G.K. Chesterton

Tears fell from my eyes onto the poster board below and mixed with the ink from the felt marker I was using to write "Missing: Gray tabby cat with white paws and green eyes."

Linda, my missing cat, had shared a close relationship with me ever since I had adopted him about two years before. Despite the fact that I had given him a female name (after an exam, our vet mistakenly told us he was female and we didn't find out the truth until much later), he didn't seem to mind. And even now, when we had taken him from his familiar South Carolina neighborhood and moved him to Virginia, he seemed to bear it well. Linda continued to faithfully greet me every day when I returned home from school. But my younger sister had recently adopted a kitten, and Linda hadn't taken this change well. The image of the hurt look he had given me after meeting the kitten was still etched vividly in my memory.

One night soon afterward, he didn't come home for his evening meal, and none of my repeated calls throughout the neighborhood brought him running. The cheerfulness of the Christmas decorations on the houses failed to excite me the way they usually did. I went to bed reluctantly, certain he would turn up first thing the next morning. But I was wrong. And after two days, I started to panic.

Frantically, I dialed the local animal shelter, but no cats fitting his description had come in. So, with my family's help, I'd made and distributed the posters and even found a local radio station willing to announce Linda's disappearance and plead for his return. Every day after school, I spent hours either on foot or bike scanning the neighborhood for him and calling his name until my voice was hoarse. Every night in bed I asked God to bring him home.

By the time Christmas Eve had arrived, Linda still had not. He had been missing for eight days. After spending the church service and our Christmas Eve dinner distracted by my sadness and anxiety, I glumly went to bed where I dutifully prayed once more that God would bring Linda home. Then exhausted, I fell into a deep sleep.

Several hours later, my clock radio blinked 11:59 P.M. I suddenly awoke. It was rare for me to wake in the middle of the night; I'd always been a sound sleeper. But as I lay in the darkness, I was fully awake and consumed with a desire to get up and look at the stars outside.

For several years, I'd had a personal Christmas Eve tradition of scanning the sky for the brightest star, which I liked to imagine was the "Christmas star." Whether it was actually the North Star that led the ancient wise men to baby Jesus in the manger, I didn't know. But I enjoyed viewing it anyway, and usually looked for it before I went to bed on Christmas Eve. As I lay there wondering why I was awake all of a sudden, I realized that I hadn't even bothered to look for it this year.

Eagerly, I leapt from my bed and peeked through the blinds on my bedroom window, but I couldn't discern any stars. Then a thought came to me with surprising strength. Try the front door. Now.

The thought of opening the door to the icy wind outside didn't excite me, but somehow, I felt, I had to find the Christmas star. So I unfastened both locks and swung the door open. Shivering in my nightgown, I scanned the sky until a silvery white dot came into view. The Christmas star! At that moment, I knew that no matter where Linda was, or if he ever returned, God still cared for me.

I stared at the star for a moment, then reached for the door to pull it shut, looking down to the front stoop as I did so. And then I saw him—Linda—thin, shivering and reeking of gasoline. He sat quietly before me. His green eyes searched mine, as if to say, "I'm sorry. Will you take me back?"

Immediately, I scooped him up. But before I closed the door, I stood with Linda in my arms to gaze once more at the Christmas star. Then I said a prayer of thanks to the God who watches over all his creation—from the most distant star to the purring cat I held closely.

~Whitney Von Lake Hopler
Chicken Soup for the Soul Christmas Treasury for Kids

41

Vavoom's Lesson in Love

You can't stay in your corner of the forest waiting for others to come to you.
You have to go to them sometimes.
~Winnie the Pooh

The Bible says that "perfect love casts out fear." I had never seen that demonstrated until I met Vavoom, a tiny calico feral cat.

Vavoom blew in with a blizzard one winter, and spent her days with two male companions in the relative warmth and safety of my crawlspace. Despite the temperatures dropping well below zero several times that January, Vavoom never showed any inclination to come into my house; I could feed her, but she insisted that I keep my distance, thank you very much! Like many feral cats, Vavoom and her friends viewed me as the enemy, a necessary evil in their environment who provided food and shelter, but who could never fully he trusted.

Spring came, and Vavoom became pregnant. She remained in the crawlspace of the house, popping out twice daily to meow at the back door for her dinner. She felt comfortable enough to ask for food, but still would flinch and run if I attempted to pet her.

Then the rain came. Lots of it. Enough in one morning to turn my back yard into a small pond, which began to drain into the crawlspace.

The power of the rainfall and wind had knocked over some potted plants I kept outside. I went out into the torrent to upright them and noticed, running toward me, a very skinny Vavoom with something small and pink in her mouth.

She had a look of urgency in her eyes and came straight toward me. She dropped her parcel on my shoe, and meowed.

It was a newborn kitten.

The kitten was hairless, premature, and turning blue from wet and exposure. I immediately picked it up and put it in the pouch of my sweat top to warm it. I picked up Vavoom without a struggle, and took the family into my utility room, where I had a cardboard box. I filled the box with soft rags, and placed the kitten into the box. Mother Vavoom jumped happily into her nest. I brought her a dish of food and some milk, sat down next to the box, and started to pet her. Instead of ducking, Vavoom thrust her head back into my hand and purred.

The next day, I found her other three kittens; they had drowned during the flooding. Apparently, Vavoom knew she could only save one, and believed I was her kitten's only hope of survival. Her desire to save her kitten's life was more important than her own fears and mistrust.

Vavoom and her kitten, George, are still part of my family. As a matter of fact, George is my brat cat — as friendly and companionable as his mother was shy and aloof. George has known only love during his life, beginning with the perfect, mother's love that saved him.

~Jean Fritz
Chicken Soup for the Soul Celebrates Cats

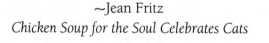

42

The China Cat

In everyone's life, at some time, our inner fire goes out.
It is then burst into flame by an encounter with another human being.
We should all be thankful for those people who rekindle the inner spirit.
~Albert Schweitzer

I stuffed the small bag of ashes into the tiny china cat and carefully glued felt to the bottom. How do I get myself into such strange situations? I wondered. Sitting at my dining room table, I stared at a bottle of glue, some scraps of felt, a pair of scissors and an elderly lady's china cat statue. I pondered the sequence of events that had led me to this.

"Dr. Bryant, can you come over and talk Mrs. Painter into putting her cat, Callie, to sleep?" As a veterinarian, I often get strange requests, and this was one of the more unusual ones. The call came from Julie, a social worker at a retirement community close to where I worked. Callie was a patient of mine, whom I had diagnosed with failing kidneys a few months earlier. Julie explained herself: "Callie looks terrible. She won't eat, and she urinates outside her box. Mrs. Painter can't care for her properly. The staff is tired of cleaning up after the cat. Will you please come and talk to her?"

After work, I drove to the retirement community and met Julie. As she led me to Mrs. Painter's room, she said, "Sometimes, she has trouble understanding, but do your best to explain what's best." Best? Best for whom?

I gently knocked on Mrs. Painter's room, rehearsing silently what I was going to say. Julie asked me not to tell her that I was being "sent." Mrs. Painter opened her door.

"Hello, Mrs. Painter, it's Dr. Bryant, from the animal hospital. I was driving by and wondered how Callie was doing, so I thought I'd stop in."

Mrs. Painter recognized me. "Oh, hello, dear! How nice of you to come!"

She led me into her room. It was small, containing a hospital bed, a vanity, a tall dresser and a bathroom that looked like one you would find in a hospital. As I looked around at her few possessions, I wondered what it must be like to narrow down a lifetime of earthly belongings so they could all fit in one room.

Mrs. Painter and I sat opposite each other. Callie was sleeping on the bed. She petted the cat gently while she spoke. "Oh, she's fine. Such good company."

Trying to get a little information—or should I say "ammunition"—I asked about her appetite and drinking habits. Mrs. Painter assured me that she was urinating in her box and her drinking habits were normal. She claimed she wasn't vomiting, and even played with her a little every afternoon. A cat in end-stage kidney failure would not be playing and eating. I didn't know what to believe. Callie was painfully thin and looked dehydrated.

Mrs. Painter said that she and her husband had lived in the independent-living section of the facility until he died a year ago. She was then sent to assisted living. Nursing care inevitably would come next. As she told me that she wasn't feeling too well lately, I could almost hear her thoughts: My cat is old; she is dying. I am old; I am dying.

Mrs. Painter gently stroked her beloved cat and said, quite out of the blue, "She is the only friend I have in the world."

I will never forget that. She is the only friend I have in the world. Sitting in that darkened room that chilly winter afternoon, with an old lady and her old cat, I silently vowed that I was never going to discuss euthanizing Callie. Not today, not ever.

As I left, I told Mrs. Painter that if she felt that Callie was not doing well, the important thing was to not let her suffer. She seemed to understand exactly what I meant. Usually, the elderly consider their lives parallel to their elderly pets' lives.

It wasn't long before I heard from Mrs. Painter. She called the day after Christmas. She was very calm and matter-of-fact. "Dr. Bryant, it's time for Callie."

Once again, I found myself in Mrs. Painter's room. Callie looked even worse than she had the month before. Her skin was stretched over her bones, and her eyes were sunken. She was semi-conscious. I gave her the painless injection, and she silently slipped away. As I wiped away tears from my own eyes, Mrs. Painter just sat on the bed and watched, dry-eyed. She said nothing.

Afterward, I sat with Mrs. Painter; she seemed far away, lost in thought. She was just sitting on the edge of her little bed, fondling a small, ceramic calico cat. When she finally spoke, it was almost as if she were talking to herself. "My husband gave me this cat for our anniversary because it looked like Callie." She handed it to me. "I want Callie cremated, Dr. Bryant. I want you to place her ashes in here and give it back to me. Would you do that?"

I looked down at the ceramic cat, representing her husband, her cat, and a life silently slipping away.

So there I sat in my dining room that January evening, watching the glue dry thoroughly on the bottom of the china cat. When I delivered the cat statue to Mrs. Painter, the loneliness in that small dark room was hard to bear. I asked Julie if we could try to find a suitable cat for Mrs. Painter. She explained that Mrs. Painter was failing and didn't have the capability to take care of another cat.

A few weeks later, I asked Julie again. She again refused. As the months went by, my thoughts would occasionally go to Mrs. Painter, and a terrible sadness would descend upon me. I pictured her in that little room with her few possessions—joyless without a pet.

Months later, I decided to visit Mrs. Painter. As I stood in the lobby and waited for the elevator, a cat appeared and sat next to me, as if she were waiting, too. When the door opened with a loud ding, I got on, and so did the cat. She calmly sat down as the elevator ascended to the second floor. The doors opened, and she sauntered out. A nurse laughed at my bemused look. "I see you've met Pumpkin," she said.

As we spoke, Pumpkin made her way to Mrs. Painter's room. The door was slightly ajar, and she walked in. Not having special privileges like the cat, I knocked. Mrs. Painter opened the door. "Well! Two of my favorite girls in one visit!" she exclaimed. I marveled at her appearance: She seemed ten years younger.

After my visit, Julie told me Pumpkin's story. A nurse had found her in the parking lot as a kitten. Soon after, she became a "resident," too. Although she visited everyone in assisted living, Mrs. Painter was her favorite. Then Julie said something that made my heart sing: "Dr. Bryant, you were right about getting another cat. Pumpkin has made all the difference in Mrs. Painter's life here."

Veterinarians live to make a difference in people's lives through their beloved pets. This time, however, it was a cat who accomplished this. Pumpkin gave Mrs. Painter something to live for.

~Mary Bryant, V.M.D.
Chicken Soup for the Cat Lover's Soul

The Wings of an Angel

Kittens are angels with whiskers.
~Author Unknown

I watch as the beautiful warm sun shines down on his gentle, young face. And the early summer breeze blows his long beautiful white hair. And for a moment... it's as if you can almost see the wings of an angel, and then I blink and they're not there.

I watch as he walks with such style and grace, each step more graceful than the last. And for a moment... it's as if you can almost see the wings of an angel, and then I blink and they're not there.

I watch as he plays with the innocence of a child. Pouncing on each wiggly toe or getting dizzy from chasing around. And for a moment... it's as if you can almost see the wings of an angel, and then I blink and they're not there.

I watch as he lies at the head of a sick, spotted child. The softness of his fur touches her itchy red skin and his musical purr becomes a soothing lullaby. And for a moment... it's as if you can almost see the wings of an angel, and then I blink and they're not there.

I watch as he looks out the window for each child to arrive home and brushes up against their legs as if to say "I've missed you," forgetting that the children are grown and have homes of their own. And for a moment... it's as if you can almost see the wings of an angel, and then I blink and they're not there.

I watch as he lies on the lap of a tired old man, whose frail callused hands gently stroke his pure white hair. And then they both sleep. And for a moment... it's as if you can almost see the wings of an angel, and then I blink and they're not there.

I watch as the warm autumn sun shines down on his aging old face. And the crisp autumn breeze gently blows his beautiful white hair. And for a moment... it's as if you can almost see the wings of an angel, and then I blink and they're not there.

Many years have passed since I last saw his face, but I will always remember how he walked with style and grace. And how he soothed the pain of each sick child or how he gave comfort just lying around. And for a moment... I close my eyes and I can almost see the beautiful, warm sun, shine down on his angel-like face, and then I blink....

And I watch as he soars with style and grace! His long white hair gently blows in the wind. And his angel-like wings, they were always there! They simply were hidden in his beautiful white hair.

~Joni Strohl
Chicken Soup for the Soul Celebrates Cats

Chapter 7

Loving Our Cats

We Love Each Other

*I have felt cats rubbing their faces against mine
and touching my cheek with claws carefully sheathed.
These things, to me, are expressions of love.*
~James Herriot

What I Did for Love

The call came at ten o'clock on a warm August night.

"Can you foster-sit a kitten who can't walk?" asked Laura, the humane society volunteer. The word kitten is equivalent to a guarantee of fostering in our house, and the fact that he couldn't walk just sealed the deal. Without a thought, we agreed to be the temporary guardians of a handicapped cat.

He arrived a few minutes later, scared, shaking and covered in his own mess.

"We found him on Grove Street," Laura said, "so we named him Grover."

Job one was to clean him up. He was tiny enough to fit in one hand, so the bathroom sink seemed a logical choice for his bath. While gently rubbing the shampoo into his smelly fur, Laura answered our as-yet-unspoken but obvious question of what was wrong with him.

"He might have been hit by a car," Laura explained. "We'll wait a couple of weeks to see if he gets better." We didn't have to ask what would happen if he didn't get better. With an all-volunteer humane society supported solely by donations, we had to make difficult but pragmatic decisions about the animals we invested our time and money in.

Over the next two weeks, we watched with pity as Grover's hind legs continually played tricks on him, first moving in odd directions, then jacking up his rear end as if it were on a hydraulic lift, sometimes resulting in his literally being end over end. He often landed with a thud in his food or water dish, either frustrated or soaking wet. On top of all that, the poor little guy had seizures whenever he tilted his head back too far. There was virtually no change in his condition during those first crucial days in our care, and we knew what that meant.

What did change, though, was our attitude. What began as pity soon grew into admiration as we recognized characteristics we often find sorely lacking in many of our fellow humans: trust, patience, persistence, courage—along with a surprising lack of what is often all too evident with those same humans, a complaining nature. It simply wasn't in him to grumble about his plight in life. Instead, he seemed inordinately grateful that we had found it in our hearts to help him.

The two weeks of waiting had not yet fully passed when we realized that even a little handicapped cat deserved a chance, whether he had been hit by a car or was simply born this way. And we were determined to give him that chance.

Over the next few weeks, life with Grover challenged our heretofore mundane routine. We found ourselves learning a new language: "Grover-speak." We quickly became adept at determining which cries meant, "I'm hungry," and which meant, "Hurry! I can't make it to the litter box in time!" The second cry always brought an instant reaction as we dropped whatever we were doing like a hot potato. Scooping him up, we would rush him to "his" room, where there waited a specially designed litter box atop a shower curtain that would catch any "overspray." He would struggle to find a comfortable position on his side to do what other cats do so naturally in a much more private and dignified manner.

All along, we knew we were just temporary caretakers of this special kitten, and so began our search for the perfect home for a little guy who many would consider imperfect.

In the meantime, we researched what might have caused this strange condition. From our research, it seemed as if Grover was born with cerebellar hypoplasia, a genetic condition caused by the mother cat contracting distemper while pregnant. Whether or not any or all of her kittens would be affected, and to what degree, appeared to be simply a matter of chance — and Lady Luck had obviously chosen to ignore Grover.

Our next step was to confirm this diagnosis. Off we went to Ohio State University Veterinary Hospital — two hours by car, each way, from our home. There, Grover was given his very first nickname, "Pud Pud," which we assumed must be short for "Puddin," in response to his sweet temperament. Several veterinarians and veterinary students observed Grover's walk, examined him, and asked us a litany of questions about his everyday activities, after which they confirmed that Grover suffered from cerebellar hypoplasia.

During this period, we received two inquiries about adopting Grover, one from a vet and one from a family two states away. We determined to find Grover the perfect new home by Thanksgiving. This brought a simultaneous sense of relief and sadness, each in equal measure. Thanksgiving was not far off, but we knew that the home he found would not be ours.

There were other things to worry about during the waiting period, though. All the sharp edges in our home that might hurt Grover as he struggled to travel from place to place had to be dealt with. We found some scrap pieces of bubble wrap and promptly wrapped the corner of the brick hearth, the "meanest" corner in the house in Grover's esteemed opinion. My observant nature soon required a trip to the office-supply store for two giant rolls of the cushiony bubble wrap, most of which soon decorated the chair legs, wall corners, lamp bottoms, desk edges and anything else that might harm our temporary boarder.

Grover was now old enough to be neutered, a decision that required another two-hour drive, this time to MedVet, in Columbus, Ohio, an animal-emergency hospital that specialized in nonroutine care. After speaking to the surgeon who would take care of Grover, and being assured that they would use every necessary precaution to ensure his safety — including the use of "people" anesthesia — we entrusted him to the capable hands of the doctor. Then came the seemingly endless wait until Grover appeared once again, totally alert and looking none the worse for wear after his brief hospitalization.

So, after adapting our daily routine to fit his, modifying an entire room so he had a space of his own, making two four-hour round trips to have him diagnosed and neutered, "decorating" our entire home in bubble wrap and moving his favorite chair in front of our bay window so he could watch the birds, Grover was adopted.

Three Thanksgivings have come and gone since Grover found his forever home — and, as I write this, he sits beside my desk in his favorite chair.

And when next Thanksgiving comes, we will give thanks again — for the privilege of sharing our lives with a little handicapped cat named Grover.

~Linda Bruno
Chicken Soup for the Cat Lover's Soul

45

Bedroom Secrets of Pets Revealed

Most beds sleep up to six cats. Ten cats without the owner.
~Stephen Baker

A long, long time ago, people slept in the house; dogs slept in a doghouse in the backyard; and cats, well, they "catted around" and slept in the barn or alley. That was before our pets migrated from the backyard to the bedroom to sleep, and from the kennel to the kitchen to eat. Now, the average doghouse has three bedrooms, two baths, a spa, an entertainment center and a two-car garage. Yes, the doghouse is our house.

Consider this: Before the arrival of our four-legged bed-partners, human bed-partners decided which side of the bed they would sleep on; we carved out property lines on the mattress. But then we decided to welcome pets into our homes, hearts and bedrooms. That was the last day any of us got a decent night's sleep.

I was reminded of this recently when, after a hectic trip, I headed home from New York to Almost Heaven Ranch in northern Idaho. Between airplane breakdowns and storms, it was a nightmare trip that took two sleepless days of travel instead of the usual one.

Fighting extreme fatigue, I finally made it home, stumbled into our log house, and headed directly to my bed, ready to slip between the flannel sheets and nestle under the goosedown comforter next to my beloved wife, Teresa. Now at long last I would be able to sleep. It sounded great in theory, but I was dreaming!

Three formidable barriers to my sleep were sprawled across the king-size bed. Scooter, our wired wirehaired fox terrier, was lying perpendicular across the bed, while Turbo and Tango, our two Himalayan-cross cats, were asleep on each pillow. I shoehorned myself next to Teresa and collapsed into deep sleep. I was sawing the timber and dreaming sweet dreams when suddenly, I was shot in the ribs with a deer rifle! At least that's what it felt like.

It was actually Teresa's elbow that had poked into my side as a last resort to stop my snoring. Sleepily, I looked across at her. She was crowded onto the tiniest sliver of mattress at the edge of the bed. The cats were wrapped around her neck and face, and our twenty-pound, flabby, fur-covered, thorn-in-the-side, Scooter, was dreamily snoring away, her feet pushing against Teresa's head. But would Teresa shove an elbow into Scooter, or disturb Tango or Turbo? Are you kidding?

Now, if I snore, Teresa's sure to find a way of letting me know it, and if I cross over to her side of the bed, she waits only a nanosecond before shoving me back onto my side or onto the floor. But there she lay, unwilling to move a muscle or twitch an eye, because she didn't want to interrupt the fur-queen's sleep!

I turned over, pulling instinctively on the down comforter to make sure that Teresa let me have my fair share of it. Yet through this sleepy tug-of-war, I was careful not to disturb my "Scooter Girl," who slept lying across me, looking warm, toasty and content.

And who needs an alarm clock when you have pets? I had managed to doze off again, but Scooter woke me up before the crack of dawn to be let outside. Again, I looked across at Teresa. Turbo and Tango were kneading her hair and licking her face to show they were ready for breakfast — now!

It was clear that Scooter, Turbo and Tango had had another great night's sleep, while Teresa and I were battling for shuteye scraps. I knew the pets would fly out of bed fully charged, while my wife and I, chronically sleep-deprived, would crawl out from under the blankets to start another day on the hamster wheel of activity we call life.

And yet... that's not quite the whole story. I knew full well that our four-legged bed partners had as usual gotten the best end of the sleeping arrangements, but I regarded it as just a small payback for the great gift of unconditional love that they give us, twenty-four hours a day, seven days a week.

So as I got out of bed, I paused to kiss Teresa's cheek, pat Scooter's furry head and stroke the cats' tails. Our bed was in purr-fect order and I had had a grrr-eat night's sleep after all.

~Marty Becker, D.V.M.
Chicken Soup for the Cat and Dog Lover's Soul

46

The Power of Love

God made the cat in order that man
might have the pleasure of caressing the lion.
~Fernand Mery

When I first saw the big gray-and-white cat in our yard, I knew right away that he was a stray. He was fierce-looking—a wounded warrior with a huge head and shoulders and a badly scarred body.

I started putting out food for him each day, and, even though you could see that he was starving, he wouldn't come near it if anyone was in sight. Because of one dead eye, which gave him a malevolent appearance, all the neighbors who saw him were afraid of him, even the cat lovers. Winter came, and he still wouldn't trust me or my family. Then, one day, it happened—a car hit him. I realized this when I saw him dragging himself through the snow to the food dish. I knew then that we would have to humanely trap him. It took some ingenuity, but we finally did it.

He spent a week with the veterinarian getting treated for his injuries, and also being neutered, de-wormed, de-fleaed, having his shots, being bathed, etc. We were eager to bring him home to join our family, but, when we arrived at the veterinarian's office to take the cat home, we were met by a very serious doctor who told us that we should put the cat to sleep immediately. Our big stray was so ferocious and mean that he would never, ever become tame, let alone a pet.

I wasn't convinced. I have always had great faith in love's power to tame even the wildest beast. I thought to myself, I've been praying for this cat since the day I first saw him. I'm not giving up that easily!

I told the vet, "I want to try. I'm taking him home." We named him Paws.

We opened the cat carrier under the bed in the guestroom, where we had put food, water and a litter box—in the farthest back corner so Paws would feel protected—and we left the room. Three days went by, and we did not see any sign of the cat. The only way we knew he was under the bed was that, when any of us walked by the open bedroom door, we heard deep growling and hissing.

I wanted to touch his heart, to somehow let him know that he was safe and loved. I devised a plan to reach him safely. I put on my husband's large hard hat and a pair of his welding gloves. Lying on the floor, I slid under the bed toward Paws, with my face to the floor and only the top of my head, protected by the hat, facing him. I reached out to stroke him, all the while gently repeating over and over again, "Paws, we love you, we love you, we love you."

He acted like the Tasmanian Devil—snarling, growling, howling, hissing, hitting his back on the underside of the bed as he tried to scratch and bite me. It was scary—but I knew he couldn't hurt me, so I just kept going. Finally, my gloved hand reached his face, and I was able to stroke him, still telling him how much we loved him. Ever so slowly, he began to calm down. He was trembling with fear as I continued to stroke him and speak to him in the same soft tone for a few more minutes. Then I slid out from under the bed and left the room.

The first step had been made. I was pleased but wondered how long this campaign would have to go on.

Several hours later, I came back upstairs and went to my bedroom. I noticed a cat on the bed, then did a double-take. It was Paws—all stretched out on the pillows and purring up a storm! I clapped my hand over my mouth. I literally couldn't believe it.

That dear cat became the love of our household. He often had three of our other cats licking and grooming him at one time, two dogs snuggled up next to him throughout the day, and, best of all, every night he would assume his special place to sleep—on my pillow with his beautiful, scarred, furry face nuzzling mine.

Although Paws finally succumbed to cancer, his legacy—my continued and steadfast belief in the power of love—lives on.

~Barbara (Bobby) Adrian
Chicken Soup for the Cat Lover's Soul

47

Conversation

*Are we really sure the purring is coming from the kitty
and not from our very own hearts?*
~Emme Woodhull-Bäche, translated

I have always been a "dog person." As far back as I can remember, there were dogs in my house. Not cats, dogs. So when two coworkers found a tiny gray kitten eating out of the Dumpster near our office building and asked me to take him in, I agreed, reluctantly. "Only temporarily," I proclaimed, "I'm a dog person." My coworkers nodded their heads knowingly and handed me the warm little bundle.

The kitten was three months old when I brought him home. Weighing in at barely three pounds, he rode peacefully in the passenger seat, atop my gym bag, and waited patiently while I went into Wal-Mart, befuddled in front of the cat items trying to decide what to buy. I knew I would need cat litter and a pan, some cat food, maybe a toy or two. I made my purchases and returned to the car to find his small gray face with green eyes soften at the sight of me. Something inside me shifted a little bit.

Don't get attached, I told myself, it's only temporary.

I took him to the vet the next day, calling him John Doe. I announced loudly in the waiting room that I was in possession of a cat in need of a permanent home. Meanwhile, I tried not to notice the warm feeling I got as I felt John Doe purring in my arms.

Several months went by with no responses to my "Cat Needs

Good Home" posters. Since he had started responding to my calls (as much as cats will respond), I officially named him Bonaparte. I thought it was a funny name and I wasn't keeping him anyway.

At some point during those months, Bonaparte started sleeping with me at night. He had a curious habit of laying down in such a way that his body always touched mine. When I shifted, he stood up, waited for me to get settled again, then lay down against me again.

I had never known cats could be so affectionate.

He performed the usual kitten antics that caused me to scream with frustration. He brought the curtains in my bedroom down so many times that I started telling friends that he was redecorating. His sudden bursts of energy that caused him to race frantically around the house in pursuit of invisible bugs left me shaking my head in amazement. He yowled every night by the front door to go out—until I got him neutered. He woke up at five every morning and parked himself on my chest; paws folded neatly under his body, staring at me intently until I finally woke up and drowsily stroked him.

Then there was the constant purring that never ceased to delight me.

When he was two years old and I had long since fallen in love with him, Bonaparte became deathly ill. He spent three months in and out of intensive care at the vet's office, and he required a feeding tube for most of that time. One night, when I had to take him to the emergency clinic, I slept by his cage because I didn't want him to wake up and not find me there. I took him to a specialist one hour from home, where he stayed for almost a month. I drove there every day to visit with him, cuddle him and brush him because he was so sick he had stopped grooming himself. The vets were grim about his prognosis. I remember standing in the hallway one morning, sobbing, begging them not to give up on him.

See, there were these cold nights that I had to get through without his warm body snuggled up against mine. The hole in my heart left by the loneliness was tremendous.

The vet finally determined that a risky surgery had to be attempted, although there were no guarantees for Bonaparte's survival. It was his last and only chance. Miraculously, Bonaparte came through, recovered and was able to come home a few weeks later.

Today he is six years old, and over the years I have brought home two other stray cats. Bonaparte worked his magic on them just like he worked it on me. They were unsure, insecure and frightened, yet practically melted in his presence. He grooms them, lays against them while they sleep, or touches noses with them as they pass in the hallway. His heart is so big that it spills out and touches the cold, hidden places in other hearts.

Somehow Bonaparte found that place in my heart. He found it before I even knew what was happening. And every night when he climbs into bed with me and arranges his body so that every part of him is touching me, I feel my heart fill with love all over again.

~Kelly Stone
Chicken Soup for the Soul Celebrates Cats

A Dickens of a Cat

*Authors like cats because they are such quiet, lovable, wise creatures,
and cats like authors for the same reasons.*
~Robertson Davies

"Gwen, I think it's ovarian cancer, and I think it's spread everywhere. I'm so sorry," my surgeon told me. "Go home and get your affairs in order. We'll operate as soon as possible."

Surgery revealed that I did, indeed, have an aggressive form of ovarian cancer. Lying in the hospital, I feared for my future. I feared I might not have a future. I feared I would be unable to care for myself. And since I was recently divorced, I feared being alone. How could I cope with chemotherapy, my job as an editor and caring for my home?

"Mom, I think you need a pet," my daughter said as she walked me up and down the halls of the hospital.

"Why do I need a pet?"

"I don't want you to be alone."

"Oh, Wendy, how can I take care of a pet? I'm not sure I can take care of me."

"Cats don't require much care."

"I'm a dog person," I answered, with an "and that is that" finality.

But that night, after she had gone home, I began to think. She and I were so focused on my cancer and whether I'd live or die that we thought of little else. Perhaps a pet would not only give me some company, but would also give us something else to focus our attention on now. Pets have always given me joy, and the doctor had already told me that the very best therapy was going to be a positive attitude.

I drifted off to sleep thinking about the kind of pet I might want. In the morning when Wendy came by, I shocked her by saying, "All right, I've decided I want a cat. I want you to go to the animal shelter and get me a tuxedo cat. Since I'm a book editor, I think I should have a very literary-looking cat. His name will be Charles Dickens. Make sure he looks the part. He should have a white bib, mittens and socks, and a mustache would be good."

She didn't make it to the shelter that day because after eleven long, tiresome days in a hospital bed, I was suddenly discharged to go home. But the next afternoon, Wendy got a "mommy sitter" and went to find my cat. I could hardly wait for her to get home. When the garage door opened, Judy, my "sitter," went to see what Wendy had chosen.

Judy carried a young, bright-eyed cat to my bed. He had the compulsory white bib, mittens, socks and a one-sided mustache. I couldn't believe it. I had told Wendy what I wanted, but I never dreamed she would find the exact cat I'd described. "Hello, Charles Dickens," I said.

He said, "Meow."

Dickens had a history. As a frightened stray, he had found his way to a Colorado Springs back porch during a rainstorm. Soaking wet and freezing cold, he shivered next to a glass door. The lady of the house had compassion. She took him in and fed him, but she could not keep him. The next day, she wept as she took him to the pound and told the attendants, "Make sure whoever gets him calls me."

That evening, after Dickens had settled in, I called her. She told me, "I'm about to have a baby, and I already have three cats. I wanted to keep him, but there was just no way. So I prayed God would send him to someone who needed him and would really love him."

In that moment, I realized that Dickens had not come to me by chance. "Your prayers have been answered," I said, and then I told her my story and ended with, "I need him, and I already love him."

All that first day and the next, Dickens went over my house with a "fine-toothed nose." He poked into every crevice and cranny, investigating everything. Then he began to sneeze and sneeze and sneeze. His nose was running, and his eyes were dull. Dickens was sick. Wendy took him to the vet.

"Is he going to die?" I asked when she brought him home.

"The vet doesn't think so. He's started him on some antibiotics and thinks Dickens is old enough and strong enough to survive."

Poor Dickens. He was very sick. He lay on the foot of my bed on a hot-water bottle for days. I had wanted to refocus our attention on something besides my illness and upcoming chemotherapy, and I surely did. All we could think about was whether Dickens would live or die.

After about eight days, Dickens had his turning point. He sprang up from the hot-water bottle with a gleam in his eye. "Well, hello, cat," I said. And I could see in an instant that I had correctly named him. He was going to be a rascally dickens all right. He crouched around corners waiting to spring at me as I passed by. He attacked my feet under the covers. He played until he dropped exhausted at my side.

Then I started my chemotherapy. Wendy went with me for the first four-day round of treatment. I didn't learn until later how frightened she had been. I didn't realize what it was costing her emotionally to see her mother in this dire situation. Neither of us knew when (or if) I, like Dickens, might have my turning point.

I tolerated the first round of chemotherapy fairly well, and I thought I could make it through the remainder of the twenty-four treatments on my own. "Go home and get on with your life," I told my daughter.

There were lots of nights during the six months that followed when I would wake from a deep sleep, nauseated beyond belief. By that point, Dickens was sleeping in the crook of my arm. When I awakened, he'd jump to the end of the bed and wait. When I would get back into bed, he would once again snuggle down beside me. This little creature God had sent my way blessed my long, lonely nights.

Some days, Dickens raced me up the stairs. At my pace it wasn't much of a race. He romped and played and made me laugh and laugh. I tolerated the chemotherapy pretty well, and I am sure one reason was because Dickens gave me a cheerful heart that was "good medicine."

Then, finally, I finished chemo. All I had to do was wait—wait and pray and hope that the cancer was in remission.

In October, my surgeon said, "We can't find any cancer from the outside, and we'd like to take a look inside." I agreed surgery would be a good idea.

This time, my son Mark came to stay with me and to take care of Dickens. After only an hour in surgery, I heard the voice of my delighted surgeon saying, "It's gone. There's no cancer anywhere."

This was my turning point! I was going to live! I went home to be greeted by a very happy cat, and while I couldn't lift Dickens (he now weighed fourteen pounds, and I was not supposed to lift anything over ten), I sat down, and he crawled onto my lap. "Well, cat," I said, "it looks like I'm going to stick around for a while. We both made it. We're survivors." Dickens didn't say much. He just stretched a little and purred and purred.

Dickens and I have a new problem now—one we like. We're getting older. We retired this year, and now I spend all my time at home with him. It's been ten years since I heard those fateful words "ovarian cancer." Today, these two survivors are living life to the fullest.

~Gwen Ellis
Chicken Soup for the Cat Lover's Soul

49

A Cat Named Christmas

Alan opened the backdoor on Christmas morning to find the yard covered in a beautiful carpet of glittery white snow. But it wasn't beautiful to Alan.

Alan was unhappy, as Alan often was, because he hadn't gotten what he wanted for Christmas. Instead of the BB gun he'd asked for, Alan had received a new bicycle. It was a shiny, red bicycle, with chrome wheels and blue and white tassles streaming from the handlebars. Most children would have been thrilled to find it sitting next to the tree on Christmas morning, but not Alan.

"You're too young for a gun," his mother had explained, trying to comfort him. But it hadn't worked. Alan pouted all of Christmas morning. When Alan was unhappy, he wanted everyone else to be unhappy, too.

Finally, after all the other gifts were opened, his father had asked Alan to take the discarded boxes and crumpled wrapping paper to the trash. As Alan tossed the papers into the barrel, a tiny, shivering kitten popped its head around the fence and greeted him with a timid "meow."

"Scat!" Alan hissed at the kitten, who ignored the command and ran anxiously toward the boy. "You mangy old stray. If I had my gun, I'd shoot you," Alan said. He slammed the lid on the trash can and headed toward the house, the kitten chasing after him.

As Alan climbed the stairs of the back porch, he heard another meow and looked down to find the kitten standing at his feet. "I thought I told you to get lost," he said angrily, and nudged the kitten down the stairs with the toe of his boot. But before Alan could open the door and go inside, there was the kitten, rubbing against his legs and looking up at him hopefully.

"You're sure not much of a cat," Alan said as he sat down on the stoop of the house and rubbed the kitten behind the ears. "And you're about the ugliest thing I've ever seen." The kitten was bone-thin from hunger and its coat was a muddle of colors—brown and black and white and orange and tan—every color a cat could possibly be. "But it is Christmas," Alan said, "and I suppose it couldn't hurt to give you something to eat." So Alan went into the kitchen and returned with a bowl of milk for the little cat.

But the kitten showed little interest in food, even though he obviously was hungry. Instead, he climbed into Alan's lap, rubbed against his jacket and began to purr. "You sure are a friendly little thing," Alan said, petting the happy kitten. And soon, Alan was happy, too. He somehow forgot to be angry about the BB gun, and the skinny little kitten didn't seem so ugly anymore.

With the kitten under his arm, Alan went into the kitchen where his mother was preparing dinner. "Look what I found," Alan beamed as he set the small cat on a rug in front of the stove and fetched another bowl of milk.

"You know you can't keep him," his mother warned, "but I guess it's okay to feed him something. After all, it is Christmas."

Alan's mother had no intention of allowing the cat to stay in the house. The kitten lapped up his milk and had fallen asleep on the rug in front of the warm stove when Alan's mother knelt down to pick him up and return him to the back porch. The little cat yawned and stretched, nuzzled against her chin and began to purr as he fell back to sleep. "You sure are a sweet little fella," she said quietly, laying him back down on the rug.

Alan's father, too, had said Alan couldn't keep the cat. But later that day, as he sat reading in front of the fire, he felt something pulling at his pant leg. When he looked down, the playful kitten sprang into his lap and knocked his book to the floor.

"Are you still here?" he asked, already heading for the backdoor with the kitten. But the cat scurried up his arm and, sitting on his shoulder, gently bit his chin and began to purr. As Alan's father took the kitten from his shoulder and held him in his hands, the kitten looked up and meowed at the man who smiled down at him. By that evening, the kitten had found a home.

"What shall we call him?" Alan asked as his mother tucked him into bed.

"Well, he's your cat," his mother said. "But since he came today, why don't you call him Christmas?"

And Alan fell asleep with the little kitten named Christmas cozily nestled at his side.

Alan grew to love Christmas very much. He was the best Christmas present any boy could ever receive, Alan thought. The two spent countless hours together during the following summer and when Alan returned to school the next fall, he would come home each afternoon to find Christmas waiting at the back door, anxious for his playmate to return.

Christmas would race Alan up the big oak tree in the backyard, or ride in Alan's wagon, or chase the tail of a kite as Alan launched it into the clear, blue sky. Christmas was Alan's best friend, and Alan was no longer an unhappy little boy.

Though it was clear that everyone in Alan's family loved the little cat, and he was always anxious to love them back, Alan knew that Christmas loved him best. But Alan's mother, as Christmas contentedly rubbed against her legs when she prepared a meal, and his father, as he sat reading the newspaper with the cat curled purring in his lap, felt that Christmas must love them best. In fact, anyone who was with Christmas for very long knew he loved them. They felt the little cat must love them better than any cat has ever loved a person. But that's the kind of cat Christmas was.

Then, one afternoon as autumn first began to give way to winter, Christmas wasn't waiting as usual when Alan arrived home from school, and the young boy knew something was wrong. He went to his bedroom to find Christmas huddled on his bed. The small cat was quivering all over and his nose was warm. Alan got his mother, and although she and Alan and his father did all they could to make Christmas well, the little cat grew worse and soon died.

Alan was devastated. And even though days stretched into weeks and soon it was Christmastime once more, nothing seemed to make Alan happy again.

Then one day, as he sat quietly in front of the Christmas tree at his grandparents' house, watching the lights flicker on and off, his grandmother asked, "Why so sad, little man? This is the season of joy."

"I'm sad about Christmas," Alan said. "Why did he come at all?"

Not realizing he was talking about the kitten who had come to Alan's house on Christmas morning, his grandmother took Alan on her lap and said, "Christmas came to show us love. That's why you should be joyful."

"But why did he have to die so young?" Alan asked. "How can I be joyful now?"

"Because the love he brought didn't die. It will always be with you," his grandmother explained.

And when Alan returned home, he was no longer sad when he looked at the tree Christmas used to climb or the wagon they used to play in. Instead, he remembered the love the kitten had brought to him. And he was happy.

And then he knew why Christmas came.

~Rand Souden
Chicken Soup for the Soul Christmas Treasury

50

Conversation with a Cat

I love cats because I love my home and after a while
they become its visible soul.
~Jean Cocteau

About eight years ago, my girlfriend Gale and I bought a cabin in Flagstaff, Arizona, to use as a summer getaway. The cabin needed extensive renovation, so during that first summer, while Gale worked in Tucson, where we lived at the time, I traveled to Flagstaff for a week or so each month to make the necessary repairs.

One warm afternoon, while I was working on the deck, I heard a meow. Looking up, I saw a half-grown cat standing thirty or forty feet away from me near our woodpile. I figured she was one of the feral cats that lived in the area. Studying her for a moment, I meowed back. Encouraged, the cat meowed again. I replied, briefly wondering what we were saying to each other. A few more mews were exchanged before she finally skittered off into the woods.

She obviously enjoyed our conversation because she came back. Every day that week, I saw her running through the yard or sunning herself in a protected spot near the woodpile.

I have always had a soft spot for cats—we had two at home in Tucson—and so I began to leave food out for her. If I was around, she wouldn't go near it, but if I was inside, she'd come and lick the bowl clean. I tried holding food out to her in my hand, but it was still too frightening for her. She needed her space, so I gave her a wide berth.

Something about this particular cat touched me. I wanted to convince her to let me pet her. I could see that a whole person was just too much for her to handle, so while she ate her dinner on the porch, I put some cat food on my fingers, lay down on the floor just inside the door, and stuck my arm and hand with the food on it out the door—in clear view from her food dish. It took a few days of this dinnertime routine, but soon she was licking the food off my fingers with no problem.

Next, I brought her food bowl out to the porch and, instead of leaving, sat near her while she ate. She quickly made the connection that the big, scary human also meant delicious food. She was wary, but her hunger was stronger than her fear.

She was fairly unremarkable in appearance. Her short, smooth coat was white with patches of charcoal gray that was almost black. Her face was mostly white, but she had a dark spot above one eye and around one ear. Her back was all dark gray except for her one unusual marking: a small patch of white, shaped like an arrowhead, in the middle of her spine.

One day as she had her nose buried deep in her bowl, I reached over and ran my hand along her back. She startled, but didn't bolt. I continued to pet her and talk to her while she finished her food.

We had made definite progress, but this was where it stopped. She let me sit near her and pet her during meals. She would even come up on the porch and hang around if I was sitting on a chair reading, but she wouldn't come inside and wouldn't let me pick her up or hold her. We'd hit a wall, and she wouldn't go an inch further.

Still, we had a connection. If I left to run errands, as soon as my car pulled into the drive, my standoffish cat would come running to greet me. I decided to name her Moki, after the Moki Dugway, a spectacular stretch of road that winds through the red rocks and desert of southern Utah. Something about the arrowhead on her back seemed to resonate with that area.

For the next few months, whenever I went back to Tucson, I paid Jessica, a neighbor's daughter, to put out food for Moki while I was gone. Jessica told me that Moki ate her food, but wouldn't let

Jessica near her. She reserved that privilege for me. And so our pattern continued: Every time I pulled into the drive that summer and fall, Moki seemed to sense my presence and came running.

Then, one October afternoon, I pulled in, but Moki didn't come. I was uneasy, but not alarmed. Perhaps she was off hunting. A little while later, Jessica's mother knocked on my door. "I have some bad news," she told me.

One evening, my neighbor explained, when Jessica came over to put out food for Moki, somehow the family dog got out of the yard and followed Jessica over to my house. Moki was waiting near the woodpile for her dinner when the dog came up behind her and attacked her. Jessica screamed at him to stop, but the dog shook Moki violently before Jessica could reach them. A moment later, the dog dropped the cat, and Moki took off, bloody and injured. She didn't know where Moki was—or how she was—but she wasn't hopeful about an injured cat's chances in the predator-filled woods around our houses.

I immediately jumped in the car and went looking along the woods by the road. I called and called, but heard and saw nothing. Moki, if she was alive, was long gone. That visit I spent part of every day searching for Moki. All that I found was some fur by the woodpile, a horrible reminder of what had occurred. Deeply saddened, I left Flagstaff a week later, sure I'd seen the last of Moki.

Winter passed, and I made one or two trips to Flagstaff to work on the cabin. There was never any sign of Moki. I was surprised at the pain I felt at the loss of this cat who had kept such an unbending boundary between us. I put the memory of Moki in a compartment in my heart and tried to forget about her.

When May rolled around again, I made another trip to Flagstaff to put the finishing touches on the cabin where I hoped Gale and I could spend some time together that summer.

Late one afternoon, as I was working inside with the door open to let in the spring breeze, I heard it: a faint meow. I dropped what I was doing and ran outside.

There she was, coming toward me as fast as she could—on

three legs. Her fourth leg was still there, but she wouldn't put any weight on it.

I knelt down and petted Moki gently so I wouldn't frighten her, but I was so happy to see her, I found myself picking her up and holding her close to me. She didn't struggle. Instead, she purred loudly as I carried her inside.

I called Gale to share the good news. She thought I should get Moki to a vet as soon as possible. That night, Moki slept with me without ever leaving the bed.

The next morning, I took her to the vet. He X-rayed her leg and said that it had been broken and had knitted badly, but he didn't recommend putting her through the trauma of re-setting it. He felt that, in time, once the leg was fully healed, she would begin using it again. I asked the vet to spay her and give her shots and worming medicines. The following day, when I picked her up at the vet's office, Moki snuggled in my arms as if she had always done so. The wall between us had disappeared.

Moki and I have remained close. In fact, there haven't been very many occasions over the last eight years when we've been apart; she even travels with us on vacations. I don't know how she survived that snowy winter, alone and injured out in the cold, but I'm glad she did. I don't know which one of us was happier at our reunion; today, I can't tell you which one of us is more attached to the other. Gale says that Moki looks at me with "Nancy Reagan eyes." Moki is clearly my cat, and I am clearly her person. And life is sweeter because of it.

You just never know where a conversation with a cat might lead you.

~Hoyt Tarola
Chicken Soup for the Cat Lover's Soul

51

Patches

W hen Bob awakened in the middle of the night, knowing he was dying, somehow, Patches knew, too. As I lay beside the man I'd lived with for more than twenty years, I felt a warm, furry creature push herself between us, inch by inch, until her nose jammed under his chin. She refused to leave, clinging to his t-shirt as if she could prevent his leaving—refusing to acknowledge that he'd already left.

That ancient, weepy-eyed calico, who seemed more human than cat, spent three days mourning, curled up on his dirty clothes in the bottom of the closet. Emerging finally to lie in the garden for the summer, she stretched in the sun, watching the birds hop by her nose.

The following winter, I packed Patches in her travel bag, and we headed down to Mexico for a few months on my sailboat in Puerta Vallarta. She checked out the pelicans and slept in the sun. Life went on.

When I flew down to Zihuatanejo to crew up the coast with a friend, to make things easier on Patches I left her with the vet in the local mall. She knew him and liked to sit in the front window, watching the baby octopus in his aquarium or flirting with passing shoppers until they came in to visit the gata bonita. For an old girl, she was a shameless hussy.

When I returned ten days later, the sad, little bundle of bones had scabs on her face from crying.

"Your husband left her. She was afraid you'd abandoned her, too.

She refused to eat," the vet told me. "The shopping ladies came in every day to cuddle her. They tried to get her to eat, but I think she wanted to kill herself."

When I picked up the scabby mess with the smelly breath, she stuck her head in my armpit. I carried her back to the boat under my cotton shirt and lay her down on the cushion in the cockpit. As I turned to retrieve my backpack from the dock, she threw herself down the three steps of the companionway and sprawled on the floor, too exhausted to make it to our bed.

I slept that night, her nose jammed under my chin, guilt fluttering around me like a wounded bird. In the morning, I felt something pulling at my tangled hair.

It was Patches. "Feed me. Feed me," she meowed as she circled on the covers. "The sun's out. It's time to watch the pelicans." Relief poured over me in a warm wave.

We sat on the dock in the morning sun, watching the pelicans bang into the sea. It was time to move on. Patches curled on my lap, then looked up at me as if she knew.

I ran my fingers under her chin. "Don't worry. I won't leave you again."

And I never did.

~Carolyn Harris
Chicken Soup for the Cat Lover's Soul

Chapter 8

Loving Our Cats

Faithful Feline Family Members

You are my cat, and I am your human.
~Hilaire Belloc

A Gentle Goodbye

everal years after my mother was widowed, she decided a cat would be the perfect companion. Since I shared my home with two cats, I was considered the feline expert. When my veterinarian told me about a litter of six-week-old kittens that had been dropped off on his clinic steps, I helped my mother pick out the perfect kitten, whom she named Cameo. From that point on, the sun rose and set on this black and white cat, who, unlike my cats, could do no wrong. Cameo quickly became my mother's pride and joy.

For the next eight years, Cameo lived as an only cat. Since Mommala and I lived near each other, we frequently exchanged visits and cat-sitting chores. When I visited Mommala accompanied by my golden retriever guide dog Ivy, Cameo would go into hiding as soon as we entered the apartment. After being unharnessed and unleashed, Ivy would go looking for a playmate, but Cameo would retreat further under the bed.

During my frequent travels, my two cats stayed at Mommala's house, and the three cats established a comfortable relationship. However, when Mommala traveled and Cameo came to stay with us, her shyness caused her to spend much of the time behind the stove or on the closet shelf. Frequently, the only sign of her presence was the emptied food bowl I set out for her at night while keeping the other cats enclosed in my bedroom. Although Ivy was gentle with cats, Cameo never learned to be comfortable around her.

At Mommala's death, Cameo's world turned upside-down. I had

told Mommala that if anything happened to her I would adopt her beloved cat. Because I had recently married and moved from New York to California, Cameo's first hurdle was a coast-to-coast flight. To my delight, she traveled with hardly a meow in the carrier I placed under the empty seat next to me. Ivy, like most guide dogs, occupied the space for carry-on luggage under the seat in front of me. Following our arrival in Fresno, Cameo had to adapt to a strange new world, including one new cat and my husband's guide dog, Kirby. It had been bad enough dealing with one golden retriever, but now there were two of these playful creatures to reckon with!

As anticipated, Cameo went undercover for three weeks. It was her passion for food that eventually drove this timid creature out of hiding and into family life.

As a blind cat lover in a multi-cat household, I identify each cat by a distinctive-sounding collar bell. For Cameo, I selected one with a tiny tinkle that seemed to go perfectly with her petite and cuddly persona. The day I heard the tinkle of her bell hitting the food bowl, I knew we were entering a new phase of togetherness.

Whenever I sat in my favorite lounge chair listening to a book on tape and knitting, I knew immediately when it was Cameo who chose to share my lap. After a while she would butt her head into my hand indicating it was time to stop these other activities and begin brushing her. Delighting in being groomed, Cameo rewarded me with purrs and kneading paws. Occasionally, I felt her body stiffen, and I'd know one of the dogs was approaching.

During the first few months Cameo was with us, when Ivy or Kirby approached, she jumped off my lap and leaped onto a table, counter or the refrigerator. Soon realizing that dogs, although large, could easily be dominated by a powerful hiss or smack, she no longer relinquished lap time and administered doggy discipline as needed.

Over the next few years, Cameo coexisted peacefully with her canine and feline siblings. When the alarm clock went off in the morning and the dogs were invited to join us, she learned to make room in the bed for the canine corps. As time passed, she thought nothing of jumping over a dog for a cuddle from a favorite human.

When progressive loss of vision forced Ivy's retirement from guide work, and my new guide-dog partner, Escort, entered the family, Cameo met this challenge with newly acquired feline aplomb.

Escort, a young, playful and energetic golden retriever, was put in his place by hisses, spitting and, if needed, a smack on the nose. Like Ivy and Kirby, he learned that this small creature could readily communicate her desire to be left alone, particularly when she occupied my lap.

Although Cameo and my beloved guide dog Ivy lived together for six years, they could not be called friends. They resembled siblings, who, for the good of other family members, had agreed to live together but basically ignore each other's foibles.

During the year of Ivy's retirement, her health continued to deteriorate. The day came when the quality of her life had worsened to the point where I knew our partnership had to end.

I made the dreaded call asking our veterinarian to come to the house to euthanize my friend, helper and companion of eleven years. When the doctor arrived, my husband, our friend Eve and I sat on the floor in a circle around Ivy to provide comfort in her last moments. At this time, Cameo was fast asleep in her favorite chair. What happened next showed me a totally new and unexpected side of her personality.

She awoke with a start, and the sound of her tinkling bell alerted me she was on the way. Jumping over Eve, she joined the circle. Purring loudly and rubbing up against her human companions, she provided the comfort we so desperately sought in this emotion-laden situation. She seemed to adopt the role of grief counselor. At one point she flung herself into my arms, sending me a clear message that she felt my pain and was there to comfort me. No more aloof feline reserve for her.

And as Cameo walked back and forth between us all, it was obvious that she was no longer indifferent to her long-term house partner. Several times she stopped and licked Ivy's face, something she had never done before. As I held Ivy in my arms and reached out to touch Cameo, I felt Cameo's tiny paw touching Ivy's large paw.

Cameo seemed incredibly attuned to the importance of touching the old dog, who was now totally blind.

But Ivy could still hear, and it comforts me to realize that the last sounds my treasured teammate heard as she slipped quietly into a gentle death were my murmured endearments and Cameo's soothing purrs.

~Toni Eames
Chicken Soup for the Cat and Dog Lover's Soul

53

Machiavelli

As every cat owner knows, nobody owns a cat.
~Ellen Perry Berkeley

Arthur, a cat of discriminating taste, largely ignored them, these oversized, fluffless males who came and went. In Arthur's opinion, they practiced less-than-meticulous personal hygiene. They bathed no more than once a day, he guessed, and rarely smoothed their hair. Not like Arthur. He twisted and ran his tongue down his dazzling white back. Arthur's personal assistant liked clean cats. Her name was Beth, or maybe Brenda. He couldn't remember. Arthur didn't concern himself with details.

They were easy to get rid of, the fluffless males. Arthur figured this out back when his personal assistant was married to Bill, or was it Bruce? Whatever his name, the husband liked to sit in Arthur's chair and sleep on Arthur's side of the bed. The worst offense, however, was the day that the husband came home smelling of some other male cat. Unacceptable. Arthur had no choice but to soil a pair of wingtips. The husband yelled. Arthur targeted some running shoes.

"Either that cat goes or I do," the husband said.

Hardly a difficult choice, Arthur thought, but his personal assistant cried and hesitated. However, she only hesitated until she found out that the other cat belonged to another woman. Arthur stayed, and the husband went.

Then came other fluffless males. Arthur let each one stay for a while—until the man did something unforgivably crass, such as calling Arthur "kitty." Then Arthur would soil a pair of shoes or a jacket or a gym bag. Arthur's personal assistant would cry and accuse. The male would defend himself. She would counter that her cat had an uncanny sense about these things. Arthur would hit the shoes one more time. Another fluffless male would disappear. Life was good.

Then came George, or was his name Jeff? The New One heard about Arthur and the shoes. When he came to dinner, he brought roses for the personal assistant and some expensive, catnip-scented bauble for Arthur. Arthur accepted the bribe, but, when he was sure the New One was watching, he would cast a long look at the shoes: leather topsiders. The New One understood that look. He smiled at Arthur, scratched his ear gently and called him "Machiavelli." Arthur didn't know what Machiavelli meant, but it sounded cool.

One weekend, the New One came over with tools in tow. From his comfortable perch, Arthur could hear pounding in the backyard. He disliked the noise and went looking for a pair of shoes, but the New One never left them lying around. Finally, the pounding stopped, and the New One opened the back door and called Arthur. Outdoors? He wasn't allowed outdoors. But the New One had screened in the back porch and built a special platform for Arthur. They sat on that porch all day: the two humans curled together, and Arthur stretched out, eyes closed, face lifted to the sun. He felt the warm, scented air ruffle his dazzling fur. I suppose, Arthur thought, this one can stay.

~Susan Hasler
Chicken Soup for the Cat Lover's Soul

54

The Gift

O
ne day a handsome black tomcat appeared at our back
door. His coat had a white bib and four snowy paws, making him look like he was wearing a tuxedo. His tail was as
crooked as a corkscrew.

My four-year-old brother Daniel and I had never had a pet. We
both instantly fell in love with the gentle black and white cat. All
that first afternoon, the three of us played together. When it got
dark, we begged our parents to let our new friend come inside so we
could feed him. Mom shook her head. "It might confuse him," she
explained. "This cat looks too healthy to be a stray. He must have a
home already."

But the next morning, the tuxedo cat was still there. He waited
patiently by the front door like a butler at a mansion. "Yea!" said
Daniel. "He wants to be our cat!"

It did seem like he was telling us something. He stuck around
all day, playing with Daniel and me outside. When we went into the
house, he jumped up on the barbecue and watched us through the
window. The last thing I saw that night were his green eyes, staring
in at me.

The next day, our parents warned us that we needed to try our
best to find his owners. My mom helped me make a flyer that said
"Found: black and white cat with crooked tail" with our phone number on it. I drew a picture of the cat on each one and we hung them
around the neighborhood.

The second day, I named him Alley, as in "alley cat." The third day, our dad and mom let us put some food out for him. The fourth day, our parents broke down and we got to bring him inside.

Alley let me carry him like a baby, from room to room. Daniel built Lego castles all around him. He followed us all around the house and at bedtime he jumped on each of our beds while we got tucked in, as if he was saying good night to us.

Alley was a dream pet.

Our family woke up from the dream about two weeks after we adopted him. That was the day a big, tattooed man appeared at our door holding one of our "Found Cat" flyers. Before anyone could say anything, Alley strolled over to the man and rubbed on his leg. It was obvious that they knew each other.

"My name's Mark Johnson," he announced, casually picking Alley up. "I see you've met my only roommate, Dewey. He kinda wanders when I'm out of town. Can I offer you good people a reward for watching him?"

"No," Dad said with a sigh. "It was a pleasure to have him as our guest." The rest of us were completely silent. At the door, Mr. Johnson turned back and faced us kids. That's when he must have seen the tears in my eyes. "Wow. I'm sorry," he said. "I didn't realize you kids had gotten so attached. Hey, I only live a few blocks away. If you two would ever like to visit old Dewey..."

"His name's not Dewey!" Daniel yelled at the top of his lungs. "It's Alley!" He ran sobbing to his room.

Mr. Johnson's eyes widened. The full meaning of his visit had sunk in at last. He slipped out awkwardly. Over his shoulder was slung Alley. Alley's unreadable green eyes looked back at me all the way down the walk.

For days, I found myself staring out of the window at the barbecue as if Alley might suddenly rematerialize there. Daniel went through spells of bursting into tears. Our parents tried to console us by keeping our family schedule full and entertaining. They even talked about going to the pound to pick out another pet.

Then one day, I heard Daniel yell, "He's back!" We all hurried into the family room. Sure enough, Alley was there by the door nuzzling Daniel, his crooked tail lashing Daniel's legs.

He had found his way home.

My heart was jumping with joy. Then Dad said, "Daniel. Sarah. He can't stay. He's not ours, remember?"

Daniel and I both looked at him like he was crazy. "But Dad..." Daniel began.

"Do we have to tell that Mr. Johnson guy?" I asked, looking into my dad's eyes.

Dad nodded his head. Even though I could tell it made him sad to do it, he looked up the name and left a message on Mr. Johnson's machine. "Your cat is here again," Dad said. "Would you please stop by and pick him up?"

I felt like this would be the last time we would ever see Alley. I figured Mr. Johnson would lock him up in his house. For the rest of the day we played with him; making cat fortresses out of cardboard boxes, dangling strings around corners, petting him and feeding him treats. Alley went along with it all, just like he expected that kind of treatment and wanted nothing less.

When Mr. Johnson arrived at 8:00, I had made a decision. I waited in the hall behind Daniel and our dad, holding Alley in my arms. As soon as Dad opened the door, I said to Mr. Johnson, "I think he wants to live with us."

"Sarah..." Dad began.

But Mr. Johnson nodded at me, letting me know it was all right. Then he squatted down, so that he would be at the same level as Daniel and me.

"You know, Sarah, I think you're right. He seems to have made a decision. I think he must like kids," he said with a wink. He set down a small cardboard box. "I didn't come to take him. I just came by to bring you these." Inside were a bowl and several cans of cat food.

"You're letting us have him?" I asked, stunned. "Like a gift?"

"Well, kind of," he said with a shrug. A tattoo-scrawled arm darted out as he petted Alley. "Bye, Dewey. I'll miss you. But I have a feeling you'll be in good hands."

And, just like that, Mr. Johnson was gone. None of us ever saw him again.

From then on, the tuxedo cat was ours. In no time at all, he became a respected member of our family. He was a fierce hunter, yet he remained extremely gentle with us. Whatever room the family was in, Alley was there. Whenever Daniel and I were ready for bed, Alley popped in to say goodnight.

Sometimes I wonder what made our cat decide to stop being Dewey and want to become Alley. We will never really know, but it gave us all an example of what giving is all about. Because the truth of the matter was that Mr. Johnson hadn't given his pet away.

Alley had given himself to us.

~Sarah Strickland as told by Craig Strickland
Chicken Soup for the Preteen Soul 2

Five Hundred Flowers

Who hath a better friend than a cat?
~William Hardwin

I am what is sometimes referred to as "a woman of a certain age." Single and childless, I have lived alone for most of my adult life. Up until six years ago, I hadn't even had a pet.

At that time, I was living in an apartment—which didn't allow pets—where I commuted an hour each way to the Los Angeles high school where I teach English. Although I had always wanted a little house of my own, with a yard and a garden, I somehow never took the necessary steps to make that dream come true. One year followed another, and as so often happens, I just continued in the comfortable, if somewhat unfulfilling, rhythm of my life.

Until "the week of the cats."

It was late May, and the school year was almost over. My classroom, which is a little bungalow, sits off by itself on the school grounds. One Tuesday afternoon, I heard a piteous meowing coming from underneath the classroom floor. It took me almost four hours to coax a small, but vocal, gray tabby kitten from its hiding place. The kitten was hungry and obviously needed help. Although I knew it wasn't allowed, that afternoon after school I took the kitten I'd named Maximus home to my apartment, smuggling him upstairs so I wouldn't get in trouble with the manager. I wondered what in heaven's name I was going to do, now that I had a kitten in my life, because from the very first I knew that whatever happened, I was going to keep him.

Two days later, one of my students, knowing that I had rescued a kitten, came to me and begged me to take her little girl kitten. She had brought it home, but her parents wouldn't let her keep the cat, a Russian blue, and she didn't know what to do. I figured I was already breaking the rules with Maximus, so what was one more? My student brought me the "little girl"—who turned out to be an adolescent boy cat: my Grey Boy.

The weekend came and went. Things were going well. I was enjoying my two new apartment-mates, and so far no one had complained or turned me in. Then, the next Tuesday, another little gray tabby kitten—an orphan, possibly Maximus' sister—was placed in my arms by a fellow teacher. I knew taking her home would be pushing my luck, but I did it anyway. When I carried Pearl into the apartment that afternoon, it was clear my life was about to change. I had a family now and needed a home to put them in.

My cats were just the catalysts I needed to finally go for my dreams. I began looking to buy a house in earnest. Within a week, I found one, and just two months later, we moved in.

It was a wonderful time in my life. I loved my new home, and coming back each day to my trio of sweet and loving cats was a joy beyond description. This happy state lasted about a year—until the morning I found Pearl dead. I wasn't sure what had killed her. I thought it might have been a stroke or aneurysm as she didn't have a scratch on her body.

I stared at her small, still figure, feeling as though my heart would break, but I had to go to work. I picked up Pearl and put her in the backyard. I would bury her when I came home that afternoon.

It was a miserable day; I was distraught, and my students were particularly unruly. When I dragged myself home after work, overcome with fatigue and grief, I wasn't sure I could actually face the sad task that lay ahead of me. Barely holding myself together, I asked my neighbor to help me dig the hole. When it was ready, I put Pearl into it and then completely broke down. As I sobbed hysterically, I was aware that Grey Boy was staring at me with an unusual amount of focus. Then I gave myself over to my grief, and Grey Boy quietly walked away.

Eventually, I fell silent. As the sun began to set, I sat at the picnic table in the backyard, staring at the ground and simply feeling the aching pain in my chest. My darling Pearl was gone, and nothing would be the same.

I looked up and noticed Grey Boy trotting toward me, holding something in his mouth. I couldn't tell what it was. He came directly to where I was sitting and, stopping a foot away, dropped the item in his mouth at my feet.

It was a single pinkish-purple flower shaped like a trumpet. Grey Boy tilted his head to look up at me and then, seeing that I had observed his gift, turned and trotted away.

Surprised, I inhaled sharply, and then sighing, I breathed, "Oh, Grey Boy." He had never done anything like this before.

The tears slid down my cheeks as I reached down and picked up the beautiful blossom. I held it in my hand and cried again, but this time my tears felt healing. I sat there for an hour, holding Grey Boy's gift and slowly recovering my equilibrium.

Pearl's death was harder on me than I ever could have imagined. For the next three months, I felt just terrible. During that period, Maximus stayed close, and Grey Boy continued to bring me flowers—about five hundred of them! On the weekends when I was home all day, he brought them morning, noon and night, and several times in between. On workdays, he would bring flowers to me before work and when I returned in the evening. It seemed whenever I turned around, Grey Boy would be coming to me to deliver another flower. He didn't stay—after he dropped the flower and saw me pick it up, he walked away.

Then, after about three months, as I started to feel better, Grey Boy suddenly stopped bringing the flowers. And he has never done it again, not once.

What touches me the most about the five hundred flowers is that during those three months, Grey Boy was grieving, too. He was quieter than usual, and I often noticed him sitting and staring at Pearl's grave. But my Grey Boy knew that I needed his help—and he never wavered from his self-appointed mission of mercy.

~Bev Nielsen
Chicken Soup for the Cat Lover's Soul

56

The Christmas Angel

Let your tears come. Let them water your soul.
~Eileen Mayhew

When my daughter Rachel was six years old, we went to the local shelter, looking for the perfect cat. We liked a lot of the cats we saw there, but we were especially taken with a mother and her kittens. All the kittens were entirely jet black, except for one. She had a small white tip to her tail, like one bright light in the night sky. We brought her home and called her Star.

Starry was a charmer. Rachel admired her proud manner and enjoyed even more the secret knowledge that it was all an act. Starry could only appear aloof for so long before leaping into Rachel's arms to be cuddled and stroked. As time went by, Rachel and Starry adopted certain routines. At night when we watched TV, Starry crawled into Rachel's lap, and stayed there, purring contentedly. Starry always rubbed her face along Rachel's chin, ending the love fest with a gentle nip on Rachel's nose. Sometimes I couldn't help but feel the injustice of this. I was the one who took care of the cat, feeding, cleaning, grooming—yet, Starry was clearly Rachel's cat. Eventually, I came to love watching their cozy bond.

My little girl grew up, went to junior high and finally high school. Starry was ten and Rachel was sixteen. Starry and Rachel were still close, though Rachel spent less and less time at home. Starry spent most of her day sitting on the sideboard in the dining room, looking out the window into the backyard. I loved seeing her as I'd pass, her glossy black coat almost sparkling in the sunlight she loved to seek out, the white tip of her tail brilliant against the shining black of her curled body.

One Sunday morning, early in November, Starry got out the door before we could stop her. When Rachel's friend came over to study that evening, she came in the door with a worried expression. "Where's Starry?" she asked.

When we told her we didn't know, she had us come outside with her. There was a black cat lying in the street.

It was Star. The cat's body was warm and she didn't appear to be injured. There was no blood or wounds that we could see. It was after hours, but our vet agreed to meet us after our distraught phone call. Rachel was upset, but holding it together. My husband Burt and I told her to stay at home while we took Star to the vet.

Burt and I picked Starry up carefully and rushed her to the vet's office. The vet examined her briefly before looking up at us and saying, "I'm sorry, but she's gone."

When we got home, Rachel could tell by our faces that Starry was dead. She turned without speaking and went to her room.

It had been a hard year for me. My father had died not long before, and I hadn't totally come to grips with the loss. Rachel and I were in the midst of the delicate dance mothers and teenaged daughters everywhere find themselves performing—circling, pulling away and coming together in odd fits and spurts. I took a chance and knocked at her door. When she said come in, I sat with her on the bed and we cried together. It was a good cry, clearing out some more of the grief I couldn't face about my father and bringing Rachel and I closer as we shared our sadness about Starry.

Life went on. Thanksgiving came and went. Rachel and I both found ourselves mistaking black sweatshirts strewn on chairs or floors for our newly missing black cat. The sideboard looked desolate, empty of the warm presence glowing with life I'd come to expect there. Over and over, little pangs of loss stung our hearts as the weeks went by.

I was out Christmas shopping, when I saw it. It was a Christmas tree ornament in the shape of a "cat angel." A black cat with white wings and a red ball between her paws. I had to get it, but bought it wondering if it would be a happy remembrance of the cat we'd loved or a chilling reminder of our loss.

When I got home, I painted a white tip at the end of the angel cat's long black tail and hung the ornament on our tree.

That evening, when Rachel came in, she flopped on to the couch. She sat staring at the Christmas tree, "spacing out" after a long day at school and after-school sports. I was in the kitchen when suddenly I heard her gasp. "Mom," she called. "Mom, come here!"

I walked in and found her standing in front of the tree, looking at the cat angel with shining eyes. "Oh, Mom. It's Starry. Where did you find an ornament with a tail like hers?"

She looked about six again. I gathered her into my arms and wonderfully she didn't resist. We stood together, looking at the tree, feeling our love for Starry and for each other.

Our charming, nose-nipping cat was gone, but now Starry, the Christmas angel, would be a part of our family tradition for years to come.

Sometimes you can make your own miracles.

~Pamela S. Zurer
Chicken Soup for the Cat and Dog Lover's Soul

57

Puffin's Gift

On a hot, stifling day in early August, I made the decision to get a cat. My shadow, a beautiful Belgian sheepdog, had passed away, and I needed a new animal to love. I'd never been around a cat, but my new landlord didn't allow dogs. Ron, my fiancé and a veterinarian, persuaded me to adopt a cat.

Reluctantly, I left my air-conditioned car and walked into a veterinary clinic that gave temporary shelter to stray cats. As I opened the door, a blast of hot, pungent air enveloped me, and I fought the urge to go home. A weary technician led me back to the cages. "Picked a bad day to come," she complained. "Lost our air a few hours ago, and now all we have is one fan."

It wasn't doing much for the cats. I looked at them in their small cages. Not a tail twitched; no eager eyes met mine, begging for a home. Some were asleep; others, limp and quiet, were paralyzed by the heat. Unable to decide which comatose cat to bring into my life, I turned to leave, feeling only a little disappointed. After all, I was a dog person.

"Meow."

I looked at the technician, and we turned back.

"Meow!" A gray paw stretched out between the bars, and emerald eyes demanded my attention.

"I'll take that one," I said without hesitation, then wondered what I had just done.

After a brief exam, they handed her over to me, and we drove to the clinic where Ron worked. He performed a more thorough exam to assure me that the cat was healthy. He showed me how to hold her, which wasn't easy because she had been on the streets for so long that she was just as scared of me as I was of her. I named her Puffin after my favorite Maine seabird, and, flush with Ron's approval, I took her home to my orderly, neat apartment in the city.

I can do this, I thought, and, after I'd closed all the windows and doors, I unlatched the door of her carrier. Puffin flew out much faster than her namesake and tore through the apartment, a blur of gray fur. It was the beginning of a very long week. The new scratching post wasn't satisfying, and she took to my old couch. When both sides were bare, she started on the legs of the antique dining-room table that had originally belonged to my parents. When she wasn't tearing through the apartment or clawing up the furniture, she was lying in wait for the inevitable moment that I opened the front door, eager for escape.

Ribbons of scratches covered my arms from our battles at the front door. After all, she had been an outdoor cat, ten months old, who already had given birth to a litter of kittens. "Give her time," Ron pleaded. But the only time I really enjoyed Puffin was at night when she curled up into a ball next to me on my quilt, purring us to sleep.

Ron and I married two years later, and the three of us moved into a condo in the suburbs, near the new clinic Ron purchased with a partner. Puffin now had two floors to roam and didn't seem as tempted to escape. But, when we settled into our new home, she began to boldly claim her territory. The second-floor landing became her perch, and I became her mouse. Whenever I tried to go upstairs, Puffin would crouch at the landing, waiting until I was within reach, then lunge at my ankles with a sharp bite. It wasn't long before I invested in a pair of Nike high-tops. I would have given anything for a gentle dog who didn't bite, scratch or attack.

Five months later, we had wonderful news: I was pregnant. It started out smoothly with the usual fatigue and a little morning sickness. Every afternoon, I returned home from teaching, put on my high-tops and prepared for my face-off with Puffin at the top of the stairs. When I reached the second stair from the top, Puffin would lunge at me, biting, as I ran into the bedroom. Safe on the bed, I pulled off my shoes and crawled under the quilt for a nap. Puffin followed suit, curling into my legs and softly purring us off to sleep.

At thirteen weeks, I had a miscarriage. Ron drove me home from the hospital late in the day, trying his best to keep up our spirits. "I just need some time to be alone," I told him, urging him to go back to work.

"You're not alone," he reminded me. "Puffin will take care of you until I get home." I looked at him incredulously, shaking my head. If only I were coming home to my dog.

Ron went back to work, and I went inside. Our home felt dark and lonely. With a deep breath, I slipped into my high-tops and started to climb. Puffin's eyes glinted green from the top of the stairs. She stood poised, alert and ready to attack. Her eyes narrowed, and I tensed. "Please, Puffin, not today," I begged, tears starting to form. It was all too much. I collapsed on the staircase and started to cry.

Puffin hesitated, then sat down. Wiping my cheeks, I slowly got up and made my way to the top, unimpeded by my cat. She let me pass, licking a paw. I walked to the bedroom, removed my shoes and fell onto the bed. Puffin leaped onto the quilt, staring into my teary eyes. I held out my arms, and, for the first time, she came to me and licked my face with her tiny, rough tongue. I smiled and rubbed her ears. She turned and purred, then snuggled into my belly, her heartbeat making up for the one I had lost. We drifted off to sleep.

Twelve years later, Puffin sleeps on our bed in a new house. Her best friend, an adopted border collie, snores softly on a pillow below. Suddenly, the door bangs open, and our five-year-old daughter, Julianne, leaps on the bed, eager to pet her cat. Puffin's green eyes narrow, Julianne laughs, and the chase is on. Little pink Nikes run as fast as they can.

~Jennifer Gay Summers
Chicken Soup for the Cat Lover's Soul

Toto's Last Christmas

Open your heart — open it wide; someone is standing outside.
~Quoted in Believe: A Christmas Treasury *by Mary Engelbreit*

Snow fell softly on Christmas Eve as I made my final patient rounds. The old cat, fragile in his downy white coat, was sleeping. Days before, his owner had dropped him off to spend the holidays with us. Sadly, she had worried he might not make it to greet her in the New Year. Indeed, the day after she dropped off the cat, I called to warn her that he was failing. Her tear-choked voice let me know she understood. "No heroics, please, Dr. Foley, but let him rest easy and make him as comfortable as you can."

Soft blankets along with a heating pad were wrapped around his frail body to keep him warm. Puréed chicken and tuna had been offered and declined, and now he slept in the deepest of sleeps. Not wanting Toto to be alone in his condition on this holiday night, I wrapped him in a large wicker basket and carried him home.

A gust of wind blew the door from my hand as I entered the house. My cat, Aloysius, greeted us while my other cat, Daphne, peeked timidly from the corner of the room, sniffing appreciatively at the cold winter air. They both knew what a wicker basket with an electric cord hanging from it meant. Aloysius retreated haughtily across the room.

Rescued as an abandoned cat from a clinic I worked at previously, Aloysius has been with me for twelve years — through vet school, my first job and my first home. Other people see him as just a cat, but for me his presence has become a constant in my life. Aloysius is the one who listens to all my tales of woe. On the down side, he is possessive and has a low opinion of anyone, feline or other, who infringes on his territory.

Daphne had come to me a timid and yet ferocious feral tabby kitten that no one could tame. Ten years of love, patience and roast beef tidbits had paid off. Now a round and sassy butterball of a cat, her heart was mine. To keep the peace in the house, however, she usually agreed with Aloysius on the subject of uninvited guests. Sensing his disdain for the fellow in the basket, she politely hissed from the corner.

"Now, now, you big bullies," I said. "This fellow is old and may be leaving us soon. We wouldn't want him to be alone on Christmas Eve, would we?"

Unmoved, they glowered from beneath the Christmas tree.

Old Toto slept on in his basket. I placed him by the table in the kitchen and plugged the cord for his heating pad into the wall. My husband, Jordan, and I prepared our Christmas Eve dinner while Toto slept, and I checked on him every once in a while to be sure he was comfortable. Daphne and Aloysius, still resentful of our guest but moved by the smell of grilling steaks, crept into the room. I warned them that Toto was old and frail and to be good hosts, they must let him be.

Toto still slept.

Dinner was ready, and Jordan and I sat at the table. Relaxing after the long work day, soon we started teasing each other about what surprises were hidden in the gleaming packages beneath the tree. Then Jordan silently nodded toward Toto in his basket, and I turned my head slowly to look at the cats.

Aloysius first, and then Daphne behind him, slowly and cautiously approached the basket. While Toto rested, Aloysius sat up on his haunches, peered into the basket and gave a long, deep sniff. Gently, he lowered himself and walked to the corner of the old cat's basket. Then he rubbed his cheek against it, softly purring. Daphne followed, leaned into the basket and, sniffing Toto's face, placed a gentle paw on his soft blanketed body. Then she, too, lowered herself and purred as she rubbed his basket. Jordan and I watched in amazed silence. These cats had never welcomed any other cat into our home before.

Leaving my chair, I walked over and looked at Toto. With the cats still positioned at each corner of the basket, Toto looked up at me, breathed once and then relaxed. Reaching my hand beneath his blankets, I felt his heart slowly stop beating. Tears in my eyes, I turned to Jordan to let him know that Toto was gone.

Later that night, I called Toto's owner to let her know that he had died comfortably and quietly at our home, with two cats beside him, wishing him a fond farewell and Godspeed on his last Christmas Eve.

~Janet Foley, D.V.M.
Chicken Soup for the Pet Lover's Soul

59

An American Cat in Paris

It is in the nature of cats to do a certain amount of unescorted roaming.
~Adlai Stevenson

When people think of pets in France, they think dogs. Dogs being served little platters of steak tartare in fine restaurants. Tiny, fluffy poodles poking their heads out of fashionable pocketbooks.

As for my wife and me, when we think back on the two years we lived on rue St. Didier in Paris, we think of a very different sort of pet. We think of Chuck. Our Rhode Island-bred, orange-and-white, tiger-striped, lazy, hungry and sometimes biting cat, Chuck.

Not long before moving to our cramped sixth-floor Parisian apartment, we were introduced to Chuck at the Providence Animal Rescue League. Unlike the kittens there who eagerly poked their paws through the bars of their cages, Chuck just sat on a little shelf in the back of his pen and looked up at us with a wounded expression. "I know you're not going to choose me since I'm a full-grown cat," he seemed to be saying, "so I'm not going to try and sell myself."

But when my wife gently lifted him out and gave him a hug, Chuck allowed himself to purr very softly, and we adopted him on the spot. A few months later, when it became clear that we would have to move overseas because of her job, most French people we talked to urged us to bring our new pal along. But our American friends did not agree.

"It wouldn't be fair to him," said one friend. "He's just getting used to life as a housecat." Still, it didn't take long for us to decide that Chuck was now a full-fledged member of the family, and where we went, he went. I think we said something like, "Chuck is used to our routines, and we don't want to break that up." Inside, we knew that it was the two of us who were used to Chuck's routines, and we badly wanted his comforting presence in a big, foreign city where we knew not a soul.

During those first few months in Paris, when we could understand little that was said to us, were afraid to speak up in stores and restaurants, and felt like strangers right down to the soles of our shoes, Chuck's new European-style habits gave us much-needed laughter and encouragement. He was delighted with French food—Friskies au boeuf, to be exact—and he cheerfully rode the bus to his veterinarian in a cat carrier that allowed curious passengers a full view of his impressive orange-and-white mane.

"Il est superb!" exclaimed one delighted French matron with a boxy hat and high-necked Chanel suit. A construction worker from Madrid gravely examined and lightly prodded him then, despite our objections, declared that "he must be Spanish." Chuck even developed a nodding friendship with a nightingale that sang its song each evening from on top of a nearby hotel. And he made us realize, seeing his round, fluffy shape up in one of our many windowsills, that we were not, in fact, alone.

We soon found out, however, that the French windows Chuck loved so much could swing wide during a windy night, as could the French doors that led to our minuscule balcony. When my wife awoke for work one morning and saw those doors banging in the wind, she instinctively began to search the apartment. Chuck wasn't in any of his usual hiding places and since the drop from our balcony was probably a fatal one, we feared and expected the worst.

The sidewalk below held no clues, nor did the neighbors we questioned in nervous, flailing bursts of English and French. We tried taping cardboard signs with a crayon drawing of Chuck and our phone number up and down rue St. Didier, but as the day passed by, we felt more and more hopeless. An indoor cat whose claws had been taken out by a previous owner, Chuck wouldn't have known what to do or where to turn if he had found himself without a roof over his head. And now it was getting dark. "Bon courage," said our concierge clasping her tortoiseshell cat Violette in strong arms, "bon courage."

The hours dragged on that night, and eventually my wife and I came to terms with the simple fact that we had lost our best friend.

"It's my fault," I said again and again. "I should have put in locks or something so he couldn't get out."

"No, it's both our faults," said my wife. "We should have let Chuck stay in Rhode Island where he would have been safe. I can't get over how empty it feels in here without him, and this is how it's going to be from now on."

The apartment seemed to hold nothing but useless Friskies boxes, sweaters with orange-and-white hair on them and cat toys that jingled as we accidentally brushed past them. My wife tried taking a bath, but it wasn't a real bath without Chuck there to jump up on the bidet and watch the water foam and gurgle as it swirled down the drain. I tried flipping through *Paris Match*, but what was the point without the fat, furry body that always inserted itself if you spread open a magazine or book.

It was early the next morning when the telephone jangled us out of sleep. "I theenk I have your cat," said the voice, and proceeded to give an address at the far end of our long St. Didier block. Though I didn't believe it could possibly be Chuck, I grabbed his basket and ran as if pushed along by little jet-puffs of hope.

I can't remember now what the building looked like or the elevator that took me to the seventh floor. All I can recall is the image of the chubby, long-haired pet we had brought to Paris from Providence lounging casually in the corner of this stranger's bedroom and looking about as pompous as I had ever seen him.

"Chuck jumped through the bedroom window of a sleeping Frenchman," was how my wife ended up describing the whole thing at work the next day, "after leaping from balcony to rooftop to balcony to balcony." Several times she and I walked along rue St. Didier pointing skyward to trace the truly impossible route. Several times we agreed that there was just no way a shelter cat with no claws should have been able to traverse so many slippery rooftops.

When visitors came to our small apartment in the weeks and months after that, they never failed to comment on the green garden fencing that was sloppily nailed over each of our lovely French windows. Most also noticed the rickety wooden gate I had hammered into place to block the door to our balcony. "Why are you obscuring these beautiful views?" they would ask. "And why did you put that fence in front of such an ornate, Parisian patio?"

When my wife and I heard this we would simply smile at each other and explain nothing. But as a certain orange friend purred safely down in the crack between two couch pillows, we would think, "Chuck has had his Paris adventure. Now it's time for him to stay put, so we can have ours."

~Peter Mandel
Chicken Soup for the Cat and Dog Lover's Soul

Loving Our Cats

Purr-fect Pets

I pet her and she pays me back in purrs.
~Star Richés

60

That's My Cat

February 1991. Operation Desert Storm is raging; our country is at war. Here at home, my house is strangely silent—the result of both the absence of my eleven-year-old son, Zach, who is spending the weekend with his father, and the void left by the death of my mother, who will never again interrupt me with an ill-timed phone call. As if war, separation and death are not enough, Valentine's Day lurks around the corner, with no lover or beloved in sight.

This is the clincher. At age thirty-seven, I have yet to experience a Valentine's Day that comes through on its Hallmark promise. For whatever reason, when February 14 rolls around, boyfriends take a hike or I receive valentines from admirers I wish had stayed secret. This year, my sense of abandonment is profound.

Out of this mire of despair, I have an idea: Forget the man. I will get a cat.

A long-haired, pink-nosed, calico female cat is what I have in mind. But, suddenly, the image of a black male cat pops into my head. Just as suddenly, I reject the thought. No black cats and no males, I decide. Black cats are too mysterious, too sleek and aloof. And male cats, too independent and too likely to spray. Bottom line: A black, male cat doesn't seem cuddly enough.

And so, on this fateful day in February, I call the local humane society and ask if they have any calico female cats. "You're in luck!" the voice at the other end of the line says. "We have a calico female kitten just waiting to be adopted."

"Great!" I say. "That's just what I'm looking for."

After hanging up, I immediately launch into a nest-making frenzy—vacuuming, dusting, cleaning and organizing. It never occurs to me that a little kitten wouldn't know the difference or even care. Mothers nest, so that's what I do.

With the home fires now burning brightly, I launch my blue Mazda in the direction of the animal shelter, all the while thinking about my mother. My mother always occupied a lot of my time, but her recent death has made her an even more frequent companion, unlimited now by the constraints of time and space.

My mother hated cats for as long as I could remember—until, that is, one walked into her life. It was Christmas in northern Michigan, and my brother Michael, my son Zach, and I had convened at my mother's house to celebrate the holidays.

There was a scratch at the door. My mother opened it. In walked a cat, a huge presence of a cat with long, black-and-brown-mottled fur coated with a dusting of snow. He entered the house like he had been there before. He had an enormous head with round yellow eyes and a broad, flat face. Looking up at my mother, he meowed, as if to say, "Merry Christmas" or "So nice to see you again." His face reminded us of a mug shot on a most-wanted poster, so we named him Muggs.

He was the only cat my mother ever loved, and he only stayed the week. When my brother and I were getting ready to return to our own homes, apparently, so was Muggs. My mother was convinced that he embodied the spirit of my brother Ricky, who had died at the age of five. Who were we to argue? Somehow, it made sense. Muggs returned the following year, same time, same place, only to leave at the end of Christmas week, this time never to return.

Driving up to the humane society, I decide to name my new cat Muggs, in memory of my mother and in deference to her hope that death isn't the end. Right now, I want to believe that, too.

I park my car in the shelter's circular driveway and crunch through the snow to the door. A spry older man in a light-blue shirt greets me at the reception counter. "Hi there! What can I do for you?"

"I've come for the calico kitten," I announce.

"I'm sorry, miss. The calico was just adopted about an hour ago."

I feel as if I have been sucker-punched. That cat was supposed to be mine. Why didn't I run over the minute I got off the phone?

"Hey!" the attendant said, brightening. "Her brother is still here."

"No," I say. "I don't want a male cat." My despondency is as thick as quicksand and just as slippery. "Okay," I say finally. "Do you have any other cats I could look at?"

"Do we have other cats?" he replies with a wry grin.

He guides me down a long narrow hallway to a room with cage after cage of cats: sleek cats, fluffy cats, dainty cats and chunky cats. Tigers, torties, white ones and gray ones. And they all just sit there, or lie there plastered against the back of their cages, staring coolly at me with complete indifference. Cats are so good at that, I suddenly remember. What was I thinking?

And then I hear something: a strange, low vibration and the tinkling of a bell. As I proceed down the row of cages, the vibration and bell get louder, until I finally identify their source. There, in the last cage at the end of the line, is a tiny black kitten, batting a plastic jingle ball around its cage and purring at the top of its little kitty lungs. Ah, I think, this must be the calico's brother. Imagine that, a black male cat.

His antics amuse me, and I find myself stirred by his show of life. But then, as if propelled by some counter-magnetic force, I turn abruptly away from his cage, searching in earnest for what I really want.

Except that, now, compared to the vibrant little one, the other cats seem even more lifeless, like four-legged zombies or feather dusters on sticks. The purring and jingling black kitten emanates a presence that tugs and beckons, reeling me in. Come see! Come see me! And so I do.

"Oh my, little one. What are we going to do?" I ask out loud, quietly, as he rubs against the bars of his cage, leaning toward my touch. As if on cue, the attendant appears and says, "Want to hold him?"

"Okay," I breathe, knowing all the while that I am losing my grip on something and sinking fast. Not into quicksand this time, but into something softer, darker, more comforting, like the sleek black velvet of this little one's body in my arms.

As the kitten crawls up my jacket and against my neck, purring loudly into my ear, I read the sign at the side of his cage:

Black male cat.
Purrs like a motorboat.
Name: Muggins.

I am not making this up.

"So, what do you think?" grins the attendant, holding the cage door open.

"I think," I say through my tears, "this is my cat."

~Mary Knight
Chicken Soup for the Cat Lover's Soul

Joy

Joy is
a cat's purr
that bursts forth
suddenly
and for no reason.
A rumble
amidst couch cushions
in late afternoon sunlight that
becomes rhythm.

~Laura Cota
Chicken Soup for the Soul Celebrates Cats

Bogie's Search for His Forever Home

If you want others to be happy, practice compassion.
If you want to be happy, practice compassion.
~Dalai Lama

I first met Bogie during a volunteer training class at Pittsburgh's Animal Friends, Inc., my community's no-kill shelter. As the facilitating volunteer spoke to the recruits gathered in the resident feline room, I couldn't help but notice the gray-and-white shorthair cat sleeping in his cage. The nametag on the cage informed me that Bogie, a four-and-a-half-year-old male, was the current occupant of cage 12. Poor thing, I thought as I knelt down before his cage to get a better look.

"Hey, little guy," I whispered, anticipating a meow or purr in response to my hello. But this cat was not happy that I woke him. Instead of purrs, Bogie hissed and spat, growling and staring at me with eyes that looked possessed. I was positive that, given the opportunity, he would have bitten my face off. I quickly apologized to Bogie, assuring him that I meant no harm. The rest of the group, distracted by this rather loud how-do-you-do, looked over at us.

The facilitator explained, "That's Bogie, the shelter's longest-term resident, and, as you can see and hear, he also happens to be our problem child."

Bogie seemed fully aware that he was being talked about, and his body language confirmed his irritation as his tail swished violently back and forth. The group chuckled at the facilitator's words, then began milling around the room, oohing and aahing at the friendlier cats that occupied the other cages. Bogie just sat there, growling.

After the training class, I began volunteering at the shelter every Sunday. Although I love all animals, I am particularly fond of cats, so I spent my time there socializing the cats—hours of playing, brushing, kissing, massaging and loving my furry little feline friends. Every cat received equal amounts of my love and attention—that is, every cat but Bogie. Bogie was strictly off-limits to volunteers because of his history of biting. This type of behavior isn't all that unusual for de-clawed cats, and poor Bogie had been a victim of that unfortunate and inhumane surgery prior to coming to the shelter. For Bogie, who felt defenseless and vulnerable without his claws, biting was the only way to protect himself against any perceived harm. As a result, Bogie was left to sit in his cage and observe all that went on around him.

Although Bogie was labeled a "Staff Only" cat, I didn't ignore him. From the moment I met Bogie, I was determined to break through his tough exterior to uncover his beautiful but hidden, loving spirit. The trick was how to go about it. My first thought was to make him feel important, so, every Sunday when I walked through the door, I would sing out his name before addressing any of the other cats. "Hi, Bogie! How are you? Boy, did I miss you Bogie!" Then I gave him his favorite fishy treats while telling him that his new family would be coming any day to take him home. I felt that it was important for him not to give up hope. I know it sounds crazy, but I believe that Bogie understood—if not my words, then at least my soft, reassuring tone. There were a few times that I actually snuck my finger though the cage bars and scratched behind Bogie's ears, until he discovered this intrusion and swiftly let me know that he did not approve. I brought Bogie a new bed and sprayed it with lavender oil, hoping that the aroma would calm him—it didn't. I brought him toys, hoping that he would play and find even the tiniest bit of pleasure in something—he was not interested. Day in and day out, he lay in that cage with his back facing the world. It was a pathetic sight; despite my efforts, Bogie had given up hope.

Because I already shared my home with five felines and two dogs, adopting Bogie was out of the question. But I had to do something — his situation tore at my heart. I began a campaign to find him a suitable home. Hoping that someone would be interested in giving him a second chance at a happy life, I told Bogie's sad story to anyone who would listen. Bogie was found wandering a beach in South Carolina. How he got there is anyone's guess. Perhaps he lost his way or maybe he was purposely abandoned. Only Bogie knows what really happened. He was rescued from the beach by a vacationing shelter employee and was brought back to Pittsburgh, where he weighed in at a frail six pounds and was diagnosed with hemolytic anemia. Medical treatment was successful, and, soon, Bogie was on the road to recovery. With Bogie's illness under control, he was eligible for adoption. The day finally came when a family adopted Bogie — only to return him days later because of litter-box aversion. Rejected, Bogie, in turn, seemed to reject the world. I told everyone that he was just waiting for his perfect person. Bogie needed someone who would be committed to working with him to help overcome the many traumas of his life, someone who actually embraced his cranky disposition and wouldn't give up on him, even if he did have an accident in the house — in short, someone who would make him feel safe and loved. I was sure that someone was out there... somewhere.

Finally, to my great joy, after a very long two years and four months of living at the shelter, Bogie was adopted in May 2002. Bogie's adjustment to life outside the shelter wasn't always easy, but his adoptive family constantly reassured him that he was finally in his forever home. The progress he made was slow, but definitely steady. Within two days, he allowed his new mom to briefly scratch him under his chin. Within a week, he was playing like a kitten, and, so far, he's only had one accident! The daily doses of hugs and kisses that he receives are healing his little heart, enabling him to trust once again.

When I think of Bogie and all the positive changes he's experienced since he found his forever home, I have to smile — especially when I see him sitting on his window perch, watching the birds while his tail swishes playfully.

That's right: I am Bogie's new mom, and there isn't a day that goes by that my formerly cranky cat doesn't thank me for giving him the chance to prove that, underneath all that attitude, he's just a big bundle of love.

~Lorra E. Allen
Chicken Soup for the Cat Lover's Soul

63

Medicine Cat

The doctors sent my mother home to die. A fifteen-year survivor of breast cancer, she had suffered two heart attacks when advanced cancer was found in her lung.

Mom had struggled to raise three daughters while holding a full-time job, yet worked hard to maintain a cozy home for her family. Growing up, I knew only two things about my mother: She had an iron will, and she loved nature. During her days of illness, she told me a third: "I've had a miserable life."

My dad was a difficult man to live with, but my mom did not complain, probably because she could not put words to her own need. But when it became clear that because of her progressive deterioration, my dad regarded her as a burden, she and I decided that she would move to my home.

I had three weeks to make a myriad of arrangements. I changed my work schedule, found transportation, an oncologist, cardiologist, hospice care, medical equipment, a caregiver and bather. My plan for Mom's final days was simple: She would live with love, and die with grace.

Upon her arrival, after an exhausting five-hour trip, Mom was examined by the home health-care nurse. The nurse took me aside and asked, "How long do you think your mother has?"

"Two, maybe three months," I said.

The nurse looked at me sadly. "Adjust your thinking," he said. "She has days, maybe a week. Her heart is weak and unstable."

My home, small and comfortable, was a haven to four cats and a golden retriever. The animals had the run of my house. During my parents' infrequent visits, they'd seen the cats prowl the kitchen counters, the dog snooze on the couch and knew the cats shared my bed. This made my father angry and my mother uncomfortable. I was worried my mother would be bothered by my pets.

We installed the electric hospital bed and oxygen machine, which frightened the cats from the bedroom. I'd moved their furniture, and they were peeved. The retriever, on the other hand, an immature dog with bad habits, was excited by all the changes in the house. She jumped up, barked and shed more profusely than usual.

One cat, however, seemed to adjust perfectly. Otto had been an ugly, smelly kitten adopted from the animal shelter, but he grew into a handsome cat. His short coat was white with black and tan tabby patches, accented by bold orange spots. The veterinarian decided he was a calico. "Unusual," she said, "because calicos tend to be female."

Otto was as smart as he was unusual. He had learned to retrieve paper balls, ran to the telephone when it rang and even gave useful hints about how to fix the toilet. Once when I was trying to repair the toilet, he kept reaching into the open tank, pushing on the float with his paw. Since I was not having any success with the repair, I decided he might be on to something. I went to the hardware store and bought a new float mechanism. It worked.

Otto was the one cat who was not afraid of the hospital bed, the oxygen machine or the medicinal smells. Nor was he afraid of the frail woman who had scolded him down from the kitchen counter. Otto jumped onto the foot of Mom's hospital bed, and stayed.

He was not startled by the nurses. He did not interfere when Mom was fed, nor when she was transferred from bed to commode and back. Whether the disturbance was from changing her bed or because of bathing, he simply waited to resume his post. With the exception of eating and using the litter box, Otto never left Mom's room.

Days passed, and Mom started to rally. "Not unusual," I was told, "a rally is often a sign of imminent death."

I grieved. But Otto would not give her up so easily. He used her improved condition to reposition himself from the foot of her bed to her side. Her thin fingers found his soft coat. He leaned into her body, as if clinging to the threads of her will to live. Though weak, she caressed the cat and would not allow me to take him.

Days turned into weeks and Mom continued to fight. Once, after the nurses had gone for the day, I heard the sound of Mom's voice coming from her room. I found her with the head of the bed raised. Otto was tucked into the crook of her elbow, listening adoringly as she read from the newspaper. I will forever cherish the memory of Mom's face with Otto's paw, claws retracted, caressing the side of her chin.

Being vigilant, I made sure juice, water and pain medications were always available. One evening I was surprised to find Mom unassisted in the bathroom, filling her empty medication dish with water. "Mom, what are you doing?" I asked.

Without looking up, she replied, "Getting a drink set up for Otto." I helped her back to bed. Mom sipped apple juice while Otto drank from the stainless steel dish. Getting that drink set up became her evening ritual.

Eventually, using a walker, Mom began to take walks through the house. She was trailed by oxygen tubing and Otto. Where she rested, Otto rested. Where she moved, Otto shadowed. It seems I had forgotten my mom was a mother. Somehow, Otto knew, and during those days he became her cat child, giving her life purpose. We had come a long way from the days when she used to chase him off the kitchen counter.

Exactly three years have passed since then. The hospital bed and oxygen machine are long gone. The medicines and nurses are gone, too. But Mom's still here. And so is Otto. And so is the bond that united them in days of sickness.

"You know, I swear that Otto knows my car when I drive up!" Mom says.

He does. Whenever Mom returns home from running an errand, he greets her car at the curb. She carries him up the driveway. They just pick up wherever they left off, with his front paws wrapped around her neck.

Happily, I prepare meals with Mom watching from a stool, and Otto next to her on the counter.

When we saw the oncologist a while ago, he patted himself on the back. "I can't believe it, Lula," he said. "I can't find your cancer and your heart is strong. When your daughter brought you to me, I thought you were a ship that had sailed."

We let the doctor think what he likes, but Mom gives the credit to Otto.

Thankfully, my mother has put off dying, and Otto continues to share his gift of love—a medicine more potent than any drug a doctor could prescribe.

~Joan M. Walker
Chicken Soup for the Cat and Dog Lover's Soul

64

Happy Endings

I t was a Saturday afternoon. As the shelter's cat-program director, I had just completed an adoption. Now, I stood in the adult-cat room, looking around. The doors of the cat cages—we call them cat condos—were open, yet some cats still lounged on the brightly colored, flannel-covered pads inside them. There were a few cats lying on the wide, sunny window ledge, watching the world outside or just snoozing contentedly. I looked up and saw Otis walking along the catwalk, a network of boards suspended from the ceiling that cats access by climbing a tall, rope-covered column in the corner that doubles as a scratching post. Moo stuck his head through the cat door from the screened-in porch, just to make sure he wasn't missing anything important. Satisfied I wasn't bearing food, he withdrew his furry black-and-white head, and, through the window, I saw him leap gracefully onto one of the chairs on the porch to resume his nap in the dappled sunlight. The scene was one of pleasant, clean, feline serenity.

What a difference a year makes, I thought. A year ago, Noah's Ark Animal Foundation's cats were all in foster care, as well as some cramped temporary housing in my own home. It hadn't been easy, but we'd made it through. It had been just one more stage in our journey—rising from the ashes of the tragedy that had nearly destroyed us seven years before.

In March 1997, local teenage boys broke into our shelter, killing seventeen cats and seriously injuring a dozen more. The story generated headlines across the country—it was even voted *People* magazine's

1997 "Story of the Year," based on the level of reader response. When the young men were found guilty of only misdemeanors, many animal lovers were outraged, feeling the boys had been let off with too light a punishment. Yet even this dark cloud had a silver lining: Using the incident as a banner, we at Noah's Ark, along with other animal-welfare organizations, were able to persuade state legislators to stiffen the animal-cruelty laws in Iowa, and in several other states as well.

But, as an organization, we experienced some tough times. The tragedy had been traumatic for all involved, and it took a while to recover emotionally. Then, five years later, we were forced to move from the facility we had been using for more than ten years. We scrambled and found a temporary home for our shelter dogs on the farm of a generous couple who supported the foundation's work. The cats were scattered in homes throughout the area.

We kept our doors open—rescuing and finding homes for as many dogs and cats as we could, as well as promoting spay/neuter education and activities. In the meantime, we were slowly raising money to buy land to build a new shelter. We were doing the best we could under the circumstances. The strain was enormous, and, privately, I wondered how much longer we could go on that way.

Then a miracle happened—the kind that makes you pinch yourself to be sure you aren't dreaming. A fairy godmother appeared, waved her magic wand, and—poof!—we had our very own brand-new shelter. Well, not exactly, but close! The administrator of a charitable foundation heard about our work. Our benefactress, who was appropriately named Miss Kitty, made a sizable donation, which—in addition to the money we had already raised—enabled us to build a shelter: the beautiful, modern, designed-for-animals building in which I now stood.

Of course, it took a lot more than a "poof!" to build the shelter. A great deal of work went into the research, design and building of our facility, because not only is our shelter clean and comfortable for animals, staff, volunteers and visitors, it is also kind to the Earth. Our building is "green," which means it is energy-efficient and has healthy interior-air quality because it was built with nontoxic construction materials and designed to take advantage of the sun for lighting and thermal power. The cats and dogs at Noah's Ark really seem to like the building. This is important because, even though we hope their stays will be brief, some animals spend a long time with us. Once we take an animal in, it remains with us until we find it a home—no matter how long that takes.

Doing rescue work isn't always fun. There is a high level of frustration because we can't save them all, and also because we worry when an animal doesn't seem to be adjusting well to shelter life or is returned after an unsuccessful adoption. Nevertheless, there are a lot of happy endings—and they are what keep us going.

I smiled, thinking of the adoption I had just completed. Kenny left this afternoon in the arms of a woman who couldn't see him, but loved him all the same. Kimberly, who is blind, immediately fell in love with Kenny, a long-time Noah's Ark resident, who had been passed over repeatedly by other potential adopters, probably because he was considered too ordinary: a black shorthair cat, no longer a kitten.

Of course, Kenny had done his part. Kimberly wanted a cat who would be drawn to her. Just a few moments after she took a seat in the adoption-room rocking chair, Kenny was on her lap, extolling his own virtues in his own way. Sometimes, I can only marvel at how these cat adoptions transpire; so often, it seems that it is the cat or kitten who adopts a human family, not the other way around. In any case, Kenny and Kimberly connected in a way that was beyond mere visual attraction. It was a particularly satisfying happy ending for me because I knew how much Kenny had to give.

Leaving the cat room, I looked around and said, "Don't worry, guys. Soon, it'll be your turn to go home with someone nice." Then I closed the door and walked through the happiest ending of all—Noah's Ark's new building, which houses our reborn spirit and provides shelter for the steady stream of animals who need and receive our care.

~Janet Mullen
Chicken Soup for the Cat Lover's Soul

65

The Cat and the Cat Burglar

I lived in New York City for many years. As a professional dancer and dance instructor, it was the logical place to pursue my career. The city had its many good points—fine museums, great theater, wonderful food and terrific shopping, but it also had its downside—high prices, crowding, noise and crime. The crime bothered me the most. As a single woman, I felt particularly vulnerable. I considered getting a dog for protection; I had grown up with German shepherds and loved them. But the idea of cramming a big dog in a tiny apartment didn't feel right. So, like every other single woman in New York, I had a few deadbolts on my door, and in the streets, I watched my back.

One day, I huddled under an awning on St. Mark's Place with a group of other people who had been surprised without an umbrella by a sudden cloudburst. A scruffy-looking guy, a street person standing in the small crowd, held up a tiny kitten and said, "Anybody give me ten bucks for this cat?"

The kitten was beautiful. She had a fawn underbelly with a chocolate tail and back, and a deeper cocoa mask with pure white whiskers. I was immediately intrigued. But a kitten didn't fit in my watchdog scenario. I wrestled with myself internally for a few moments before digging into my purse and scooping out all the cash I had on me—seven dollars and a few coins. I needed a dollar for the subway home, so I said, "Will you take six dollars for her?"

He must have realized that this was his best offer, or else he was so desperate that he just took whatever he could get, because we made the exchange and he left.

I named my new roommate Seal because her whiskers looked like a seal's. She seemed happy in my small apartment, and I enjoyed her company immensely.

One night, after I'd had Seal for about two years, I woke up in the middle of the night to a loud noise. Loud noises are not unusual in New York, even at 2:00 A.M., so I settled back down and attempted to sleep again. Immediately, Seal jumped on my chest and started stomping on me with all four feet. This was not kneading or playful swatting, and I realized Seal was trying to alert me to something. She jumped off the bed and I followed her. We both crept in the dark toward the kitchen. I watched Seal and when she stopped at the doorway to the kitchen, I stopped too. Keeping her body hidden, she poked her head around the corner of the doorway, and I did the same.

There we saw the figure of a man outlined against the frame of the broken window.

He was in my kitchen.

I refrained from emitting the high-pitched and therefore obviously female scream that was welling in my chest. I made myself inhale an enormous breath. Exhaling, I imagined the opera star, Luciano Pavarotti, and a sound like "WHAAAA" blasted out of me. I think I was planning on saying, "What do you think you are doing?" But I didn't need to. Even to myself, I sounded like a linebacker, and that guy was out the window and crawling like the human fly along the brick wall of the airshaft outside my kitchen as fast as his burglar legs could carry him.

After that night, I felt more confident about living in New York City. I kept a bat near my bed and practiced grabbing it and using it from every angle I thought might be necessary.

Seal and I became a team. I found myself trusting her more and more. If I heard a noise, I'd look at Seal. If she seemed curious or concerned, I'd investigate it. If not, I'd ignore it too. She became a source of security for me.

Seal is still around. She's eighteen years old and still spry. I have a bigger place now and I'm toying with getting a German shepherd, but not for protection. Seal and I have that one handled.

~Laya Schaetzel-Hawthorne
Chicken Soup for the Pet Lover's Soul

66

Nurse Mima

When I was a small child, I spent months in the hospital with severe headaches for which the doctors could find no cause. It was finally determined that I suffered from migraines and would most likely be on medication for the rest of my life to control them.

In college, I was unfortunate enough to see a doctor who claimed that my headaches were all in my mind and took me off all my medications. The headaches I suffered during this time were debilitating, forcing me to remain in bed for days with the windows covered and the air conditioner on high. During these periods, I would be constantly nauseated and dizzy, unable to read or even type because my hands shook so badly.

After suffering through a particularly bad episode in which I lost partial vision in one eye, I was finally given a prescription for an injection to try when I had my next headache. I was returning from the drugstore after picking up the prescription when I first met Mima.

I heard a soft meow from under a nearby car and squatted down to see who was there. Lying under the oil pan was a wreck of a calico cat, crying piteously to anyone who would listen. Her fur was missing in patches all over her body, and she was covered with fleas, which I could see crawling across the bridge of her nose. At first, I thought her legs might be broken because they stuck out from her body at such sharp angles, but when I called to her, she pushed herself up on them and moved toward me. I realized they only appeared to stick out that way because of how emaciated she was.

Once she saw that I had no food, she darted back under the car and resumed meowing. Afraid of what might happen to her if I left her out there too long, I ran into the house and brought back the only thing I could find that she might eat. I broke the cheese into pieces and put it under the car for her, then got back into my car and drove straight to the pet store.

A name, a pet carrier and a trip to the vet later, I brought her into my house for the first time. Frightened and confused, she darted under my bed and was not seen for days. The only indication that she was all right was the rate at which the cat food was disappearing!

Those first weeks, Mima stayed as far away from my husband and me as she possibly could, slinking out from behind the toilet or between the cabinets when we came near them, and pressing herself flat on the ground when she couldn't get away fast enough. I decided after three weeks of failed attempts to simply stroke her head that she would probably never be an affectionate cat, but comforted myself with the knowledge that at least she wouldn't starve to death on the streets.

About a week after that, I was sitting on the couch, crocheting a blanket as a peace offering for Mima, when, suddenly, one of the worst headaches of my life came upon me. My hands shook so badly that I had to simply drop the yarn and hook on the floor as I stumbled toward the bathroom, my stomach churning. Mima was, as usual, behind the toilet and streaked past me as I entered the room.

Somehow, I managed to make it to the couch again, where I lay flat on my back with a cool, wet washcloth over my face. My head felt like it was going to explode, and I wished my husband were home from work. By this time, I was in so much pain that I couldn't remember his phone number and was having trouble even thinking. I found myself praying just to fall asleep.

All of a sudden, something poked me in the ribs tentatively. I opened one eye and saw Mima cautiously kneading her paws against my stomach, her face a mask of concentration. I reached out for her, and, as she rubbed her head under my palm, the only coherent thought I now remember having was that she was incredibly soft. With Mima's warmth in my arms, I fell asleep easily—and remained asleep for several hours.

When I woke up, Mima was lying on my chest, her chin resting on my neck as she dozed peacefully against me. One paw was out-stretched and pressed on my cheek as if she had been stroking my face while I slept. Hoping that she wouldn't run away, I ran my hand down her back and was delighted to hear a small, rusty purr start in her throat.

As she opened one green eye, I realized that my headache was gone. I sat up quickly in surprise, and Mima slid onto my lap. She yowled at me, annoyed at having lost her place, and I cuddled her in my lap. For a moment, it looked like she was going to bolt away from me, but she changed her mind and set about making a nest on my legs.

Since that day on the couch, Mima knows when I am about to have a headache. She coaxes me onto the couch with her, then pro-ceeds to crawl up onto my chest and lie down on me with her face just a few inches from mine. Before I know it, her purring has lulled me to sleep, and the pain soon fades away.

Over the years, Mima has proved to be better medicine than anything the doctors have prescribed, and our bond continues to deepen each day she is in my life. I feel very fortunate to have Nurse Mima to care for me, and, in return, will continue to repay her in the only way I know how: by making her life safe, happy and secure.

~Natalie Suarez
Chicken Soup for the Cat Lover's Soul

67

A French Cat

*It is impossible for a lover of cats to banish these alert, gentle, and
discriminating little friends, who give us just enough of their regard and
complaisance to make us hunger for more.*
~Agnes Repplier

R ecently, my husband Gene and I traveled throughout Europe.
We rented a car as we always do and drove along the back
roads, staying in quaint, out-of-the-way inns. The only thing
that distracted me from the wonder of the trip was the terrible longing I felt for our cat Perry. I always miss him when we travel, but this
time, because we were gone for more than three weeks, my need
to touch his soft fur and to hold him close became more and more
intense. With every cat we saw, the feeling deepened.

We were high in the mountains of France one morning, packing the car before resuming our trip, when an elderly couple walked
up to the car parked next to ours. The woman was holding a large
Siamese cat and speaking to him in French.

I stood watching them, unable to turn away. My yearning for
Perry must have been written all over my face. The woman glanced
at me, turned to speak to her husband and then spoke to her cat.
Suddenly she walked right over to me and, without one word, held
out her cat.

I immediately opened my arms to him. Cautious about the
stranger holding him, he extended his claws, but only for a few seconds. Then he retracted them, settled into my embrace and began to

purr. I buried my face in his soft fur while rocking him gently. Then, still wordless, I returned him to the woman.

I smiled at them in thanks, and tears filled my eyes. The woman had sensed my need to hold her cat, the cat had sensed that he could trust me, and both, in one of the greatest gifts of kindness I have ever received, had acted upon their feelings.

It's comforting to know the language of cat lovers—and cats—is the same the world over.

~Jean Brody
Chicken Soup for the Pet Lover's Soul

68

The Ins and Outs of Cats

The cats are in, and they want out,
So they begin to dance about.
They stroke my chin and then they pout
Because they're in, and they want out.

They purr and mew and tantalize
and kiss me, too, and vocalize.
What can I do but theorize
That I am duped by their sweet eyes?

So out they go, I hold the door.
I hope they know they must endure
the rain and cold. But they are sure;
So out they go. I hold the door.

Yet very soon, I hear their cries.
(I will presume they caught no mice!)
Here's one, now two, back to entice.
It is their due, and I'm so nice.

The cats are out, and they want in.
They start to shout; no discipline.
But have no doubts, 'twould be a sin
To keep them out when they want in.

So open door, and in they come.
They're coy, demure — I'm overcome.
I'm never bored and never glum;
I can't be poor with cats for chums.

And so it goes, the cats are in.
They want to go where they have been.
And so it goes, the cats want out
'Cause that's what cats are all about.

~Betsy Stowe
Chicken Soup for the Cat Lover's Soul

69

Babblers Anonymous

During my college days, I began cultivating myself to fit the image I held of an aspiring author. I fancied myself a connoisseur of language and shuddered at others' misuse of it. Most of all, I scoffed at people who spewed drivel at babies or, even more loathsome, at pets. Although neither babies nor pets were part of my life, I felt quite certain that when they were, I would be a role model for mothers and animal lovers everywhere.

Then one day my friend Marcia called and asked if I would take in a stray cat. "He's cold and scared," she said. "He's been living on my neighbor's garage roof. Someone dumped him from a car."

Cats are sensible animals, I thought. I had always admired their regal bearing and independence. Besides, Charles Dickens, H. G. Wells and Mark Twain had all owned cats. I imagined a cat curled at my feet as I typed, perhaps inspiring my creativity to new heights. I invited Marcia to bring over the stray.

As Marcia approached my apartment, I heard rather than saw the cat. He protested loudly until she set the carrier on my living room rug. The moment she opened the door of the carrier, a skinny black cat streaked out, raced into the bedroom, jumped into the bathroom and bathtub, leapt out, then charged back into the living room and onto my lap.

"I've got to run," Marcia said, grabbing the carrier and stepping outside in one smooth move. "Yell if you need anything."

By this time, the cat was kneading his paws on my stomach in frantic rhythm, much like a boxer jabbing a punching bag. "You're not shy," I said wryly. Although the cat was bony, his coat shone blue-black in the lamplight. His mustard-yellow eyes blinked at me momentarily before he resumed his activity.

"I guess I need to call you something." I choked on my words. Listen to me, I thought. I'm talking to this animal as if he understands.

"Ralph," I continued, despite myself. "Ralph is a nice, no-nonsense name." No cutesy Boo-Boos or Fluffys for me.

That night I set down the rules of cathood. Ralph would not be allowed on my bed. He would sleep on the rug in the living room. He would learn to respond appropriately to simple, one-word commands. For my part, I would speak to him like the intelligent animal he was.

After a two-night cycle of putting Ralph on the floor and awakening to find him beside me in bed, I gave in on that rule. I told myself that this was for my good rather than his, because his purring relaxed me, and his warm, fuzzy body felt wonderful against my back.

As the week wore on, we seemed to understand each other perfectly. I made sure not to speak to Ralph other than as master to animal. Then one morning, I accidentally stepped on his tail. Such a pitiful wail! I scooped him up and held him close.

"Oh, Mommy's so sorry!"

I looked around. Who said that? Oh, no! It was happening. I was beginning to talk like one of them.

Over the next few days, I desperately tried to curb my maternal feelings. I decided to squelch the Mommy business first, but nothing else seemed appropriate. Master was a bit much. Kathy? No, too familiar—I would lose my authority. "Mommy" best summed up my role. So grudgingly, I became Ralph's mommy... but I promised myself I would make no further concessions.

Then one night Ralph was sick on the carpet. After cleaning up, I hugged and stroked him.

"Poor baby," I cooed. "Him was sick."

Him was sick! I envisioned my English professor tightening a noose around his neck. As Ralph napped, I reviewed my worsening condition. I could no longer deny the facts. I was rapidly becoming a pet owner-babbler.

During the next few weeks, I resolved to control every word that came from my lips, but the unthinkable happened. Such aberrations as "You is a widdle baby boy" flowed freely, as though the evil spirit of grammar atrocities possessed me every time I looked at Ralph. Worse yet, he seemed to expect such talk.

One night I decided to go cold turkey. I placed Ralph on my lap so he faced me. "Now," I began, consciously resisting the babble, "you're a sensible, intelligent animal. You want an owner who treats you as such, don't you?"

Ralph's eyes never moved. I read understanding there, encouraging me to go on. "Henceforth, I will treat you with the dignity and respect such a noble cat deserves."

Ralph's mouth was opening. So intent was his stare that for one insane moment, I thought he would speak. He yawned in my face.

"You silly, pweshus baby," I said, laughing and cuddling him to me.

Now the rules are gone. I never had the authority anyway. Only love and the babbling remain. Does anyone know of a Babblers Anonymous?

~Kathleen M. Muldoon
Chicken Soup for the Pet Lover's Soul

Loving Our Cats

Great Cat Moments

There are no ordinary cats.
~Colette

70

When Puss Comes to Shove

If animals could speak, the dog would be a blundering outspoken fellow;
but the cat would have the rare grace of never saying a word too much.
~Mark Twain

Cat owners like to describe their felines in superlatives. One person has the smartest cat in the whole world; another boasts of the biggest or the loudest cat in the whole world. I have Humphrey, the ugliest cat in the whole world.

Humphrey was a little crumpled when I got him. He was sitting in the middle of the road, suffering from a nasty case of failure to grant the right of way. His head was crooked, his jaw broken and one eye looked straight out into the twilight zone. The little fella had enough road rash to be an honorary Hell's Angel. He was the hurtin'est cat in the whole world.

I didn't think he would make it, but after four months and three hundred dollars he was doing quite well. He almost died three different times, but he never gave up. His head is still shaped like the last potato at the fruit stand, and the vet had to grind some teeth to let his mouth close, but Humphrey just wouldn't quit. He's got an eye on one side and a fur-lined depression on the other, and part of his nose is still out on Route 16, but that doesn't faze Humphrey. He's a cat, and he's tough.

Obviously I like cats, but a lot of men don't. Cats are not macho. Cats are not rough and tough. Cats, I am told, are sissies.

But let me tell you something, cats can rearrange your face and hand you your lips. Ask my dog.

My dog weighs eighty pounds and has a smile like the keyboard on Dracula's piano. He has too many teeth and not enough jowl. He's not afraid of anything. Except cats. So many ill-tempered Toms have tap-danced on his face, his nose looks like a country fair after the tractor races. Among the legions of slit-eyed mouse-molesters that trouble Shep's dreams, Humphrey ranks pretty high.

Some years ago, Shep and I were living with the afore-mentioned "puddy," a second cat named Bugsy Moran, and Lynn, the nice lady who saw dutifully to their every desire.

The five of us were happily ensconced in a modern, well-appointed duplex. Among the more admirable features of the place was a thick, springy carpet that covered every inch of floor space except for a small area inside one bedroom closet.

One still day in the dead of summer, it was oppressively hot. Flowers were limp and lifeless. The ice cream man wore a greedy smile. As for Shep, the combination of lying on a thick rug and wearing one at the same time was too much for him. He retreated to the uncarpeted closet and stretched out on the cool cement, secure in the assumption that, among the fur-bearing four-by-fours present, his rank, guaranteed by his size, would ensure that he was undisturbed.

Bugsy had pushed Lynn's knickknacks aside and was resting peacefully on the third tier of a teak bookshelf. But Humphrey was having a problem. Generally, on warmer days, Humphrey sprinted down the hall, through the bathroom door and leaped into the tub, where he played with the faucet drips before passing out till dinner was served. Unfortunately, on the previous day, without Humphrey's knowledge, Lynn had filled the bathtub with water. The result was an abrupt feline behavior modification involving a very wet cat and a slightly torn shower curtain.

As the morning melted into afternoon, Humphrey got more and more annoyed. He paced the house glancing nervously into the bathroom and longingly into Shep's closet space. Faced with the choice of confronting twenty gallons of cold water or eighty pounds of hot canine, Humphrey opted for the latter.

Lynn and I were sorting laundry on the bed. She was marveling at how each of my socks was unique, when Humphrey stalked into the room and positioned himself in the open closet doorway at the edge of the carpet. One of Shep's eyes opened momentarily. He blinked uneasily in the face of Humphrey's baleful stare, then, seemingly reassured by his five-to-one size advantage, drifted back to sleep.

After several long minutes the cat stood up and stretched thoroughly like a Kung Fu priest preparing for combat. Carefully, Humphrey took one step toward the sleeping black hulk. Shep's ear twitched, and again both eyes popped open. An almost inaudible rumble came from deep in the dog's throat. Humphrey sat down and waited.

After several moments, Shep's eyes closed again. He groaned and shifted to a more comfortable position. I know what he was thinking. Cats are afraid of dogs. Right?

Shep is not tall or long. He's thick. Almost his entire body is protected by dense fur and heavy muscle. He has only one window of vulnerability—his feet. The ferocious and powerful Shep has delicate tootsies. Very slowly Humphrey stretched his mitt out as far as it could reach. It gently touched against Shep's front paw.

Shep's foot jerked immediately in toward his body. His head came up as he showered Humphrey with a long and ominous snarl. The cat held his ground.

After a minute, Shep's head sank slowly to the floor. His eyes began to droop, but each breath was exhaled as a low, moaning growl. Again the cat stretched his paw into enemy territory. This time Shep's rear leg was the victim. With a sharp and frightening roar, Shep jerked upright and tried to tuck all four feet under his body. His ears lay flat against his neck and a ghoulish row of gleaming white teeth were exposed and at the ready.

Humphrey pulled his head back and squinted. Behind the still-extended paw his face wrinkled. Shep continued growling and snapping his teeth. Humphrey moved in closer and reached one of Shep's exposed toes. Shep jumped to his feet and crowded against the closet wall, growling and glancing nervously about. Humphrey moved in quickly and began hitting at the backs of Shep's rear legs, like an elephant trainer at the circus.

Shep trampled some high-heeled shoes and bellowed uselessly as he beat a hasty if not honorable retreat. Humphrey sat down in the middle of his conquered territory and proceeded to wash his ears.

In some corner of the universe, I'm sure a scoreboard lit up: Cats—1, Dogs—0. Cats may not be macho, but just ask Shep if they're sissy.

~Joe Kirkup
Chicken Soup for the Cat and Dog Lover's Soul

71

Comedy Pet Theater

The cat is above all things, a dramatist.
~Margaret Benson

Imagine a theater production featuring performing kitty cats. Sound crazy? Let me tell you how it happened.

I was born in what is now called Russia, the fourth generation of a circus family. My parents were dog trainers. Although I loved animals and learned from my parents how to work with them, I wanted to be a juggler. I started my training as a juggler when I was six years old, trained for the next six years, then began performing with a circus when I was twelve. At sixteen, I was asked to join the Moscow Circus — a dream come true for any circus performer — and toured with them for four years, even traveling to America. After winning many awards for my performances, including World's Best Juggler, I felt that I had progressed as far as I could as a straight juggler and decided to train as a clown. Not long after that, I returned to America and was hired by Ringling Brothers, eventually performing in a Las Vegas act.

By this time, I had brought my wife and daughter to America. We wanted to complete our family with a pet, so I went to a pet store to buy a cat. I was shocked by the price they were charging for a cat. I couldn't afford it. Then a friend told me to go to the animal shelter to adopt a cat.

Adopt a cat? What did that mean? And what was an animal shelter? In Russia, I hadn't been aware that there were animal shelters. It seemed like such an American concept: to have pet stores where people bought cats and dogs, as well as shelters for the animals when the same people no longer wanted them. Still, I went to the shelter and found a beautiful, white longhair kitten to adopt. We named her Sugar.

Like all kittens, Sugar was endlessly entertaining. She pounced on everything and seemed to especially like chasing her own tail. We were constantly laughing at her behavior. I suppose that is what gave me the idea to include her in my clown act.

As a novice clown, I was not as confident as I was with my juggling skills. I felt I should have a back-up joke, in case any part of the clown act was a flop. After watching Sugar, I came up with an idea for a back-up routine: I would reach for a bag on the stage, and, when I opened it, Sugar would jump out. I would clutch my head over the mistake of the wrong bag while Sugar entertained everyone with her cute cat antics!

When I tried it, it worked! In fact, it was wildly successful—audiences loved seeing Sugar onstage. And Sugar seemed completely comfortable with her role as chief tail-chaser. The audience and stage lights didn't seem to faze her.

And, so, my Comedy Pet Theater was born. I saw that audiences were very excited to see performing cats. Although dogs are more commonly trained, I knew cats could definitely be trained as well; they just needed a different approach.

To start, I found out what the cat liked to do naturally, then incorporated some show business into that activity. For instance, some cats love to climb, others love to jump and still others like to chase things. With the appropriate props and staging, the cat's natural behavior took a fascinating turn. The other secret was to have lots of cats onstage, because not every cat wants to perform every time. Onstage, if I walked up to a cat, looked into the cat's eyes and got no connection, I knew to move on to another cat. When I got that connection, the magic and fun would happen. I could tell that the cat was up for doing the special thing that cat loved to do anyway.

My reputation grew, and I began receiving phone calls from other places asking me to perform. A man called me from Los Angeles and offered a large fee. He asked me about my dog act—I had added a few trained dogs to the Comedy Pet Theater by that time—and then he asked if I performed with cats, too. I said yes. He replied, "Great! How many?" I told him six cats, and then he sent me a contract to sign.

The day before I was to leave for L.A., the same man called and asked me about my transportation—how was I getting the cats to L.A.? I told him I was driving my Ford Escort with the cats in the back in their carriers.

There was a moment of puzzled silence, then he said, "How are you going to fit six big cats in a Ford Escort?"

Then it hit me. He thought I was a big "jungle cat" act. "These are house cats," I told him.

At first, he hit the roof! He had advertised a circus act with trained dogs, juggling, a clown and big cats. Then we decided that, of course, the show must go on, and we would use the audience's expectation to comic advantage.

When the cat act was announced, we made a big fuss about how unprecedented the stage setup was: no nets, no cages, no audience protection at all. We really built the tension, so that, when the "cats" came out onstage, the audience went wild. It was a huge success—to everyone's relief.

Since then, many new animal performers have joined my Comedy Pet Theater. In America, all animal acts must be regulated by the local humane society to make sure that there is no cruelty, abuse or neglect occurring. I have become good friends with the local representatives of the humane society because, not only do I treat my cats, dogs, birds and rats as the family pets that they are, but I always add to my act by adopting from the shelter! I even like to plug adopting pets from shelters in all my shows.

Today, we divide our time between Las Vegas, Branson, Missouri and touring. Each of my animal performers is a beloved pet. We travel together, perform together, and eat, drink and rest together. It is a true "family circus"!

~Gregory Popovich
Chicken Soup for the Cat Lover's Soul

72

Moving Together

You enter into a certain amount of madness when you marry a person with cats.
~Nora Ephron

I was on a hillside whipped by wind, soaked in dew, beyond disgusted, all because of that wretched cat. I'd only opened the door for a moment. I'd been groggy with motel sleep, eight hundred miles from our last night's bed, so I wasn't thinking clearly.

I had been in the rented box of a room, and I needed something real to look at for a few moments. But when I opened the door there was nothing but sky and highway—gray on gray with scrub bush in-between.

I closed the door just as Lisa was coming turbaned out of the bathroom.

This was the big trip, her return to Winnipeg from Montreal where she had what she repeatedly called "the best year of my life."

My mail and phone campaign had coaxed her to return. Now, packing hopes, memories and her smoky tortoiseshell cat into my station wagon, we were heading back west together. She had been reluctant to leave, dawdling for sips of café au lait, strolling down the boulevard of St. Denis to sigh au revoir and kiss her friends on both cheeks as they eyed me with deepest suspicion.

It was a little later that we discovered the cat was missing from the motel room. "I only opened the door for thirty seconds," I pleaded.

"That's all it takes," she snapped.

That's all it took to feel like a complete failure. Eternal vigilance, the price of loving a woman with a cat.

Moreover, it was no ordinary cat. Not when it had been raised by Lisa, the social worker. Its every response had been scrutinized. A nap in the pantry was a sulk, a scratch on the hand was a plea for attention, a walk out the window onto the second-story ledge was a suicide attempt and cause for Lisa to cancel our date.

"I should have seen it coming," she'd said. "Chloe's been alone too much."

And how would Lisa analyze this blunder during our very act of moving together? A cat's jealous rejection? A dark flaw in my character? This could affect our future together. I had to find that cat.

We called out in cat sounds along the bushes. I prodded the underbrush. It opened into a jungly ravine. Where would I go if I were a cat?

"She's gone!" Lisa cried into the wind. "I just know she's gone! I loved her so much!"

If only I had a reputation for being reliable—for locking doors and mailing letters, finding my car in a parking lot—but I didn't.

Ashamed, I stared into bush and vines thinking how Chloe was really just a vulnerable creature, frightened of the car, anxious in the cage. She just wanted some peace. I could empathize. A quiet rabbit hole, soft leaves. She could sleep for days. And so could I.

But we were late. We had to meet the movers. We had family waiting and friends taking time off work to help. We had jobs.

I crashed into the ravine. Never mind the branches and nettles. Scratches were good. Blood could draw sympathy.

Could that cat really want to linger in this wilderness? She was a consumer cat, supermarket-wise in the ways of Kat Chow and Miss Mew. What did she know about hunting mice and sparrows?

Then I stumbled through the tangles and discovered another world. It was a housing development—streets with names like Buttercup Bay and Peony Drive and children on skateboards staring at my muddied clothes.

"Hi, kids." They looked suspicious. "I lost my cat." They stayed frozen. "I'll give you fifty bucks to find her."

Sudden acceptance. "Wow! Was it black?"

"She's smoky tortoiseshell grey. She has a hot-pink collar with toy sunglasses attached."

"I saw her!" hollered one of them. "She was right here. I knew I should have grabbed her!" The boy was furious with himself. Never again would he let a cat get away. He'd pack his garage with them for years to come. The kids scrambled into full alert.

I found Lisa and told her Chloe was spotted up the hill from the motel. She suddenly came to life. "That tramp!" she said. "What's she doing way up there?" Where there is anger, there is hope. Where there is hope, there is action. We put up reward posters, knocked on doors, phoned the local vet and police. As the day wore on, we left a reward if she was found later, hired someone to drive her to the airport, arranged plane fare and a flight cage.

We finally ate. The fast-food franchise overlooked the development. We watched children on skateboards and bikes cruising the lanes below. Some were checking shrubs, trampling a flowerbed. It was comforting.

We were both pretty quiet. Lisa finally spoke, "She was a good cat."

"Lisa, it's not over."

"She can live here okay. As long as she finds someone to care about her."

"I wish we could find her," I said. "I'd give more than money."

Lisa lowered her eyes. "I've been bargaining in my head. 'Give me back Chloe and I'll be better to my mother. I'll do volunteer work.'" And then she added, looking straight at me, "And I'll stop blaming you."

My secret thought welled up. "I've been making all this into a test. Lose the cat, lose Lisa. Find the cat, keep Lisa. I'm almost ready to give up everything — the move, the house, whatever. I guess I can't handle tests."

Lisa cupped her hand as if she were speaking to me through a microphone. "This is not a test. I repeat. This is not a test." We smiled to each other. "I'm not coming back for you," she said. "I'm coming back for us."

Dusk was settling in. The hills were gray — smoky, tortoiseshell gray. Chloe was nowhere, but it felt as if she were everywhere.

We were already packed so it didn't take long to clear the motel room. I only had to call the radio stations and leave an announcement about Chloe. Lisa took out the last bag.

That was when Chloe appeared. She simply walked out from under the bed, blinking in the light. She had been asleep inside the box spring all that time. It seems there was an opening we couldn't see. Lisa shrieked. The cat fled back into the mattress but we pulled her out. Then we left in a run.

As we pulled out of the motel driveway, we saw a pack of kids heading up the hill towards us. They probably had cats with them. At least two or three. We didn't stop to check. We already had everything we needed.

~Sheldon Oberman
Chicken Soup for the Cat and Dog Lover's Soul

73

The Cat's Bill of Rights

I am the cat, and I have certain inalienable rights:

I have the right to walk over your face anytime I wish, day or night.

I have the right to observe and comment on any and all bathroom behavior. Further, I have the right to be highly offended by any closed door.

I have the right to smell your shoes to determine if you have been fraternizing or cavorting or frolicking with any highly questionable animals.

I have the right to assist in any food preparation, cooking, cleaning or eating event that may occur in the home.

I have the right to wake you at three in the morning if I find my food dish is not to my satisfaction.

I have the right to tip over any water container I deem unsuitable for consumption.

I have the right to curse at squirrels and birds that may dare to pass my windows.

I have the right to inspect any grocery items that come into the home. Further, I have the right to inhabit any paper bag or cardboard box that you bring home for as long as I wish.

I have the right to nap at any time and place I darn well please, without the distraction of being called or moved just because you want to sit down, wash your hands or use your computer keyboard.

I have the right to sleep on top of any appliance that is warm.

I have the right to assist in any changing of bed linens and to chase the phantom creatures that hide beneath the sheets.

I have the right to look aloof when scolded for mistaking your toes for one of those pesky phantom creatures that hide beneath the sheets.

I have the right to kill paper-towel rolls that otherwise might sneak up on you at night.

I have the right to your complete attention anytime you sit down to read or work.

And, finally, I have the right to be loved, petted, pampered and entertained, for, as you know, the best things in life... purr.

And, should you err in your ways, I will graciously forgive. After all, you are only human, but I love you anyway.

Signed,
~The Cat

~Michael Ruemmler
Chicken Soup for the Cat Lover's Soul

74

The Cat Doctor

Oh, my friend, it's not what they take away from you that counts.
It's what you do with what you have left.
~Hubert Humphrey

D r. MacFarland, a veterinarian who goes by the name The Cat Doctor, has a practice in my hometown, where we bring our cat, Ragamuffin. At one point, we had to put Ragamuffin on a strict diet of prescription food, sold only at the vet's office. One time, when I went there to get a refill, I saw one of the saddest sights I have ever seen—a cat whose hind quarters were paralyzed and could get around only by dragging his back legs behind him.

I asked the receptionist about the cat. She told me his name was Slick, and that some people had found him by the side of the road a couple of years earlier and brought him in. The poor little guy had been shot and left for dead. The Cat Doctor treated him and when he recovered, they decided to keep Slick as the office mascot.

At first, it just broke my heart to see him pull himself around the office, using just his front legs. But Slick has such spirit, that each time I saw him, I seemed to notice his difficulties less and less.

Not too long ago, Ragamuffin became ill and I had to take him to the vet. The cat was scared to death to leave our house. Although he was in horrible pain from his illness, he put up a terrific fight. He fought his way out of the cat carrier three times before I could secure it.

I finally got Ragamuffin into the car and headed over to see The Cat Doctor. Ragamuffin howled and cried the whole way. Even as I carried the carrier into the office, my cat was putting up a fight. He was terrified of being in this strange place filled with new cat and people smells.

As I looked around, I noticed Slick sitting on a little cat bed across the room, oblivious to all the commotion I'd brought into his kingdom. He ignored us, continuing to groom himself.

Setting the carrier down on the floor, I tried not to listen to Ragamuffin's strident pleas for help as I filled out the proper paperwork.

Then suddenly it got quiet. Really quiet. No more screaming. No more howls. I cocked my head to listen as I continued to calculate Ragamuffin's weight in my head. Still, silence.

A sudden fear rushed over me as I realized that the front door to Dr. McFarland's office was still open. Omigosh, I thought, Ragamuffin must have gotten out of the carrier and run outside! I dropped my pen and turned to bolt out the door. I hadn't taken more than two steps when I stopped short—captivated by the scene before me.

Ragamuffin, still in his cage, had his pink nose pressed up against the bars. He was exchanging a calm little cat greeting with Slick, who had managed to crawl all the way across the room to comfort the agitated Rags. Slick, with his paralyzed hindquarters splayed behind him, pressed his nose to the bars as well. The two cats sat quietly, Slick continuing to soothe Ragamuffin's fears in a way only another cat would know how to do.

Smiling, I realized that there was more than one Cat Doctor around this place.

~Norma and Vincent Hans
Chicken Soup for the Cat and Dog Lover's Soul

75

The Funeral

The old stone church is a fixture at what has become a busy intersection in my growing town. The church's crumbling foundation houses the catacombs, accessible to both rodents and the colony of feral cats that took up residence years ago. The cats keep the rodent population under control, but no one monitors the cats' numbers closely. Parishioners occasionally feed the strays, and one kind woman has tried to trap, tame and adopt out some of the many kittens that the colony produces.

I pass the church daily on my way to and from work, always marveling at the array of cats adorning the steps and stone walls, or sitting atop gravestones. With six cats of my own, I can't adopt any more, no matter how much I want to.

The cat colony has its own social hierarchy, based on the principle that only the fittest survive. At one point, one red male tabby appeared to be the patriarch. With ripped ears and scars across his wide face, he swaggered around the neighborhood, secure in his position as top cat. Challenges to his authority—from subordinate colony members or the neighborhood's indoor/outdoor house cats—were met fiercely. Screaming vocalizations, slashing claws and sharp bites kept the red tabby in power. He might not have been popular among the local male cats or their owners, but his prowess was legendary among the female cats. Many red kittens appeared during his reign.

Returning home extremely late one evening, I heard the squeal of brakes and then the revving of an engine as a car peeled out somewhere ahead of me. Rounding the corner where the church stood, my headlights illuminated a still, red form in the middle of the road. With emergency flashers on, I stopped in the middle of the now, deserted street. Before I could get out of my car to check the cat, a black-and-white cat came dashing out of the catacombs and rushed to the tabby. With a tentative paw, it gently touched the prone cat, sniffing him from head to tail. The tabby never moved; neither did I.

The black-and-white cat sat down next to the tabby's body, threw back its head and howled. Within seconds, cats came pouring out of the church foundation, dozens of them, of every size and color. In a well-ordered procession, each one circled the body and its black-and-white guardian, then headed back under the church. As the last of the cortege disappeared into the catacombs, the black-and-white cat continued its vigil for a few more minutes, gazing at the tabby. Once again, it reached out and touched the tabby with a paw, then followed the others.

Stunned at what I'd just witnessed, what I can only describe as a feline funeral, I sat silently crying, awed by the display and saddened by the red cat's death. Not wanting to leave him for the road department's inglorious disposal, I took the tabby home and buried him alongside my own departed pets. I wish I'd been able to bury him in the church graveyard, but I'm sure he's happy two blocks over, where his spirit can still wander his familiar territory forever.

~Linda Mihatov
Chicken Soup for the Cat Lover's Soul

The Education of Jeeves

I had been told that the training procedure with cats was difficult. It's not.
Mine had me trained in two days.
~Bill Dana

It's inevitable whenever cat lovers get together that the topic of litter boxes comes up—the merits and drawbacks of various brands of kitty litter, the best locations for the boxes, the problems certain cats have using the litter box and of course the debate over whether those new electronic self-cleaning models are really worth the price. It is an awkward moment for me, for I have nothing to say to my fellow feline fanciers on this subject, except to mention as humbly as I can, that my cat, Jeeves, is toilet-trained.

This announcement always causes a stir. Some people laugh, while others scoff. After insisting that it's true, I explain that Jeeves uses—and flushes—the toilet like any other civilized apartment dweller. I ignore the head-shaking and envious mutterings, for it is a privilege and a joy to live with this refined gentleman of a cat.

I must admit, though, there were times while Jeeves was being taught this marvelous feat, when my husband Tim and I realized that training a cat is not as simple as it seems.

One of those moments came in the final stages of Jeeves's mastery of the toilet. It had been a long, involved process. We'd started by setting the litterbox on top of the toilet, and then in various stages, we'd graduated to putting a spare toilet seat over the litterbox. It was a simple matter to eventually remove the litterbox completely—the cat recognized the toilet seat and voila!

Now we were attempting to introduce the ultimate nicety: learning to flush. We tied a string with a small empty film canister on the end of it to the toilet handle. The small canister was punctured all over and inside it we placed kitty treats. When the cat pulled on it, thereby flushing the toilet, he received a treat. This was straightforward enough, and Jeeves was really getting the hang of it.

It was a Sunday morning. Tim and I were sleeping late, a luxury for us on our constantly busy schedule, when we were awakened by a noise. As we slowly surfaced from sleep and our brains began to register what we were hearing, we realized it was the sound of the toilet flushing—and flushing—and flushing. Over and over again, the toilet gurgled and whooshed. Tim staggered sleepily from bed and made his way to the bathroom to investigate what we assumed was faulty plumbing.

Instead, when he opened the door, he saw an imperious Jeeves, paws wrapped around the film canister, pulling the string again, looking for all the world like a monarch using the royal bell pull to summon a servant to his bedside.

"Ah, there you are, my good man," he seemed to say. "Now, where's that treat of mine?"

My husband dutifully fetched a treat and the porcelain Niagara Falls was finally silenced.

Back in the bedroom, Tim recounted to me what had just happened. Up till this point, we had been feeling pleased with how successfully we were training our cat. It was then we sensed the hollowness of our victory.

The cat was doing what we wanted him to do, yet it was clear that somewhere along the way, we'd lost the upper hand. I began to wonder if we'd ever really had it.

To this day, it remains a mystery just who has been conditioned to do what, but one thing is certain: Cat training can be a very tricky business.

~Debbie Freeberg-Renwick
Chicken Soup for the Cat and Dog Lover's Soul

The Cat in the Bag

Mirth is God's medicine. Everybody ought to bathe in it.
~Henry Ward Beecher

Aunt Faye and her cat Sophie were inseparable. In fact, though Aunt Faye never had any children, Sophie was like a child to her.

I have to admit that the cat was amazing. Sophie always knew when Aunt Faye wasn't feeling well. In fact, Sophie even knew when Aunt Faye's feet were cold at night. Because that cat would snuggle up at her feet in bed, Aunt Faye used to call Sophie her "bed warmer." My aunt was sort of hard of hearing, so when anyone came to the door of her apartment, Sophie ran to the door to alert her.

Good old Sophie the cat was getting on in years. My aunt would call me from time to time to ask me to drive Sophie and her to the veterinarian. In fact, I think she took better care of Sophie than herself. If Aunt Faye didn't feel well, she wouldn't go to the doctor; she would just take an aspirin. But should Sophie sneeze or cough with a hairball in her throat, we were on our way to the vet almost immediately.

So it came as a bit of a shock when Aunt Faye called me crying hysterically. "Sophie is dead! My little Sophie is dead!"

Between sobs, Aunt Faye explained. "You know I don't sleep so good at night. So the doctor gave me some sleeping pills. I didn't like the way they smelled so he told me to put a drop of vanilla extract into the bottle to make the pills taste like candy. So this morning when I was cooking in the kitchen, Sophie got into my bedroom and accidentally knocked over my bottle of sleeping pills. They must have smelled good to her because she ate almost every last one of them. The empty bottle was on the floor next to her."

Aunt Faye was still crying uncontrollably. "You know how long my Sophie and I have been together?" Not even waiting for my answer she said, "We've been together for twelve years. Yesterday, I even bought her a new cat food. They said this cat food was softer for older cats... her teeth have started to fall out like mine. Do you know how much Sophie meant to me?"

I sympathized with her.

"Now what can I do?" she sobbed.

"Look Aunt Faye, there isn't much you can do. Put Sophie's body in a paper bag, and place it in the garbage can in the basement. The sanitation department will take her away."

"What?" she screamed. "My Sophie in a garbage can? She was like my child. Since your uncle passed away, she's been my closest friend for all these years. I can't just put her in the garbage!"

"Okay," I said. "I'm working very late tonight so I won't be able to get over to your house. However, if you'll feel better about it, take a taxi to your veterinarian and ask him to have Sophie taken to the animal cemetery. I'll provide the money for the plot and the burial."

The tears continued. "Will I be able to visit her from time to time?"

"Sure. I'll take you to the pet cemetery any time you want to go."

"How can I take Sophie to the vet? Her carrying case fell apart a few years ago."

"Put her in your old suitcase. It's not too big and Sophie will fit perfectly."

"Will there be a funeral?"

"No, dear. The vet calls the people from the pet cemetery. They'll put Sophie in a little casket and take her to the cemetery."

"Okay," she muttered with a broken heart. "It will be dignified?" she asked.

"Yes, it will," I said.

That was it. I felt bad for her, but there was nothing more I could do.

About six o'clock that evening, Aunt Faye called me at my office. "Arnold, I have something to tell you." Strangely, I sensed excitement in her voice.

"What now?" I asked. "Did you go to the vet?"

"I did just like you said. I put Sophie in my suitcase. I was standing by the bus stop waiting for a cab, so I figured, why spend money for a taxi when I could certainly take the bus? So I put the suitcase down next to me and started to look into my purse to see if I had the exact change. While I was looking in my pocketbook, some teenage boys came up behind me. One threw me to the ground and grabbed my suitcase with Sophie inside!"

"Oh no, Aunt Faye! Did you get hurt?"

"Just a few scratches. Nothing serious. I yelled for the police, but nobody came. So what could I do? I figured this was the way my relationship with Sophie was supposed to end. So I went home."

"I don't believe this!" I said, trying to hold back my laughter. "Can you imagine the expression on those kids' faces when they opened the suitcase and found a dead cat?"

She started to laugh. Aunt Faye was actually laughing!

"Wait, wait—that's only part of the story. Sophie came home! She really wasn't dead! I only thought she was dead because she was lying so still when I found her in the bathroom this morning. Being jostled back and forth in that suitcase must have finally roused her. When I got back to the house, she was waiting at my door!

"Arnold, thank you for all your help. I prayed for Sophie to enter heaven, and she came back to me."

The next time I went to visit Aunt Faye, she had a little sign on her front door that read, "This is heaven."

~Arnold Fine
Chicken Soup for the Golden Soul

The Cat Man

Life + a cat... adds up to an incalculable sum.
~Rainer Maria Rilke

I sure love to fish. There is nothing more relaxing than being high up in the mountains and breathing in that fresh, cool air. My favorite fishing spot is a lake near a little four-building, one-gas-station town located high in the mountains of California, three hours from my home. Each year, as soon as the winter snow melts, I load my fishing gear into the station wagon and head out for a day of trout fishing.

Many years ago, during one of my trips, I crossed the small dam that had been built to create the beautiful mountain lake, pulled over to the side and began to unload my fishing poles. Suddenly, I heard a gunshot ring out, whistling as it flew over my head. I was quite surprised to hear someone shooting a firearm, as this was a restricted area: No hunting was permitted. Besides, in all my years fishing in the area, it was the very first time that I had ever come in contact with anyone, except for a few logging trucks that passed by.

I ducked down behind my automobile and carefully looked around, but I didn't see anyone.

Bam! Bam! Another two shots were fired.

Zing! rang the bullets as they hit against the large boulders. Still, I could see no one.

Then four young men came walking down the dirt road. One raised his rifle and fired off a shot. A cat ran across the road and into the bushes.

"Hey! What the heck are you doing?" I asked as they approached me. "This is not a hunting area."

"Just shooting at a darn cat," said the larger boy.

Slowly, another one of the boys raised his rifle and fired another shot at the cat, who was still hidden behind the large rock.

"Come on, guys. Why kill something for no reason?" I asked.

"What's the cat worth to you?" asked one of the boys.

"How about ten dollars?" I said.

Bam! Another shot in the cat's direction.

"How about a hundred dollars? That's what it's going to take," said the largest of the four boys, taking another shot in the cat's direction.

For weeks, I had been saving money to buy some type of used boat and motor so that I would not have to fish from the bank. I had about $110 in my wallet and maybe another twenty in my pocket.

"Okay, I'll give you a hundred dollars for the cat. Just don't kill it. Please," I said.

I pulled out my wallet, took the money from the secret compartment and put it on the hood of my brown station wagon. The four boys walked closer and stood looking at the money.

A very serious look came over their faces. The biggest boy reached down and picked up the money and put it into his pocket. As the four boys disappeared around the bend of the road, I began to look for the cat. Several minutes later, the boys, in an old pickup truck, drove past me, heading back up the mountain toward town.

It took me more than an hour to get the cat to trust me enough to let me catch her. I petted her for five minutes or so, then put her into my vehicle, along with my fishing gear, and drove back up the mountain to the little store.

I asked the owner if he knew if anyone in the area had lost a cat. He walked out to my vehicle and looked at the cat. He told me that the old man who lived next door had lost his cat about a week ago. The old man was very upset because it was his wife's cat. His wife had died several months before, and the cat was all that he had left.

The owner of the small store went to the telephone and made a call. When he returned, he poured a hot cup of coffee for each of us, and we talked for about ten minutes. I heard the door open behind me, and I turned around. A gray-haired man, all hunched over, who looked to be at least a hundred years old, slowly made his way to the corner. He sat down in a rocking chair, but didn't say a word.

"It's his cat," the owner told me.

The old man tapped his walking cane three times on the floor. The owner came from behind the counter and walked over to where the old man sat. The old man whispered something to the owner, then handed him a piece of paper. The owner took the old man by the arm, helped him up, and the two of them walked outside to my station wagon.

I watched through the window as the old man reached in, picked up the cat and hugged her to his chest. Then the two men walked to a mobile home next door and went inside.

Several minutes later, the storeowner came back.

"I had best be hitting the road," I told him.

"There's a reward for finding the cat," he said.

"I don't want a reward," I replied, but the man held out a piece of paper, and I took it from him. I opened the folded paper and saw that it was a personal check made out to "cash" in the amount of $2,500. I raised my eyebrows in surprise.

"Don't worry, that check's no good. Old man's been off his rocker since his wife died," said the owner of the store.

I folded the check again and threw it onto the counter so that he could throw it away. Then something inside me told me to keep the check. Retrieving it, I tucked it into my shirt pocket.

"I guess only an idiot would think that a cat is worth paying that kind of money for," he said, laughing out loud.

"Yeah! Only an idiot would think that," I said, laughing, too.

I walked out the door, got into my station wagon and drove home. The boys and their guns had made me decide to postpone my fishing trip.

When I arrived home, my wife handed me a note from a friend of mine. It said that he knew a man who would sell me his boat on a monthly payment plan. I telephoned the man with the boat. After discussing the boat, I asked him how much he wanted for it.

"Twenty-five hundred dollars. Three thousand if I have to finance it for you," he replied.

I told him that I would call him back in about an hour.

Taking the check out of my pocket, I telephoned my bank. I told them the story and asked if there was any way to find out if the check that the old man had given me was good. I gave them the numbers from the check, then waited for them to call me back. Ten minutes later the phone rang.

"Mr. Kiser, the check is good," said the woman at the bank, laughing.

"What's so funny?" I asked her.

"Well, when I called the other bank to ask if the check would clear, the gentleman there laughed. He told me that the old man who gave you the check is extremely wealthy. He owns most of the logging companies that operate in that area of California."

And that wasn't the only surprise.

That evening, I drove over to see the boat, motor and trailer that were for sale. When the tarp was removed, the boat was like new. It was a great deal; I knew I wanted it. But, when I saw the boat's name, I decided—right there and then—that it was meant to be. Painted on the back of the boat were the words: "The Cat Man."

~Roger Dean Kiser
Chicken Soup for the Cat Lover's Soul

79

The Cat Lady

The cat is domestic only as far as suits its own ends.
~Saki

I have lived in my neighborhood for twenty years. It seems to me that I've spent at least ten of those years looking for a lost pet, either mine or one I'd seen listed in the newspaper's lost pet column.

Recently, I was at it again, going door-to-door looking for one of my own lost kitties, a little black cat named Nicholas who'd slipped out the door before I could stop him. I made my rounds, visiting with all the neighbors, describing Nicholas. Familiar with this routine, everyone promised to keep an eye out and call me if they spotted him.

Two blocks from my house, I noticed a gentleman raking leaves in the yard of a home that had recently been sold. I introduced myself and presented my new neighbor with the plight of the missing Nicholas, asking if he had seen him.

"No," he replied, "I've not seen a little black kitty around here." He thought for a moment, looked at me and said, "But I know who you should ask. Several of my neighbors have told me that there's a woman in the neighborhood who's crazy about cats. They say she knows every cat around here, probably has dozens herself. They call her 'The Cat Lady.' Be sure to check with her."

"Oh, thank you," I said eagerly. "Do you know where she lives?"

He pointed a finger down the street, "It's that one."

I followed his finger and started to laugh.
He was pointing at my house!

~Patti Thompson
Chicken Soup for the Cat and Dog Lover's Soul

80

Operation Feline Justice

Cats are notoriously sore losers. Coming in second best, especially to
someone as poorly coordinated as a human being, grates their sensibility.
~Stephen Baker

From the moment the cat carrier door swung open in our living room, Clyde the cat established his territory. He jumped out, hissing, and hopped up and down on the living room sofa. Certain that he had cowed the enemy into submission, he set out on his patrol through the house, establishing a watchtower atop the refrigerator and a safe house among the towels in the linen closet.

Clyde was the undisputed feline ruler for several years; he even grew a little soft, letting the human civilians pet his belly when he was sure no other animals could spy him. One day, another cat carrier arrived in the living room. Clyde was on a routine patrol of the perimeter when he spotted it. He circled around it, sniffing, and when he heard the tell-tale meow, he knew that times had changed. Operation "Feline Justice" must begin.

Clyde knew he couldn't proceed with a direct attack. The humans would send him scurrying from his adorable nemesis with a swat on the rear end. This wouldn't be dignified for the undisputed ruler of the house. But something had to be done, especially once the interloper had discovered his safe house and was found sleeping on the best towel in the linen closet.

The humans had a box that they put food into. They would push a few buttons, and minutes later the food emerged hot. Clyde spied on them from atop his perch on the refrigerator. He began to stand in front of the machine, pushing buttons with his paw to see what would happen. For days, nothing. Then, the door popped open and the light came on. Clyde waked in, pretended to sniff around, and, with the patience of a veteran soldier, waited. Soon the interloper hopped up on the counter and walked into the machine. And in a flash, Clyde was out. He pushed button after button, waiting for something to happen. Then... disaster. The humans.

"Why's the microwave open? Clyde, what are you doing? Bad cat! Don't play with that!"

Clyde ran to his former sanctuary, the linen closet, and waited until the coast was clear. He need only bide his time. There was another box, a box in which the humans dried out their clothes, and it had that interloper's name all over it.

~Elizabeth Emily Butler-Witter
Chicken Soup for the Soul Celebrates Cats

81

Wild Turkeys and Cat Calls

After studying wildlife in the hot, harsh African bush for twenty-three years, my husband Mark and I were sun-weary and snow-starved. We decided that it was finally time to trade our tattered desert tent for something more substantial and less sandy. So we relocated to a small, wild valley in northern Idaho.

Surrounded by mountains and forests, dotted with glacial lakes and lined with rocky streams, this land was the opposite of our African home, but we welcomed the change. Rather than observe lions, elephants and giraffes, we watched moose, white-tailed deer and black bears crisscross our meadows. But of all these animals, we became especially attached to the wild turkeys.

Several years before we arrived, the Idaho Fish and Game Department introduced wild turkeys to the area. These charismatic birds are not indigenous this far north and cannot survive without handouts during the long, frigid winters. We inherited a flock of about forty birds on our land, and we gladly participated in the Department's program of providing food for them in the winter. I took this job very seriously, and clad in my new wardrobe of fleece, wool and down, I waded into the deep snow every morning and evening to feed the turkeys.

About the same time that I adopted the turkeys, Mark surprised me with two kittens for our anniversary. He knew that after watching lions and leopards for so many years in the bush, I longed for a cat of my own that I could cuddle. However, due to the high density of coyotes and the occasional cougar, the cats weren't safe outside at night. Every evening when I fed the turkeys, I would call, "kitty, kitty, kitty," and they would scramble into the warm security of our cabin.

The turkeys soon learned that shortly after I called the cats, I spread the corn onto the snow. All the toms and hens would come running from the woods whenever they heard me. And they were not the only ones. The white-tailed deer and the crows also thought that "Kitty, kitty, kitty" meant, "Soup's on!" So whenever I called the cats, we would have forty turkeys, fifteen deer and numerous crows munching in the yard.

Perhaps I was a bit overenthusiastic in my feedings. In a few years we had more than eighty turkeys glaring at us through our windows if I was late with their food. These "wild" birds would prance around the picnic table and perch on the porch, flapping their wings until I emerged with the bucket of corn.

During mating season, the toms, wanting to impress the females, became very vocal. "GOBBLE GOBBLE GOBBLE" echoed through the forests and meadows for most of the day. The slightest noise would set them off, and to our amazement, whenever I called, "kitty, kitty, kitty," they would respond, "GOBBLE GOBBLE GOBBLE."

One day a local sportsman drove down our road and stopped his rifle-racked pickup at our cabin. He had noticed our large flock of turkeys and wanted a closer look.

"You can call 'em, you know. I'm pretty good at it," he said. "Old trick I learned from years in the woods. Ya wanna see?"

Before we could answer, he pumped up his chest, twisted his fingers into some kind of complicated knot, puckered his lips and produced a loud "GOBBLE GOBBLE GOBBLE." Sure enough, the turkeys answered rather weakly from the woods: "Gobble Gobble Gobble."

"Oh, yeah?" I replied. "Watch this."

In my sweetest voice, I called, "Kitty, kitty, kitty."

And from the woods came a resounding thunder:

"GOBBLE GOBBLE GOBBLE." Then, more than eighty birds came running toward us as fast as their scrawny legs could carry them.

Later, I told Mark that I hoped I hadn't offended the old guy.

"I wouldn't worry about it. Just wait until his friends catch him in the woods during turkey season, calling, 'Kitty, kitty, kitty!'"

~Delia Owens
Chicken Soup for the Nature Lover's Soul

Chapter 11

Loving Our Cats

Hero Cats

The most I can do for my friend is simply be his friend.
~Henry David Thoreau

82

A Mother's Love

God could not be everywhere, so he created mothers.
~Jewish Proverb

I am a New York City fireman. Being a firefighter has its grim side. When someone's business or home is destroyed, it can break your heart. You see a lot of terror and sometimes even death. But the day I found Scarlett was different. That was a day about life. And love.

It was a Friday. We'd responded to an early morning alarm in Brooklyn at a burning garage. As I was getting my gear on, I heard the sound of cats crying. I couldn't stop—I would have to look for the cats after the fire was put out.

This was a large fire, so there were other hook and ladder companies there as well. We had been told that everyone in the building had made it out safely. I sure hoped so—the entire garage was filled with flames, and it would have been futile for anyone to attempt a rescue anyway. It took a long time and many firefighters to finally bring the enormous blaze under control.

At that point I was free to investigate the cat noises, which I still heard. There continued to be a tremendous amount of smoke and intense heat coming from the building. I couldn't see much, but I followed the meowing to a spot on the sidewalk about five feet away from the front of the garage. There, crying and huddled together, were three terrified little kittens. Then I found two more, one in the street and one across the street. They must have been in the building, as their fur was badly singed. I yelled for a box and out of the crowd around me, one appeared. Putting the five kittens in the box, I carried them to the porch of a neighboring house.

I started looking for a mother cat. It was obvious that the mother had gone into the burning garage and carried each of her babies, one by one, out to the sidewalk. Five separate trips into that raging heat and deadly smoke—it was hard to imagine. Then she had attempted to get them across the street, away from the building. Again, one at a time. But she hadn't been able to finish the job. What had happened to her?

A cop told me he had seen a cat go into a vacant lot near where I'd found the last two kittens. She was there, lying down and crying. She was horribly burnt: her eyes were blistered shut, her paws were blackened, and her fur was singed all over her body. In some places you could see her reddened skin showing through the burned fur. She was too weak to move anymore. I went over to her slowly, talking gently as I approached. I figured that she was a wild cat and I didn't want to alarm her. When I picked her up, she cried out in pain, but she didn't struggle. The poor animal reeked of burnt fur and flesh. She gave me a look of utter exhaustion and then relaxed in my arms as much as her pain would allow. Sensing her trust in me, I felt my throat tighten and the tears start in my eyes. I was determined to save this brave little cat and her family. Their lives were, literally, in my hands.

I put the cat in the box with the mewing kittens. Even in her pathetic condition, the blinded mother circled in the box and touched each kitten with her nose, one by one, to make sure they were all there and all safe. She was content, in spite of her pain, now that she was sure the kittens were all accounted for.

These cats obviously needed immediate medical care. I thought of a very special animal shelter out on Long Island, the North Shore Animal League, where I had taken a severely burned dog I had rescued eleven years earlier. If anyone could help them, they could.

I called to alert the Animal League that I was on my way with a badly burned cat and her kittens. Still in my smoke-stained fire gear, I drove my truck there as fast as I could. When I pulled into the driveway, I saw two teams of vets and technicians standing in the parking lot waiting for me. They whisked the cats into a treatment room—the mother on a table with one vet team and all the kittens on another table with the second team.

Utterly exhausted from fighting the fire, I stood in the treatment room, keeping out of the way. I didn't have much hope that these cats would survive. But somehow, I just couldn't leave them. After a long wait, the vets told me they would observe the kittens and their mother overnight, but they weren't very optimistic about the mother's chances of survival.

I returned the next day and waited and waited. I was about to completely give up hope when the vets finally came over to me. They told me the good news—the kittens would survive.

"And the mother?" I asked. I was afraid to hear the reply.

It was still too early to know.

I came back every day, but each day it was the same thing: they just didn't know. About a week after the fire, I arrived at the shelter in a bleak mood, thinking, Surely if the mother cat was going to make it, she'd have come around by now. How much longer could she hover between life and death? But when I walked in the door, the vets greeted me with big smiles and gave me the thumbs up sign! Not only was she going to be all right—in time she'd even be able to see again.

Now that she was going to live, she needed a name. One of the technicians came up with the name Scarlett, because of her reddened skin.

Knowing what Scarlett had endured for her kittens, it melted my heart to see her reunited with them. And what did mama cat do first? Another head count! She touched each of her kittens again, nose to nose, to be sure they were all still safe and sound. She had risked her life, not once, but five times—and it had paid off. All of her babies had survived.

As a firefighter, I see heroism every day. But what Scarlett showed me that day was the height of heroism—the kind of bravery that comes only from a mother's love.

~David Giannelli
Chicken Soup for the Pet Lover's Soul

83

Saving Private Hammer

Nobody can do everything, but everyone can do something.
~Author Unknown

My company, Team Hammer, crossed the border into Iraq in April 2003 as the lead element of the 4th Infantry Division. As the last maneuver battalion, we jumped from hotspot to hotspot in central and northeastern Iraq until September, when we finally set up operations at an airbase in Balad, fifty miles north of Baghdad.

It was in November that I first noticed three kittens running around the base. Someone told me that they had been born under a shipping container about six or eight weeks earlier. There were dogs around the base—drawn by the food—but no other cats. Two of the kittens behaved like typical ferals and weren't interested in being around us soldiers.

That wasn't the case with the third kitten. He made himself conspicuous by constantly being underfoot in the large tent we used as a dining facility. You couldn't miss the little cat. He was as playful a kitten as I had ever seen—in fact, we called his antics "dinner theater." He chased after anything and everything, pounced on boots and batted wildly at anything that dangled. He was a complete clown and a welcome distraction from the battles raging around us. We named him Hammer, and he became our mascot. When I told my wife about the cat, she sent me a bright-red collar and "dog tag" for Hammer. It read: Pfc. Hammer, HHC 1/8 Infantry, Balad, Iraq.

Hammer was involved in almost everything that happened on the base. He ate with us, slept with us, went on missions with us. We fashioned a harness and leash out of parachute cord to keep Hammer safe when he left the base with us. He loved riding in the truck and was always one of the first to jump in when the door of a truck was opened. During artillery attacks, soldiers tucked Hammer inside their body armor for safekeeping. Everyone vied for the chance to have Hammer sleep with him; usually, the one who fed him at night got to have the warm and furry feline as a bunkmate.

For me, Hammer was a little piece of home. Our family had five cats at the time, and it felt so good having a cat with me — a living, breathing, purring daily reminder of my loved ones back in the States.

Even the "cat haters" loved Hammer. One of those was a soldier who had been badly injured. We snuck Hammer into the hospital to visit him. He was in the ICU and hooked up to a lot of monitors. He was so surprised. We put Hammer in his arms, and, although he wouldn't admit it, it was obvious Hammer made him feel better. The monitors gave him away. We could see that his blood pressure and heart rate improved while he held the cat.

Just down the hall were two Iraqi children who had been burned when the clay oven in their home had exploded. We brought Hammer to see them, and, although they couldn't speak English, their wide smiles and sparkling eyes made it clear that the cat was a special and welcome visitor.

Hammer was special to a lot of people. We called him our on-site stress therapist. When we returned from a mission, tired, dirty, stressed and jittery from all the adrenaline pumping through our systems, Hammer was there for us. He jumped into laps, rubbed against ankles and did whatever it took to get our attention. We knew we'd have to go out again in four or five hours, and it was important to relax. Hammer was the greatest at taking our minds off things and helping us feel comfortable and at ease.

Hammer was the pest-management officer for our base as well. Although he no longer had to hunt for food — we kept him well-fed—he continued to keep the mouse and rat population under control, which was important for maintaining our fresh food supplies. Hammer was simply doing his part.

As the weeks went by and the time approached for our company to return home, I couldn't imagine leaving Hammer behind. Everyone agreed that he was part of our company. He had done so much for our spirits; we wanted him to come back to the U.S. with us. At the end of January, I started sending e-mails and making phone calls—trying to arrange for Hammer to leave Iraq with the rest of Team Hammer in March.

It was a nerve-racking time for me. When Jordan closed its borders, our best chance of shipping Hammer home was lost. We set our sights on getting Hammer sent home via Kuwait City and the International Veterinary Hospital. Unfortunately, this would take funds we didn't have.

Alley Cat Allies and Military Mascots responded to my plea, and, with their help, we began asking for private donations to get Hammer home. But the time for our departure was fast approaching, and our plan for Hammer wasn't coming together as quickly as I'd hoped. I was getting worried—I knew Hammer's chances for survival were slim to none if we didn't get him home. It was coming down to the wire, and we began trying to find safe places for Hammer to stay in Iraq. We even had a wild plan to try to get a private plane chartered for the little guy.

Then the call came: The money was there! I was told to bring Hammer to Kuwait City to get his health certificate in preparation for his long journey home.

The final obstacle was getting Hammer across the border. The border patrol stopped every vehicle and searched it for contraband. Taking an animal across the border was in the gray area—some border guards would allow it, and others wouldn't. If the patrol were one of the ones who wouldn't, they would make us leave Hammer on the side of the road. But since this was Hammer's only opportunity to leave Iraq, we felt it was a chance we had to take.

Driving to the border, I was nervous. Hammer, in his handmade harness and leash, was oblivious to any tension and looked out the window at the passing countryside. As we pulled up to the border, we stopped, and the border-patrol guards began their search of our truck. Hardly daring to breathe, we watched as they made their way to the seat where Hammer was perched. They looked at the cat, but didn't say a word. They finished their search and signaled us to drive on. As we left the checkpoint, we breathed a huge collective sigh of relief and all high-fived each other—including Hammer. We'd made it!

In Kuwait City, we brought Hammer to the veterinary hospital where he was vaccinated, neutered and thoroughly vetted. Our company had to leave Kuwait before Hammer was ready to go, but he was scheduled to take a KLM flight to San Francisco and then on to Denver, where I would meet him at the airport.

Once home, I kept in touch with the hospital in Kuwait, and, finally, Hammer was okayed for departure. He was met in San Francisco by a volunteer from Pets Unlimited, a nonprofit veterinary hospital and shelter. The volunteer kept him overnight and then accompanied him to Denver. Pets Unlimited even donated a soft-sided carrier for Hammer to travel in.

When Hammer and his escort arrived in Denver, my family met them at the airport. The volunteer told me that Hammer had been quiet for the whole trip, but, as they walked toward us and Hammer heard my voice, he immediately began to purr.

It was an emotional reunion for me. Mostly, I felt relief. We had done it: Hammer was home—and he was safe. I held my old friend in my arms and savored the comfort of being together again.

For the most part, Hammer has adjusted well to civilian life. Although he was a cat who had lived with a lot of danger and learned to take it in stride, he found some things in his new surroundings pretty scary. He had never been around little children before, and his first encounter with my three-year-old grandson sent Hammer scurrying under the bed for cover. He soon accepted that these miniature people were all right, and today he has no fear of anyone who visits us.

He has also come to realize that our hamster, Zeus, is not a rodent that needs exterminating, but one of the family. As Zeus rolls around the house in his "hamster ball," Hammer watches with interest, but with no predatory gleam in his eyes. The other cats and dog have accepted Hammer, and he fits in well with the pack.

Some habits die hard, though. When it's time for bed, Hammer, used to sleeping with the enlisted men of Team Hammer, heads for what we call the "boys' room," where he, another male cat and my teenage son all bunk down together for the night.

Half a world away from Iraq, Private First Class Hammer is still on duty—lifting spirits and making people smile.

~Rick Bousfield
Chicken Soup for the Cat Lover's Soul

84

The Captain

I believe cats to be spirits come to earth.
A cat, I am sure, could walk on a cloud without coming through.
~Jules Verne

In the middle of Iowa, on acreage just on the outskirts of a little town, sits an old farmhouse. Inside the house there are lots of couches and soft comfortable chairs, hand-built perches and scratching posts, kitty doors that lead to outside pens with grass and trees and lots of sunny spots to stretch out in. Every day volunteers come to groom and pet and feed freshly cooked food to the many cats who have this farmhouse all to themselves. There is also a small staff who keep the cats' house sparkling clean.

There are dogs there, too. Out back behind the house, near the garden and the orchard, are large dog kennels with insulated and heated doghouses in them. Volunteers come to walk and feed and "love up" the rescued dogs who are brought there when their time is up at the city pound.

As you can tell, the Noah's Ark Animal Foundation runs an unusual kind of no-kill sanctuary. Yet it is a state-licensed animal shelter, officially run as a non-profit charitable organization for over a decade.

For many years I dreamed of running a shelter for lost, stray and abandoned animals. But I wanted the shelter to be comfortable and home-like. Plus, I wanted to feed the animals healthy high-quality food and treat any ailments with natural remedies. Noah's Ark has been that dream-come-true for me. It has been wonderful to watch as the often malnourished animals who come to the shelter start blossoming with health. Their shining coats and bright eyes make all the hard work worthwhile.

Their personalities blossom, too. Some of the cats assume the role of official greeter, strolling out to inspect anyone who comes to visit.

Freddy, a large and beautiful gray Persian, was one of these greeters at Noah's Ark. In fact, I called Freddy "the Captain." He was not a cuddly cat, being far too macho for that, but he was a friendly sort and no one came to the shelter who was not subject to the Captain's inspection, and perhaps a rub or two against the leg. Freddy had been at the shelter six or seven years and had become a personal favorite of mine.

One Saturday morning, I received a frantic call from one of the volunteers who had gone to feed the cats that morning. Something terrible had happened—I had to come over right away.

Nothing could have prepared me for what I found when I arrived at the shelter. During the night, someone had broken into the locked shelter and gone on a killing spree, using blunt instruments to murder and maim over twenty-five cats.

The shock was devastating, and I was almost numb as I called the police and other volunteers to come and help me care for the injured, gather up the dead and attempt to put the shelter back into some semblance of order. As the word quickly spread, a local church sent a crew of ten men to help out, including two of the ministers. It was the compassionate and conscientious labor of all these volunteers that got me through the worst moments of that morning.

After about an hour, I had a panicked thought. What about the dogs? Running out to the kennels to check, I was immensely relieved to find them all unharmed. Two of the dogs in our care, Duke and Dolly, are Rhodesian ridgeback–mastiff mixes, enormous and powerful-looking dogs with the hearts of puppies—when it comes to people they know and love. For once I was glad they looked so formidable, even though it's probably why they haven't found homes yet, for I was sure that was why no stranger had been foolish enough to take them on.

When I returned to the house, volunteers were placing the cats that had died in a cart for burial. I felt the tears come to my eyes as I recognized so many of my little friends. Then I saw the gray body, partially covered by a towel.

"Not Freddy," I moaned. "Please don't let it be Freddy." But the Captain was nowhere to be found, and I had to face the fact that Freddy was gone.

I felt physically sick when I thought that it was probably his friendly, trusting nature that had killed him—walking right up to people who had evil intentions toward this sweet and innocent animal.

The outpouring of concern and sympathy from supporters in our community was amazing. And after the local paper reported the incident, the national news services picked up the story, and soon calls and letters flooded in from all over the country. People even drove from neighboring states to adopt the survivors of the attack.

It was a painful time for me. I felt the grief of losing so many beings I had come to love, and I was bewildered by the senselessness of the whole thing. Three young men from the local high school were convicted of the crime.

The incident caused a tremendous uproar in our little town. The violence that ravaged the shelter was the subject of intense debate. A small but vocal minority felt the victims were "just cats," so what was the big deal? But the majority of people, outraged animal lovers, demanded justice.

I felt dazed, trapped in a bad dream that wasn't going away. Nothing could bring back the cats that had died. As we went about the sad business of looking for the terrified cats who had escaped to hide, and of caring for the traumatized and injured cats who remained, I mourned my friends, especially Freddy.

A few days later, as I was stepping out of the house, I saw a large gray Persian coming slowly toward me. I scared us both by yelling "Freddy!" at the top of my lungs. It couldn't be—but it was. He was wobbly and shaken, no longer the suave and debonair greeter of old, but he was alive! I scooped him up into my arms and held him to my chest, my tears falling on his head as I hugged and stroked him. Freddy had come back.

In the chaos of that terrible morning, I had confused Freddy with another gray Persian, lying dead, half-hidden by a towel, on the burial cart. Freddy had been one of the lucky ones to make it outside and escape the others' appalling fate.

Miraculously, it took only a few weeks for Freddy to come around. Eventually, he even resumed his duties as official greeter.

In my grief after the incident, I had felt like giving up—I just hadn't had the heart to continue. It was the gray cat's courage and willingness to trust again that helped mend my own shattered spirit. Ultimately, my love for Freddy and others like him made me decide to continue Noah's Ark's life-saving rescue work in spite of what had happened.

Today, if you visit our shelter, you will be greeted by a large and confident gray cat walking proudly forward to meet you. His green eyes miss nothing as he inspects you from head to toe. If you pass muster, then you may feel his large bulk pressing affectionately against your shins. For the Captain, I am happy to report, it's business as usual.

~David E. Sykes
Chicken Soup for the Pet Lover's Soul

85

Etcetera, Etcetera, Etcetera

"LUCILLE! Get over here right now!"

Silence.

The cross voice boomed again, "LUCILLE! What are you doing?"

Lucille, my small, quiet mother, looked puzzled. "Hanging up the diapers," she answered.

I opened the back door and laughed. "Mom, that guy across the alley is yelling for Lucille, his dog. Not you." I adjusted my newborn baby on my shoulder and walked to the back gate. "Make sure this gate stays locked because that dog is ornery."

I lay the baby down in her buggy and watched my six-year-old daughter put our Siamese in her doll buggy. The cat's clear blue eyes looked worried, but he remained on his back wearing a doll's nightgown and bonnet like a good baby should. When I was little, I remember my elderly neighbor's warning: "It's not good to have Siamese cats around small children. They have a mean streak, you know." She dropped her voice, "And cats will suck the breath out of a baby. Anyone with small children should think about getting rid of a cat."

No way would I dream of getting rid of our cat! Etcetera was an important member of our family. Even naming him had been a family decision. We all enjoyed listening to my record of Rodgers and Hammerstein's musical *The King and I*. The kids particularly liked the part when the King of Siam says, "Etcetera, etcetera, etcetera." And that was how our pretty, fine-boned Siamese kitten became Etcetera.

Etcetera grew up with our children. He demonstrated his good nature by never complaining and sometimes even taking the blame for their antics. The boys ended up with very sticky hair after devouring a whole package of gum. When I asked how this happened, they assured me that our cat had chewed the gum and deposited it in their hair. Another time, the owner of a pair of wet underpants told me, "Etcetera did it!"

Etcetera showed his patience by being the load carried in a big dump truck in the sandbox. He morphed into a ferocious lion and sat still for the construction of a building-block fence around him. He purred contentedly while a chubby little arm anchored him down during naptime. Was this the same breed of cat that had a mean streak?

When the new baby was two weeks old, Grandma Lucille went home, and I settled into raising our four children. One morning, during the baby's bath time, I heard frightened cries from the kids playing outside. I wrapped the baby in a towel and opened the back door. I noticed that the back gate stood open. Without warning, Etcetera whipped past me out of the house — eyes wild and tail straight out.

He made a beeline to the sandbox, where I now saw the children had been cornered by Lucille. Etcetera pounced. Lucille's threatening growl stopped. Lucille, the loser in round one, streaked out the gate yelping. Etcetera, the victor, climbed into the dump truck for a ride. After meeting our attack cat, Lucille wouldn't be over again anytime soon. I shut and locked the back gate, dried tears, watched the road building begin in the sandbox and listened as praise for our cat filled the air.

"Wasn't Etcetera brave?"

"He saved our lives."

"He flew faster than Superman."

"Our little cat's tougher than that big dog."
Etcetera, etcetera, etcetera.

~Sharon Landeen
Chicken Soup for the Cat and Dog Lover's Soul

86

Smokey

I have studied many philosophers and many cats.
The wisdom of cats is infinitely superior.
~Hippolyte Taine

My daughter had her parenting cut out for her. Only two days after my grandsons Josh and Jarod, identical twins, were born, my daughter brought them home from the hospital. The babies weighed only about four pounds each, and my daughter had dressed them in Cabbage Patch nightgowns, the only clothes she could find to fit them.

For the next five days, we all pitched in. The household revolved around these two tiny creatures. They ate every two hours, and we spent virtually the entire day in some stage of feeding them: making bottles, emptying bottles, cleaning bottles, changing diapers, preparing more bottles. After the twins had sucked down the last of their 8:00 P.M. bottles and we had changed them and tucked them into bed, we would head to the kitchen for a cup of coffee and a much-needed break. What we needed was a full-time, paid staff. What we had was Smokey, the family cat.

Smokey had been fascinated with the twins since the day they came home. He spent more time at their side than we did, watching them curiously or napping near their beds. We watched him cautiously at first, making sure he didn't hurt the babies, but though he never left their side, he never got too close to them. He seemed a loyal caretaker.

One evening, though, we briefly doubted our trust. We were

unwinding in the kitchen when Smokey let out a blood-curdling howl, like an animal killing its prey. We raced into the twins' room, and the sight that greeted us filled us with terror. Smokey was almost sitting on Josh, the smaller twin, butting the baby's little body with his head and literally rolling him around the crib. As we ran to save Josh from what we thought was serious injury or worse, Smokey suddenly lay down and started softly mewing, almost moaning. That's when we discovered that little Josh wasn't breathing.

I immediately started CPR while someone else called 911, and an ambulance raced Josh to the hospital. It turned out that both boys were highly allergic to milk. Their bodies had reached their limit in milk intake, and because Josh was smaller, he had gotten sick sooner. Mercifully, Josh had not been without oxygen for very long. Smokey had realized that Josh had stopped breathing and alerted us just in time. Josh would be fine. In fact, the doctor said Smokey had definitely saved Josh's life.

Over the following months, the family settled into an amiable routine. Then late one night, Smokey jumped into bed with my daughter and son-in-law and started to bite and scratch them. More annoyed than puzzled at the cat's strange behavior, they got up to shut him into the bathroom for the night. But Smokey dodged their grasp and darted upstairs to the twins' older brother John's room. When my daughter followed in the chase, she found John so ill that he couldn't move or call for help. "My chest," was all he could say. When he underwent emergency heart surgery, the doctors found that his aorta was almost totally blocked.

Smokey, the hero-cat, now holds a special place in our family. He may have been content to be your typical family pet when the house was half-empty, but as it filled up with children, he decided he better promote himself to a mothering position. When it comes to raising a houseful of kids, Smokey figures it doesn't hurt to have some extra help.

~B. A. Sutkus
Chicken Soup for the Mother's Soul 2

87

Bumpus

If a friend is in trouble, don't annoy him by asking if there is anything you
can do. Think up something appropriate and do it.
~Edgar Watson Howe

The big, Maine–coon-type cat was found by firefighters on Father's Day 1996, his long orange fur matted and scorched. He lay, barely alive, in the charred remains of the wildfires that plagued Alaska that year. Even though he must have been in great pain, the cat purred the moment he was touched. When the vet first saw the badly burned cat, he began to cry. He had never seen a living animal with such extensive injuries. The fire had claimed his rear feet and all his front toes. The vet was afraid this latest fire victim might not live long.

But the cat was a survivor. Bumpus, as he came to be called, seemed unaware of the odds against him. Once he began to heal, Bumpus struggled persistently to learn to walk again. Eventually, to everyone's astonishment, the cat succeeded.

Bumpus became a favorite with the rescue volunteers who helped the clinic staff care for him. After facing so much ruin, devastation and death left in the wake of the fires, the presence of this friendly, spirited cat boosted morale and helped the rescuers continue their work.

One of the volunteers, a woman named Sharon, fell in love with the big orange cat. When she was finished in Alaska, she couldn't face leaving him behind, so when Bumpus was well enough to travel, he came home to live with her in Missouri.

Besides doing emergency rescue work, Sharon volunteered at her local humane society. Her specialty was fostering sick or injured kittens in her home and nursing them back to health.

Not long after Bumpus came to live with her, Sharon took in a litter of badly wounded kittens who required special medical attention—two of them eventually needed to have a leg amputated. After the surgery, one of the two-month-old kittens, a female named Minus, came home from the vet, charged out of her carrier and jumped right up on the bed. She didn't even seem to notice she was missing a front leg.

But her brother, Cheerio, named for the circular patterns on his solid orange coat, was traumatized by the operation. Unlike other amputees Sharon had fostered, Cheerio seemed depressed at having lost a limb. He cried constantly, and when he tried to walk, Cheerio always fell and ended up doing a somersault. He took his frustration out on the carpeting, biting and growling at anything around him. At other times, he hid under the bed, refusing to come out.

When Sharon saw how depressed Cheerio was—even his eyes were dull—she worried he might sicken and die. She had to do something, but what? Her eyes fell on Bumpus, serenely grooming himself in a sunny spot on the floor. He's been through this, she thought. Maybe he could help.

Sharon had isolated the injured kittens in one room in an attempt to keep them less active. When she opened the door to the kittens' room for Bumpus, he made a beeline for the crying kitten, quietly talking to him the whole way. He walked right up to the kitten and, wrapping his furry front paws around Cheerio's damaged little body, held him like a child holds a doll. Then Bumpus began rubbing his head against Cheerio's head and licking the kitten's face. Immediately the crying stopped—and the purring began. The little three-legged kitten, who could not warm to the love of a human, immediately responded to the love of another orange cat—a larger version of himself—who had suffered in this way, too.

Over the next few days, Cheerio and Bumpus became insepa-rable. Though Cheerio didn't want his littermates around, he stuck close to Bumpus. Often when Sharon looked in on them, she found

Bumpus and the kitten curled up together on the bed—the same bed that Cheerio had refused to jump on, hiding under it instead.

Thanks to Bumpus's therapy, Cheerio regained his cheerful disposition and eventually went to live with a devoted new family.

Since then, Bumpus has become Sharon's secret weapon. Any time she has a problem with a kitten, she sends the big cat in and waits for the inevitable miracle.

Bumpus works his magic on people as well. Sharon often takes him to visit children in the pediatric oncology ward at a local hospital. The children are deeply affected when they see what the fire did to Bumpus and witness how his strong will to live has helped him. They reach out eagerly to pet the big, brave cat. And his purring presence seems to quiet their fears.

Sharon doesn't wonder how Bumpus does it, because she's always known. This wonderful cat possesses an enormous quantity of the healing spirit—more than enough to share.

~Janine Adams
Chicken Soup for the Cat and Dog Lover's Soul

88

Ringo, the Hero Cat

We adopted our red tabby Manx, Ringo, from a litter of kittens found in a shed outside my mother's nursing home. His mother, who had half a tail, was feral. We fell in love with Ringo when he was only ten days old. He had brilliant red fur, a tiny stump of a tail, bright-blue eyes and a high-pitched, squeaky mew. How could we resist? At the time, we already had three cats and had made up our minds not to get another.

Had we stuck to our promise, we would not be alive today.

Ringo was special from the beginning. He had a wonderful personality and loved nearly everyone who came to visit. An expressive cat, he could move his little bunny puff of a tail in any direction he wanted, depending on how he felt. That red pom-pom tail could speak a thousand words. He was a delight to live with—and, as we were about to discover, a hero, to boot.

Throughout the late spring and summer of 1995, my husband Ray and I developed troubling symptoms, including dizziness, headaches, high blood pressure and oversleeping. Ray was recovering from heart surgery, and I was laid up with a cast on my leg. Naturally, we thought these symptoms were part of our illnesses. We were wrong.

One hot August afternoon, we had the air conditioning going full blast, and the doors and windows shut tight. Ringo, who was inside with us, started slamming his body against the front door of our house and wouldn't stop. In addition, he meowed loudly, over and over. I had never seen him act this way before. Finally, I hobbled over and let him out.

Once outside, he continued his loud meowing, acting as though he wanted to come back in. Again, I had never seen him act this way. His unusual behavior let me know that I was to follow him. I thought he was going to take me to one of his favorite spots; instead, he led me to the south side of our house, a place on our property that we don't visit too often. Only our air conditioner and gas and water meters are there, hidden behind large bushes. Ringo began to dig in the jagged lava-rock landscaping, about three feet in front of the gas meter. Normally, a cat wouldn't dig among these sharp stones as the edges could easily hurt a paw. Then he lifted his head, opened his mouth and wrinkled his nose to let me know that something smelled awful. When I leaned down next to Ringo, the smell of natural gas nearly bowled me over.

I called the gas company immediately. They sent out an emergency crew, who told us that we were at explosive levels around our foundation. A pilot light or a spark outdoors was all that stood between us and oblivion. In addition, the gas had permeated the walls of our home and traveled up into our bedroom. Our doctor said that if we escaped being killed by a deadly explosion, we would still have succumbed to methane poisoning.

When the plumbers came, they found the leak about three feet in front of the gas meter—right where Ringo had dug. An old steel coupler had split open, and the crack was growing larger as a result of rust and corrosion. Ringo had smelled the escaping gas four feet beneath our landscaping. He led us to the gas leak that we couldn't smell—and the meter didn't register. What a nose for trouble!

After we aired out the house, our health improved rapidly. For his outstanding heroism, Ringo received the American Humane Association's Stillman Award. Only ten cats in nearly a hundred years have received this honor. While many pets have saved their families by insisting that they leave a hazardous situation—saving the pet's own life in the process—it is highly unusual for any animal to lead his family outdoors to alert them to the source of a lethal problem.

Ringo, our guardian angel, is gone now, but his extraordinary love and heroic actions will remain with us always.

~Carol Steiner
Chicken Soup for the Cat Lover's Soul

89

The Cat Who Needed a Night Light

Courage is not the absence of fear, but rather the judgment that something else is more important than fear.
~Ambrose Redmoon

On a warm August day, a dainty little cat named Dolores was receiving a special award: the American Humane Association's William O. Stillman award for bravery. The association gives the award to people who risk their lives to save animals from danger, and to animals who face down danger to save the lives of people. Either way, the winners are heroes, whether they're take-charge, fearless sorts of people, or extroverted, devoted pets like Dolores.

Dolores hadn't always been an extrovert. And she hadn't seemed very devoted to anyone, either. In fact, she'd been what most people call the quiet type. When she first came to live with her owner, Kyle, Dolores rarely had anything to say. And most of the time, she didn't like being touched.

Kyle didn't know why Dolores was so standoffish. And he didn't understand something else about her: why she always became upset whenever the lights were turned out. But Kyle didn't care. Something about the cat's quiet, unassuming manner appealed to him. So, at night, he just left all the lights on in the apartment where he and Dolores lived, even when it was time to go to sleep. And if Dolores wanted to keep her distance—well, he could respect that. Maybe, if he was patient, Dolores would someday decide to come to him, to talk to him, to be friends.

So for the next year, Kyle loved Dolores for exactly who she was. He let her keep her distance, and he didn't ask for more than she could give.

Then, one May evening, everything changed. The night started like any other. And, at evening's end, Kyle checked—as usual—to make sure all the lights in his apartment were on. Then, he went to sleep.

Sometime later he woke with a start. Something was jumping on his head! Paws were scratching his face! And, when he opened his eyes, his apartment was no longer brightly lit; instead it was filled with black smoke. But he could see who was doing the jumping and scratching: Dolores.

The little cat was all Kyle could see. But she was enough.

Together, the two made their way to the only available exit from the apartment—the back door. Kyle felt his way along the walls. At the same time, he felt for Dolores with his feet and followed her. Finally, the pair reached the back door. Kyle pulled on the knob to open the door, only to have the knob fall off into his hand. The door remained firmly shut.

Making his way to the door had taken every bit of strength and oxygen Kyle had, and he collapsed to the floor. But, once again, he felt those insistent paws scratching his face. Kyle mustered his last bit of strength to hurl himself against the door, break it down and run outside to fresh air and safety. Once there, he looked around for the cat who'd saved his life.

She wasn't there.

With sickening clarity, Kyle realized that Dolores was still inside the apartment. He ran to one of the firefighters.

"My cat's still inside my apartment!" he exclaimed. "Can you find her?"

The firefighter promised to try.

Now all Kyle could do was wait. He knew Dolores's chances

weren't good, but still—maybe, just maybe, she would be found alive.

An hour or so later, the firefighters brought the blaze under control. And one firefighter brought Kyle a bundle wrapped in a towel. Kyle held his breath. Inside the bundle was Dolores—eyes seared shut, hair singed, but alive.

The firefighter explained that Dolores had collapsed just inside the door and that a fireman had stumbled on her when he entered the apartment. After removing her from the apartment, paramedics gave the cat CPR and oxygen before bringing her to Kyle.

The fire changed Kyle's life dramatically. He'd lost all his clothes, furniture and other possessions, and had to go live with his mother for a while. His cat had changed, too.

The once-quiet Dolores was now a talker who meowed and purred almost constantly. Even more surprising was her new desire to be touched and cuddled—preferably while she was lying on Kyle's lap.

Now, just four months later, Dolores was being recognized for her bravery. But Kyle knew he'd gotten a bigger prize. He'd never asked for more than Dolores could give—and then found she was willing to give him everything she had.

~Susan McCullough
Chicken Soup for the Cat and Dog Lover's Soul

90

Simon

O nly fifty-three animals in the world have ever received the
Dickin Medal, an award presented to animals connected
with the British armed forces or civil defense who have
displayed "conspicuous gallantry or devotion to duty." The medals,
named for the founder of the People's Dispensary for Sick Animals
(PDSA), Maria Dickin, were given to the animals for their heroism
during World War II or in conflicts directly following the war. The
recipients were eighteen dogs, three horses, thirty-one pigeons and
one cat. That one cat was Simon, of His Majesty's Ship Amethyst.

In the early morning of April 20, 1949, the British warship
Amethyst was anchored in China's Yangtze River. The crew included
a small black-and-white cat named Simon.

All seafaring ships need cats. Mice and rats love to live on ships,
creeping in on hawser cables, jumping aboard from docks, coming in along with freight shipments. Mice and rats damage ships,
raiding the food storage areas and chewing fabrics to make nests
for their young. They also carry viruses, which can be passed on
to crew and passengers by mosquitoes or fleas that bite infected
rodents and in turn bite a person. Having Simon on board was better than 100 rat traps.

That April morning, the captain was waiting for daylight to continue his voyage up the dangerous river. The Chinese Nationalists,
in control of the river, had forbidden all night traffic. Civil war was
ready to explode at any moment, and the captain of H.M.S. Amethyst

had been ordered to sail upriver to Nanking to protect the British embassy there.

Shortly after dawn, before the Amethyst could escape, the Yangtze river became a war zone. Explosions shook the air. Shells screeched over the ship, and one rocket and then another crashed into the ship. When the shelling stopped a short time later, many British sailors lay dead on the Amethyst's deck. A large number of crew members were wounded, including Simon. The disabled Amethyst was trapped right where she was, and it looked as if the British ship would be stranded for political reasons for quite some time. When the captain checked their stores of food, water and fuel, he found supplies enough for about two months. Surely they would be able to escape before then, he thought.

Life on the Yangtze settled into a dull, hot, humid procession of boring days of sweat and ship repair. Simon recovered from his injuries sufficiently to continue his duties as chief rat-catcher.

One day during this time, the ship's doctor saw Simon limping past the sick bay on his way to the hold to look for rats.

"Why don't you come in here and visit these chaps?" the doctor asked, and held the door open. Simon walked inside, where row on row of cots each held an injured lad.

"I'm going to try something," the doctor told his attendant. He picked Simon up and carried him over to a bed in the corner, where Seaman Mark Allen lay with his eyes closed. The boy, who was only sixteen, had lost both legs below the knee in the shelling. For four days, since regaining consciousness, he had refused to talk or eat or even open his eyes.

The doctor set Simon on the boy's bed. Simon sat looking at him, but the boy's eyes remained closed. The doctor moved Simon onto the boy's chest and placed the limp hand on the cat's back.

"Somebody's here to see you, Mark," said the doctor.

Mark opened his eyes just a little. When he saw Simon's steady gaze, he opened them further. The corners of his mouth quirked ever so slightly.

"I have a cat at home," he said. "But I'll never see him again." He pushed Simon away and turned his face into his pillow.

The next day the doctor took Simon to see Mark again and left him sitting on Mark's bed. Simon crawled up on Mark's stomach and began kneading, as he often did before settling down. Mark opened his eyes. His thin hand reached out and stroked Simon's rough fur. The boy began to sob.

The doctor hurried over. "Cook's got some good vegetable soup in the galley. How would you like me to get you a bowl of it? Simon will stay here with you."

Mark nodded ever so slightly. He stroked Simon, who settled down by him and began purring.

From that day on, Mark began eating and gaining strength. Simon visited every day. By the time a month had passed, Mark was able to get around the ship in a wheelchair.

Day after day passed; the days turned into weeks. The thermometer rose to 110 degrees Fahrenheit every day below decks. Between the heat and the severely limited rations, life on the ship became almost intolerable.

The crew looked thin and pinched about their mouths as their energy deserted them in the sweltering heat. Only one sailor kept up his daily activities with spirit and good will: Able Seaman Simon. He patrolled the ship, visited the sick, killed mice and rats, and made life bearable for his fellow shipmates. He never complained about the heat or his health.

On July 19, the temperature reached 110 degrees on the decks and 118 degrees in the engine room. Even Simon walked the decks very slowly. They wouldn't be able to last much longer. Their stores were almost depleted and there was barely enough water to drink, a terrible hardship in the unrelenting heat. The ship was fixed now, but they were held hostage by the warring Chinese and could not sail without again risking serious damage to the ship and her crew.

By the start of August, they couldn't stay where they were any longer. They decided to make a run for it under cover of darkness. It was a serious gamble, but they had no other option.

A combination of weather conditions, some cleverly executed deceptions and sheer good luck enabled the ship to escape. On

August 3, the Amethyst, free at last, sailed down the China coast to Hong Kong. Hundreds of British citizens waited on the docks to cheer the ship as she steamed into the harbor.

Soon after, one of the ship's officers wrote to the PDSA in England to nominate Simon for the Dickin Medal. While they were docked in Hong Kong, a reply came—the awards committee unanimously conferred the Dickin Medal on Simon. The presentation ceremony would occur after the Amethyst returned to England. In the meantime, they sent a tricolor collar for Simon to wear and made an announcement to the world press: "Be it known that from April 22 to August 4, Simon of the H.M.S. Amethyst did rid the ship of pestilence and vermin with unrelenting faithfulness. Throughout the incident Simon's behavior was of the highest order and his presence was a decisive factor in maintaining the high level of morale in the ship's company."

Simon became an instant hero. The little black-and-white cat's photograph appeared in hundreds of newspapers and magazines. For weeks, Simon received more than 200 pieces of mail a day. Simon seemed unimpressed with the attention. He posed reluctantly for pictures and continued killing rats.

While en route to England, Simon picked up a virus. Weakened from the wounds he had suffered during the shelling, the cat died. The ceremony to honor Simon, scheduled for when they reached England, turned out to be his funeral.

The PDSA Pet Cemetery has an arched wrought iron gate with the words "They Also Serve" stretched over the entrance. On the day of Simon's funeral, a small casket covered by a Union Jack stood surrounded by baskets and sprays of flowers in the special cemetery.

As the ceremony was about to begin, a handsome young man in a navy uniform with H.M.S. AMETHYST on his cap walked slowly through the gate and joined the small crowd of people grouped around the open grave. He used crutches, but he stood tall and the shoes on his feet shone in the sun. It was Mark Allen, the sailor who perhaps more than anyone owed his life to Simon.

And as they buried the little hero of the Amethyst, it seemed fitting that it was Mark's strong, young voice that rang out in the morning air: "The Lord is my shepherd, I shall not want..."

~Rosamond M. Young
Chicken Soup for the Pet Lover's Soul

Chapter 12

Loving Our Cats

Saying Goodbye

*When you are sorrowful look again in your heart, and you shall see
that in truth you are weeping for that which has been your delight.*
~Kahlil Gibran

91

Angel Cat

I knew her for less than twenty-four hours, but she will live in my heart forever. I can't recall her name, so I call her Angel Cat.

I met Angel Cat during a sad time in my life, exactly one month after my beloved sixteen-year-old tortoiseshell, Couscous, was put to sleep. I adopted Cousy when I was a creative-writing student in Boulder, Colorado. Walking home from class one spring day, I headed up Pearl Street, Boulder's main drag that had recently been converted into a pedestrian mall. Pearl Street was always lively, and that day was no exception. I passed a street musician strumming a Bob Dylan tune; a mime dressed all in gold, his face spray-painted to match; a clown handing out red balloons; and a snake-wielding belly dancer. But none of these acts were half as interesting as the drama unfolding on the corner.

A young boy stood outside an ice cream parlor with a large cardboard box at his feet. Overhead, he held a hand-lettered sign: "Free Kittens." A woman who must have been his mother, and who reminded me of Cruella de Vil, hovered beside him yelling, "I don't care what you do with them. You are not bringing those kittens home."

Without a moment's hesitation, I pushed my way through the crowd that had gathered, knelt down and scooped up the smallest kitten in the box. "I'll take this one," I said, "and I'm staying here until we find homes for the rest." Relief washed over the boy's face; his mother continued to scowl.

That first night, after Couscous and I split a can of tuna for supper, I crawled into bed and settled her on the soft flannel blanket I'd placed at my feet. As soon as I turned out the light, Cousy crawled up to my pillow, walked in a circle on top of my waist-length hair until it was flattened down to her liking, and then curled on top of it with her head on my shoulder. Her baby purr serenaded me to sleep and more than made up for the stiff neck I woke up with the next morning.

Couscous was my constant companion from the time I was twenty-four until a few months before my fortieth birthday. She was there when my first book was published. She was there when I met my spouse. She was there when my grandmother died. At the end of her life, she was suffering from an enlarged thyroid, cancer and congestive heart failure. I knew putting her down was the kindest thing I could do. Still, it wasn't easy.

Two weeks after Cousy died, I was scheduled to go on a book tour. I kissed my spouse goodbye and, with a heavy heart, flew to California. The tour was a big success. Not only did it help me sell many books, it also distracted me from my sorrow—during the day, anyway. After my work was done, alone in a different hotel room every night, I closed my eyes, saw Cousy's face and cried myself to sleep.

At the end of the tour, my dear friend Lili picked me up in San Francisco and drove me to her home in the country for a short visit and some much-needed R&R. It was late afternoon when we walked into her house. Orca, Lili's black-and-white cat, ran up to greet us. Seeing Orca, a cat whom I knew well, comforted and saddened me at the same time.

"Doesn't your housemate have a cat?" I asked Lili as we prepared supper.

"Yes, a sweet, little sixteen-year-old calico," Lili answered. "But you won't see her. She won't come out when my housemate is out of town. She's a one-woman cat."

"Here, kitty, kitty." I looked under the couch, in the closets and behind dressers, eager to meet the cat who was born in the same year as Couscous. But the little calico was nowhere to be found.

That night, Lili and I put on cotton nightgowns and climbed into bed like two young girls having a slumber party. Orca lay down in the doorway, standing guard against potential intruders. As soon as Lili turned out the light, something landed on the bed with a heavy thud.

"Hi, Orca," Lili mumbled. "Settle down now."

I let out a deep sigh as a great sadness engulfed me. I didn't have to explain anything to Lili. Being a cat person, she understood, and, without a word, handed me a tissue to wipe away my tears.

A moment later, something else landed on the bed with a thud, though a softer thud this time. "Who's that?" Lili whispered.

"Must be your housemate's cat," I whispered back.

"Impossible. Orca would never let her in here. They don't get along." Lili sat up and turned on the light. There, at the foot of the bed, was the sweet old calico, staring at me.

Lili was amazed. "I don't believe it," she said. "I've lived here for over two years, and Orca has never once let her into my bedroom, let alone up on the bed. She must like you." Lili turned from me to Orca. "Be nice," she said sternly. Orca merely purred. "What a good cat you're being," Lili crooned to her pet. "I'm very proud of you."

"Hi, pretty girl," I said to the little calico, who blinked her big yellow eyes slowly in reply. I lay back down, and, as soon as Lili turned out the light, the little calico crawled up to my pillow, walked around in a circle on top of my waist-length hair until it was flattened down to her liking, and then curled on top of it with her head on my shoulder. Her ancient purr serenaded me to sleep and more than made up for the stiff neck I woke up with the next morning.

I cried myself to sleep that night as I had every night for the past month, but these tears were different. Joy mixed with my sorrow, for I understood that Couscous had sent down a message from Kitty Heaven through this angel of a cat. Couscous wanted to let me know that she was all right, and that I would be all right, too. And, even though she was no longer with me, she was never far away.

Angel Cat was still on my pillow when I woke up the next morning. She stayed close to me as I ate breakfast, packed my bags and got ready to leave. It was hard to say goodbye to her. She died a few months after my visit. After Lili gave me the news, I decided it was time to get another cat. My spouse and I adopted Princess Sheba Darling, a white Turkish Van with gray markings on her head and tail, and Precious Sammy Dearest, an orange-and-white tom. I like to think Couscous and Angel Cat are looking down at the four of us from high above, purring with approval.

~Lesléa Newman
Chicken Soup for the Cat Lover's Soul

92

Sheba

What greater gift than the love of a cat?
~Charles Dickens

I first met Sheba in 1956. I was a third grade student at the Round Meadow Elementary School. She was a seven-week-old kitten in a pet shop window. She caught my eye immediately. I had always wanted a kitten, or at least that's what I told myself when I saw her there on display.

At first, she didn't even notice me standing there. I tried tapping on the glass, but her concentration remained elsewhere as she gave full attention to the task at hand. A thousand generations of hunting and stalking instinct were brought to bear as she successfully brought down her quarry—her sister's tail.

I tapped again. She stared at me for a moment, and the bond was made. Following a brief discussion through the glass, we concluded that we were made for each other. I vowed to return later in the day to take her home with me.

Unfortunately, I soon found that the road to kitten ownership was not without obstacles. Mom and Dad didn't think much of my plans. It seemed that they knew quite a lot about the subject of acquiring pets. "Who ever heard of paying money for a cat? A kitten is something that you can get for free at any barn. Besides, we're dog people."

I wasn't sure what that meant but, even at eight years old, I could see that the only true stumbling stone here was the finances.

You see, Sheba came with a stiff price tag, two dollars and fifty cents. "A lot of money for something that you can get for free anywhere."

Getting my own way this time was not going to be easy. However, I felt up to the challenge at hand and, after a day of typical little kid whining and a chunk of "birthday money" that came from Uncle Lou, Sheba was mine.

I was an instant hit with her, and the feeling was mutual. She slept on my bed every night. We had long and meaningful conversations when no one else was around. In fact, it was Sheba who was largely responsible for my deciding somewhat early in life to pursue a career as a veterinarian.

Through junior high, high school, college and veterinary school, she remained a close feline friend. Many important decisions regarding my career as well as my personal life were influenced by conversations, whether real or imagined, with Sheba.

Though she lived with Mom and Dad while I was busy getting married, raising a family and practicing the profession that she influenced me to join, she remained a close friend and seemed to enjoy visits from me, my wife and kids.

Undoubtedly, it was her influence once again that got me thinking about opening a veterinary hospital for cats only. She seemed to love the idea when we "talked" about it, and I knew from past experience that her judgment was flawless, so I set off down a new career path. In June of 1978, my new hospital, The Allentown Clinic for Cats, opened its doors.

Sheba was twenty-two years old on opening day when Mom and Dad brought her to see me and the beautiful new hospital that she had inspired. They hadn't warned me in advance that there was a second reason for the visit.

Sheba looked horrible. Apparently she had become quite ill that week. I did a thorough exam and was forced to a bitter conclusion. You see, I had been in practice long enough to know when a situation was hopeless.

It seemed fitting that in the new hospital, Sheba was the first cat whose suffering we could ease. We had the last of our long conversations as she fell gently asleep in my arms.

~Michael A. Obenski, V.M.D.
Chicken Soup for the Cat and Dog Lover's Soul

93

A Cat's Gift of Faith

When you're used to hearing purring and suddenly it's gone, it's hard to silence the blaring sound of sadness.
~Missy Altijd

He was a marmalade tabby kitten with sapphire eyes that I adopted from the Massachusetts SPCA. Fitting perfectly in my palm, he promptly chewed his way into my thumb—and my heart. "You're a feisty little peppercorn, aren't you?" I yelped, and so he got his name.

Described by many as "an extraordinary cat," Peppercorn grew from diminutive to nearly three feet long—measured from orange-whiskered nose to pumpkin-tipped tail—punctuated by burnt-orange eyes that could stare you down. I learned that he was an excellent judge of character. A quick once-over, and he would sum you up with a flick of his tail, then either deign to advance for a pat or glower at you from the sofa armrest.

My apartment was his oyster—as was the warm spot on my neck or next to my tummy at night. He had an uncanny ability to sense my moods: He lashed his tail when I was angry and cuddled up to me when I was down. When he wanted to know what I was thinking, he meowed and gave my hand a gentle paw pat. We would mutter at each other throughout the day, often to the profound consternation of my non-cat friends.

To me, Pep was a four-footed person. I loved him as a furry son and believed he loved me with the same fierce loyalty.

And so, at age twelve, when he began to pass blood in his urine, and the doctor diagnosed bladder cancer, I was confronted with the unbearable possibility that my "little love" of a cat was not going to live forever—or even the seventeen-plus years for which I had hoped. And I found myself praying for his life, even though my belief in God could be best described as "casual"—as in, he might exist, he might not, but why take a chance?

A week after his surgery, Peppercorn seemed to be gradually recovering. As I bustled around getting ready for work, it was the first day in weeks I had felt positive about his future. I knelt down to give him a head scratch as he slowly followed me around. He pushed his head hard against my hand, rumbling away with his unique triple-noted purr, which I have never heard any other cat make, before or since. "I love you, my little love," I said with a final stroke. "I'll see you tonight." As I walked out the door, I glanced back and saw him silhouetted against the sunlight, aglow in orange and gold.

He lay stretched on the floor when I got home. The vet surmised that a blood clot had broken loose, and that Pep had died instantly. My heart died with him, and no amount of crying would help. I railed against everything for taking away my beloved cat. As I placed flowers on his headstone, inscribed with his nickname "my little love," I asked why this had been done to me. I believed it showed that there was no God and challenged anyone to prove me wrong.

The weeks oozed by as I came back to the empty hollow of my home, staring at the litter tray, food bowls and scratching post that I could not bring myself to put away.

One night, after I had sobbed so long that my eyes were dry, I dreamed of Peppercorn—if it was a dream. It was not like any other dream I had ever had; they are always fragmented snippets of images, with no rhyme or reason, and no continuity.

In my dream I stood in my living room, and Pep marched up to me, the picture of feline health, eyes alight with happiness. I scooped him up, felt his weight in my arms that had so longed to hold him again, stroked his soft fur and felt the three-noted purr rumbling against my chest. "Pep, oh Pep! I dreamed you were dead," I told him as I wept and laughed into his neck. His purr deepened, and he patted my cheek with his paw, as he always had.

After a bit, he wriggled, asking to be put down. Reluctantly, I did so, and he turned and strode to the front door, glancing over his shoulder for me to follow. At the door, he asked to be let out. "You're not allowed outside," I reminded him, puzzled and afraid. He gazed at me, and I knew I had to open the door, as much as I did not want to.

Outside, a beautiful summer's day garlanded everything with sunlight, overarched by a brilliant blue sky. Peppercorn gazed up at me for a long moment, curling himself about my legs one more time. Then he walked away over the grass. I began to sob, reaching for him, begging him to come back.

He paused, turning to look back at me once more. Then, before my eyes, he gently changed from his familiar shape to a glowing ball of golden light. I stared as he rose from the grass and up into the heavens, then disappeared into the sunlight.

I jerked upright in bed in the early morning light, struggling to hold on to the dream, resisting chill reality. I still could feel the sensation of him in my arms, hear his beloved purr. And slowly, as I sat there, I realized that the raw wound that was my heart didn't hurt the same way it had for months, soothed by Peppercorn's final visit to me.

He had been permitted to return and tell me he was okay, allowed to let me glimpse what he had become. We had been granted the final goodbye that had been denied before.

And, in that gesture of compassionate love, I felt the hand and the grace of God—Pep's final and greatest gift to me.

~Claudia Newcorn
Chicken Soup for the Cat Lover's Soul

Friends

Twenty-one years ago, my husband gave me Sam, an eight-week-old schnauzer, to help ease the loss of our daughter, who was stillborn. Sam and I developed a very special bond over the next fourteen years. It seemed nothing that happened could ever change that.

At one point, my husband and I decided to relocate from our New York apartment to a new home in New Jersey. After we were there awhile, our neighbor, whose cat had recently had kittens, asked us if we would like one. We were a little apprehensive about Sam's jealousy and how he would handle his turf being invaded, but we decided to risk it and agreed to take a kitten.

We picked a little, gray, playful ball of fur. It was like having a road runner in the house. She raced around chasing imaginary mice and squirrels and vaulted from table to chair in the blink of an eye, so we named her Lightning.

At first, Sam and Lightning were very cautious with each other and kept their distance. But slowly, as the days went on, Lightning started following Sam—up the stairs, down the stairs, into the kitchen to watch him eat, into the living room to watch him sleep. As time passed, they became inseparable. When they slept, it was always together; when they ate, it was always next to each other. When I played with one, the other joined in. If Sam barked at something, Lightning ran to see what it was. When I took either one out of the house, the other was always waiting by the door when we returned. That was the way it was for years.

Then, without any warning, Sam began suffering from convulsions and was diagnosed as having a weak heart. I had no other choice but to have him put down. The pain of making that decision, however, was nothing compared with what I experienced when I had to leave Sam at the vet and walk into our house alone. This time, there was no Sam for Lightning to greet and no way to explain why she would never see her friend again.

In the days that followed, Lightning seemed heartbroken. She could not tell me in words that she was suffering, but I could see the pain and disappointment in her eyes whenever anyone opened the front door, or the hope whenever she heard a dog bark.

The weeks wore on and the cat's sorrow seemed to be lifting. One day as I walked into our living room, I happened to glance down on the floor next to our sofa where we had a sculptured replica of Sam that we had bought a few years before. Lying next to the statue, one arm wrapped around the statue's neck, was Lightning, contentedly sleeping with her best friend.

~Karen Del Tufo
Chicken Soup for the Pet Lover's Soul

Ring of Fire

Give sorrow words; the grief that does not speak
whispers the o'er-fraught heart and bids it break.
~William Shakespeare

My friend Kathy and I are both therapists. For the last ten years, we have met twice a month to offer each other support and guidance in our work and in our lives. Recently, we discussed grief.

A client of Kathy's felt that he should be "further along" in the grieving process. It was two years after the death of his much-loved father, and he said he was still afraid he could get lost in the pain if he really let himself feel it. Instantly, the image formed in my mind of grief as a ring of fire, frightening to approach and painful to step through. And so, for most of us, like Kathy's client, the temptation is to ease on down the denial road, pretending that the loss really wasn't so great.

Working with my own clients, I make no distinction between the loss of a human or animal companion. Love is just love, no matter what body it wears. In fact, my own primary guides in learning about grief have been animals. I have grieved for humans as well, but those relationships are much more complex, and their endings can contain a mixture of many other feelings along with the grief. My feelings for my animal loved ones are far less conflicted, and so their passing has been experienced much more simply and clearly as a piercing sadness.

Five members of my animal family are now buried underneath the towering white pine in my front yard: four cats and my rickety, eighteen-year-old miniature poodle. A thirteen-year-old orange cat with a scarred white nose and serrated ears named George is the most recent. He was my dear companion and guide in life, and has continued in these roles since his death.

To deal with my grief at George's death, I've used the same process that I recommend to my clients. First, I had a picture of George in his prime enlarged and framed. The picture sits on an end table next to the chair I usually use. Several times a day, I relate to the picture in some way and, thereby, to his memory. I brush the back of my hand across the photo in the same way that I used to brush his cheek. I pick up the picture and hold it. Or I just speak to it, saying, "I love you" or "I miss you." I visit with George and enjoy the thought of him.

Then, maybe once or twice a month, I step through the ring of fire and let the grief burn me. I feel completely my love of this special friend—and my loss. And, in these feelings, we meet again as intimately as we did in life. I feel my throat tighten and the tears come, and it is as though the water coming from my eyes acts as a conductor for the energy that connected us. In my sadness, George is alive to me once more.

As soon as I step inside the ring of fire, I can remember George very clearly: his chin on my pillow and his paw cupped in my hand as we slept. I can feel it! I can see the scars on his nose and the little bites in his ears, remnants of his time on the road before he accepted me as his life assignment. I can hear the chirp of his singing purr during one of our many conversations. I can see the little spot of black fur in the corner of one eye, so unusual on an orange-and-white creamsicle cat. These details bring him to life again, details I cannot remember—even so soon after his death—unless I allow myself to step into the grief.

But there is even more treasure inside the burning ring. I find that, when I let the grief in, I am not only in contact again with my beloved, but he becomes my guide in his new world. He shows me a place where life never ends and limits never bind. He allows me to know that there is no death. In life, we live as single drops of rain. George and the other loved ones who have passed show me the ocean we become.

Unfortunately, this holy state doesn't last, and I find myself back outside the ring, feeling cold and alone. Grief is composed mostly of slogging through lonely patches. Much of the time, I just want my animals' warm and squishy fur-bodies back!

I remember when my twenty-one-year-old cat Ivan died. Three days after his death, I found myself walking around the house saying, "Okay. This hasn't been too bad. I've been good. I've been brave. Three days is just about enough. I want my cat back. Now!"

Once, after the death of Simon, another of my elderly and ailing foundling cats, he and I were having a "conversation" late at night. Suddenly, I dropped into the grief and said, "I just miss you. I want you here."

And he answered, "I am here. Every time you hold another cat, I'm right there."

And, you know, I've noticed since then that he really is! I can feel him or Ivan or George—any of them that I want to hold—in the warm, yielding body of the living cat in my arms!

Still, I don't know anyone who isn't afraid of grief. It burns—so we tend to push it away. But by not attending to it, we allow it to become an undertow in our lives, the weight pulling us downward.

The road of life isn't straight. There are sharp turns. We're going to have losses. And, if we're going to experience them, and they're going to hurt, we might as well go for the diamonds in the coal. Our loved ones can show us the way through the ring of fire—if we let them.

~Sara Wye
Chicken Soup for the Cat Lover's Soul

Mama-Cat

A meow massages the heart.
~Stuart McMillan

When I was nearly four years old I was just a mere bit of a girl. Curly hair framed my happy little freckled face, and my lively blue eyes looked at everything in curious anticipation of delights yet to be. One beautiful September day, my mother stretched out on the sofa and called to me. She asked me to bring her a cool, wet cloth for her forehead. She said she had a headache. I was happy to do such a grown-up thing and felt very important as I brought her the cloth. With that done, I skipped outside to play in my yard.

I never saw her again. My mother died of polio three days later — just one week before I turned four years old. The loss was total, irreversible and devastating. And I could not change it. No matter how I cried. No matter how good I promised to be. No matter how many threats I issued. No matter how desperately I wanted her back. My mother was gone — never to return to me. Never again to hug me close, or brush my hair, or tuck me in bed, or sing softly to me as I drifted off to sleep in perfect peace. Nor would she ever again gaze at me with love. And tragically, all too soon after she died, she began to fade from my memory. It was difficult to remember what her face looked like — or remember the tender gaze that always transmitted how much she loved me.

I was tormented by the idea that perhaps my mother left me

because I was bad. I couldn't remember what I had done, but I must have done something to cause her to leave. That burden weighed heavily on my heart. There was no peace for me. Only dreadful longing and unutterable guilt.

Soon after her death, while trees were still dressed in scarlet and gold — before the leaves had floated to the ground and left limbs bare, I overheard the mailman speak to a neighbor of mine. He called out as he passed her home, "Those are sure cute kittens." Although I had been withdrawn and listless, the idea of seeing kittens drew me to the neighbor's home. I avoided being seen by anyone as I entered the backyard. There in a wooden tool shed was a box that held a beautiful white cat who had recently given birth to kittens. She was tucked away in the corner of the neat, dry shed. It was a cozy place. The mother cat snuggled close to her babies. It reminded me of the times I had snuggled close to my own mother. The grief that had engulfed my heart began to ease a little at the sight of the mother cat. I wanted my mother, but I could not have her anymore. After a few minutes, my four-year-old mind came up with a simple plan. I would become a kitten.

And this beautiful mother cat would be my second mama. And since she was a mother herself, I reasoned, I could talk to her about my own mother. I knew she would understand. The eyes of the mama cat seemed to transmit the sweetest love to her kittens, and it reminded me of the special loving look my own mother used to gaze at me with. For the first time since my mother died, I smiled.

Each day I would visit Mama-cat. She liked being gently stroked by my little hands. Her fur was silky and soft and somehow comforting to me. Mama-cat purred loudly and talked to her babies in soft meows. She began to include me in her circle of love, too. She would gaze at me and purr loudly whenever I was near. I knew what she was saying — a four-year-old just knows these things — she was saying, "I love you, my babies," and I knew she included me in that, too.

I talked to her about my mother and how much I missed her. Mama-cat always seemed to understand. I could not speak to anyone else about the confusing jumbled-up pain that was in my heart, but I could talk to Mama-cat. She always listened patiently, and she seemed to be very wise.

My heart began to heal during the days that followed as Mama-cat showed me how much she loved all of us. I was absolutely certain that when I was with my Mama-cat I was a kitten. I believed if someone were to glance into the tool shed he or she would not see a child — they would see me as a kitten, so strong was my imagination as a four-year-old.

As time passed, and the kittens grew bigger, they no longer listened to the mother cat as well as they should have. They would ignore her worried meows to behave and stay close. They would race in and out of the tool shed and even climb way up a tree. I could always tell when Mama-cat was worried. My own mother used to get the same worried look when I would climb too high on my swing set after being told not to. She would rush over, lift me down and chide me for not listening to her. Then she would kiss me, smile and extract a promise that I would be more careful, though the following day I would be back up on the top of the swing set again.

In watching how much Mama-cat loved her misbehaving kittens, I came to understand the profound truth that my mother didn't leave me because I was bad, nor had she stopped loving me when I disobeyed her. Knowing that eased the ache in my heart.

For one very special season, I took refuge in the innocent land of make-believe. Within my young mind, I was one of the kittens this mother cat loved. That Mama-cat loved me was certain. That she eased a profound loss was also true. And her tender acceptance of me helped me fix the memory of my mother in my mind forever. When Mama-cat snuggled against me and comforted me, it was always a reminder of when I had snuggled in my mother's arms. Mama-cat was always glad to see me, just as my real mother had been. She would gaze at me with love — as my real mother had done.

No one else looked at me that way anymore. No one else was glad to see me. No one else worried about me, yet Mama-cat did, I was sure of it — just as my real mother had done. Mama-cat helped me keep the sweetest memories of my real mother from fading.

Many years later I became a mother. When my son was an infant I would hold him in my arms and gaze at him with tenderness. As he grew older, each year brought more delight, and my heart would fill with love. And sometimes, my heart would wander back to the tender memory of my own mother's love—and to a Mama-cat that helped a lonely, motherless little waif of a girl come to terms with loss. In my mind, even now, I can still see the face of my own mother and her tender loving gaze. And I can still see the sweet loving acceptance in the eyes of Mama-cat.

~Lynn Seely
Chicken Soup for the Mother & Daughter Soul

Dharma

Nearing the lake on that warm September morning, I heard a tiny mewing sound. My first inclination was to ignore the cries. I've been through enough lately, I thought; I can hardly take care of myself.

Three months earlier, at age thirty-seven, I had been diagnosed with breast cancer. Because the cancer was in more than one place, the doctor had recommended a radical mastectomy. It was scheduled for later that same month. I still remember the shock and denial I felt when I overheard my husband Gary telling someone on the phone, "She's probably going to lose her breast." Those words seared through me like a knife. No. No! I silently cried to God, I'm too young for that.

A few weeks later, while I was recovering from the mastectomy, the surgeon called with more bad news: "The cancer has spread to your lymph nodes. Chemotherapy offers the best chance for survival." All I could do was sit there stunned, thinking, Oh God, I'm going to die.

I was terrified of dying. Many of my friends draw comfort from their beliefs about the afterlife or reincarnation. But I had trouble blindly believing in things I couldn't see or touch. I wanted proof. I prayed for God to show me the truth about death.

With the fear of dying in my heart, I decided to go on an aggressive clinical trial that included a combination of high-dose chemotherapy and a five-year follow-up with a hormone blocker.

The chemotherapy wiped me out completely. Even with the antinausea drugs, I was sick every time. Two months into the treatment, it was all I could do to get dressed and keep a little food down every day. In addition to working, my husband was doing his best to care for the house and me. Wonderful as he was, it was hard on both of us. I was irritable and lonely most of the time. This short walk to the lake was my first time outdoors in a while.

Meow! Meow! The insistent pleas continued.

No, I really can't care for an animal right now, I thought as I passed by. Suddenly, ear-splitting shrieking and squawking filled the air. Four blue jays were dive-bombing the bush where the mewing sounds were coming from. Shooing the birds away, I ran and looked under the bush. Standing on wobbly legs was a tiny three-week-old orange tabby, with bright blue eyes, mewing his little head off. Gathering him up into my arms, I headed to the lake in hopes of finding his owner or else convincing someone to take him home.

The wind whipped all around us as the shaking kitten cuddled close, still scared to death. We sat together by the lake trying to find him a home. Asking a number of people and finding no takers, I decided to take him home temporarily until I could find him a home of his own. Still feeling exhausted from the chemo, I spent most of the day on the couch with the little kitty curled up on my chest purring. Later that evening, as my husband was leaving to go to a meeting, I asked him to take the kitten with him. "Try and find him a good home," I said, placing the kitten in a box. Little did I know, my heart had already been stolen.

An hour later, I beeped my husband. "Have you found him a home yet?" I asked.

"I was just giving him to someone," Gary replied.

"Don't," I said without hesitation. "Bring him home. I need him."

When Gary and the kitten returned home, the little orange tabby curled right back up on my chest like he'd never left.

For the next week, while I was bedridden, Dharma and I were constant companions. He just loved snuggling, sometimes trying to get right up under my chin. He didn't even notice my lack of hair or uneven chest. It felt good to love and be loved so unconditionally.

I chose the name Dharma because in India it means "fulfilling one's life purpose." Cancer-recovery research has shown that finding and following one's bliss or purpose supports the immune system and increases chances of survival. For me, I hoped this would include two deep-seated desires: writing and being of service to others. Dharma's name reminded me of that intention and so much more.

Arriving home from my biweekly doctor visits, I immediately picked him up like a baby and carried him around the house with me. I even carried him to the garage while I did laundry. We were inseparable. With Dharma around, I wasn't so needy and grouchy with Gary. And, boy, did Dharma purr loudly! It was so comforting to hear and feel the love he expressed so freely.

As he grew, fighting, biting and clawing furniture became his favorite pastimes. We have a fenced-in backyard, so when he got too wild for me, I would let him play out back with other neighborhood cats.

Dharma also loved chasing butterflies. Last spring, I planted purple Porter's weed specifically to attract them. The whole backyard, with its multitude of colorful butterflies, was one big playpen for Dharma. I don't think he ever caught any, but I spent countless afternoons sitting on the back porch watching Dharma live his bliss. So free. No cares. My spirit soared as I watched him live his life so fully, and I decided it was time I do the same.

Late that December, I scheduled my final reconstructive surgery and let my office know I would be back to work in February.

Then, three days after my final surgery, the unthinkable happened. Escaping from the backyard, Dharma was hit by a car and killed instantly. My life, too, seemed to end at that moment. I was devastated and no one, not even Gary, could console me. I sat there on that same couch where Dharma and I had shared so much love and cried and cried for hours. Why, God, why? I asked in desperation. I wanted to turn back time and never let him outside. With all my might, I willed it not to be so. And still it was so.

Finally, Gary asked, "Do you want to see him?" Although I had never wanted to see a dead animal in the past, I answered, "Yes." Gary then placed Dharma in a towel in my arms, and I held him and wept. We decided to bury him in the backyard by the Porter's weed.

While Gary dug the hole, I held Dharma one last time, telling him all he meant to me and how much I loved him. I thought back on all the gifts he brought me in just the short time he was with me: unconditional love, laughter, a playful spirit, a reminder to live fully and a sense of my life's purpose.

My husband said, "You know, I believe Dharma was sent by God to help you through a very rough time. Now that you're through the worst of it, it's time for Dharma to move on and help someone else."

"Do you really think so?" I asked, wanting so badly to believe it was true.

"Look at the timing," Gary said. "You hadn't been to the lake in months and the one day you venture out, you find Dharma blocks from our house in dire need of help, and in rescuing him you get rescued as well. All of his gifts can't be a coincidence. There's definitely a reason he was put in your life when he was and also taken out when he was. He was your little angel."

"Thanks," I said, letting my husband's healing words wash over me.

Watching Dharma lying so peacefully in my arms, I got the much-needed answer to my prayer about death. I realized that he would go on in me forever, the same as I would in the lives of everyone I touched. I believe Dharma gave his life so that I might know peace. When Dharma died, I awakened spiritually. I am no longer afraid of death. Through Dharma, God showed me there is nothing to fear. There is only peace. And love.

We buried him at the foot of his butterfly bush and on his headstone I wrote, "Dharma—My Little Angel." Now, whenever I sit on the back steps, I see Dharma chasing butterflies for all eternity.

~Deborah Tyler Blais
Chicken Soup for the Unsinkable Soul

98

My Mother's Cat

When my nineteen-year-old mother died two weeks after giving birth to me, I inherited her cat, Paprika. He was a gentle giant, with deep orange stripes and yellow eyes that gazed at me tolerantly as I dragged him around wherever I went. Paprika was ten years old when I came into this world. He had been held and loved by my mother for all ten years of his life, while I had never known her. So I considered him my link to her. Each time I hugged him tightly to my chest, I was warmed by the knowledge that she had done so, too.

"Did you love her a lot?" I would often ask Paprika, as we snuggled on my bed.

"Meow!" he would answer, rubbing my chin with his pink nose.

"Do you miss her?"

"Meow!" His large yellow eyes gazed at me with a sad expression.

"I miss her, too, even though I didn't know her. But Grandma says she is in heaven, and she is watching over us from there. Since we are both her orphans, I know it makes her happy that we have each other," I would always say, for it was a most comforting thought to me.

"Meow!" Paprika would respond, climbing on my chest and purring.

I held him close, tears welling in my eyes. "And it makes me so very happy that we have each other." Paprika's orange paw reached up and touched my face gently. I was convinced he understood me, and I knew I understood him.

At that time, we lived in the country of my birth, Hungary, and I was being raised by my maternal grandparents because World War II had taken my young father away, too. As I grew, the war intensified. Soon, we were forced to become wanderers in search of safer surroundings.

In the spring of 1944, when I was eight, Paprika and I snuggled in the back of a wooden wagon as we traveled around our country. During the numerous air raids of those terrible times, when we had to scramble to find safety in a cellar, closet or ditch, he was always in my arms—I absolutely refused to go without him. How could I, when one of the first stories I was ever told as a child was that of my dying mother begging her parents to take care of her cat as well as her baby?

After Christmas in 1944, when we were almost killed in a bombing of the city we were in, Grandfather decided that we would be safer in a rural area. Soon, we settled in a small house neighboring a cemetery. Here, Grandfather, with the help of some neighbors, built a bunker away from the house. In the early spring of 1945, we spent one entire night in the bunker. Paprika was with me, of course. Once again, I refused to go without him.

Warplanes buzzed, tanks rumbled, and bombs whistled and exploded over our heads all night while I held on to Paprika, and my grandmother held on to the both of us, praying the entire time. Paprika never panicked in that bunker. He just stayed in my arms, comforting me with his presence.

Finally, everything grew still, and Grandfather decided it was safe to go back to the house. Cautiously, we crept out into the light of early dawn and headed toward the house. The brush crackled under our feet as we walked. I shivered, holding Paprika tightly. Suddenly, there was a rustle in the bushes just ahead. Two men jumped out and pointed machine guns directly at us.

"Stoi!" one of the men shouted. We knew the word meant, "Stop!"

"Russians!" Grandfather whispered. "Stand very still and keep quiet."

But Paprika had leapt out of my arms when the soldier shouted, so, instead of listening to Grandfather, I darted between the soldiers and scooped him up again.

The tall, dark-haired young soldier approached me. I cringed, holding Paprika against my chest. The soldier reached out and petted him gently. "I have a little girl about your age back in Russia, and she has a cat just like this one," he said, smiling at us. I looked up into a pair of kind brown eyes, and my fear vanished. My grandparents sighed with relief. We found out that morning that the Soviet occupation of our country was in progress.

In the trying weeks and months that followed, Paprika's love made things easier for me to bear, for he rarely left my side. He was my comfort, my best friend.

By the fall of 1945, Grandfather, who had spoken up about the atrocities taking place in our country, had gone into hiding to avoid being imprisoned as a dissident by the new communist government. Grandmother and I prepared for a solemn Christmas that turned into my worst nightmare when I awoke on Christmas morning to find Paprika curled up next to me as usual—but he was lifeless and cold. I picked up his limp body, and, holding it close to me, sobbed uncontrollably. He was nineteen years old, and I was nine.

"I will always love you, Paprika. I will never give my heart to another cat," I vowed through my tears. "Never, ever!"

"Paprika's spirit is in heaven now, with your mama, sweetheart," my grandmother said, trying to comfort me. But my heart was broken on that terrible Christmas Day in 1945.

Grandfather stayed hidden until the fall of 1947, when we were finally able to escape our communist country by hiding among some ethnic Germans who were being deported to Austria. In Austria, we landed in a refugee camp where we lived for four years. These were difficult times for me, and I longed for Paprika often. I saw other people's cats and knew it would be so comforting to feel a warm, furry creature purring in my arms. But my loyalty to Paprika—mixed up in my mind with loyalty to my mother—never wavered. I had made a vow, and I would keep it.

A ray of hope pierced this darkness when, eventually, we were accepted for immigration to the United States. In September 1951, we boarded an old U.S. Navy ship. We were on our way to America.

That year, we spent our first Christmas in the United States. The horrors of war and the four years of hardship in a refugee camp were behind us now, and a life filled with fresh possibilities lay ahead. On that Christmas morning, I awoke to a tantalizing aroma wafting through the house. Grandmother was cooking her first American turkey. Grandfather, meanwhile, pointed to one of the presents under the Christmas tree. This gift seemed alive, for the box was hopping around to the tune of "Jingle Bells," which was playing on the radio. I rushed over, pulled off the orange bow and took the lid off the box.

"Meow!" cried the present, jumping straight into my lap and purring. It was a tiny orange tabby kitten, and, when I looked into its yellow eyes, the vow I had made in 1945 crumbled like dust and fell away. I was a new person in a new country. Holding the cat close, I let the sweetness of love fill my heart once again.

That Christmas day, I do believe my mother smiled down at us from heaven approvingly, while Paprika's spirit purred joyfully at her side.

~Renie Burghardt
Chicken Soup for the Cat Lover's Soul

99

The Cantor's Cat

It's really the cat's house — we just pay the mortgage.
~Author Unknown

I magine the head soloist, the music minister and the associate pastor of a house of worship. Now imagine one person taking on all those functions. That's about half of the job of a cantor.

Cantors commemorate every stop on the Jewish life-cycle. We chant the blessings that bring a child into the congregation; that celebrate the arrival of those children to young adulthood; that bind two lives together; and that pronounce a person's journey from life into death. We rejoice with the celebrants, as well as mourn with the bereaved. But how do we respond when somebody loses a loved one with four legs instead of two? And how do we handle this situation when it happens to us?

Some years ago, a silver tabby named Petey plopped into my life. We were a team from the get-go. Petey was large and cuddly and had the charming ability to hold hands with me, using a firm, tensile-pawed grip.

When I met my future husband, Mark, I was about to ask him the important question — did he like cats? — when he mentioned Julia, his own tuxedo puss. The first time Mark and I sat together on my sofa, Petey stretched out to his full length in order to sit on both our laps simultaneously. Then he looked at me with a face that said, "Can I keep this one?" And so our household numbered two cats, and two people who were allowed to live with them as long as they paid the rent.

On the first Sabbath in our first home, we suddenly noticed Petey and Julia sitting on the kitchen floor, watching our every move. We lit and blessed the candles together. They stayed at attention during kiddush and motzi, the prayers before the wine and food; and then they walked away. The following Friday, using the Yiddish word for Sabbath, we hollered, "Hey, Shabbos cats!" and they came into the kitchen and sat quietly during the blessings as they had the previous week.

Jewish law mandates caring for the animals in one's household, including feeding them before we feed ourselves. Being good Jewish pet lovers, we ran our household accordingly, and all of us thrived on the love that grew from this four-way relationship.

Many happy years passed. At fourteen, Petey started to lose his luster but none of his love. However, like an old man who doesn't quite understand why life doesn't continue on the way it did when he was young, he had his crabby moments. Still, he was my beautiful boy, and we all moved to Albuquerque from New York when I took a pulpit out West. Both cats seemed to thrive on the changed atmosphere and seemed extremely happy in their new home.

One Monday, some months after the move, I took Petey to the vet to try to find out why he couldn't keep his food down. The doctor prescribed an enzyme powder, and Petey valiantly continued to eat, but to no avail. By Friday night, he was miserable. No matter how hard we tried to make him comfortable, he cried like a baby with the effort of walking, of settling in my lap, of pressing next to the windowpane's cold glass. We ached for him and for ourselves. Clearly he was saying goodbye, but he wasn't about to go easily.

At last, too exhausted to fight any longer, he slept fitfully in our bed between Mark and me. He held my hand between the still-strong grip of his paws as I held him in my arms and whispered my thanks and my love. All night long, I struggled between fighting to keep him and facing the reality of letting him go. In the morning we rushed him to the vet, but Petey had other ideas. He died as soon as we got him inside the office.

His death destroyed us. The price of love just then was the deepest pain imaginable as we wept uncontrollably. To make matters harder, Sabbath services would begin in two hours. How could I serve professionally when my heart had just been ripped in two? Only those who have had an animal in their home can fully understand that loss, no matter how much they sympathize with it. Would the rabbi and the congregation understand my sorrow over a cat?

But begging off was out of the question. We needed to be with our congregation in our spiritual home that morning.

When I arrived at the synagogue, Mark mourned in my study, calling friends and family who knew and loved Petey. I went to the rabbi and told him what had happened. His eyes were gentle and full of understanding, and I felt the genuine quality of his words of comfort. To my surprise, he said, "Do as much as you can this morning, and I will fill in when you falter. You need the support of your congregation today. And I think we should let people know what's happened after the service." His support buoyed me enough to manage through the service. My notes soared, but my customary ebullient sparkle was severely diminished. The rabbi knew that this would be noticed, and we would meet the consequent inquiries with honest answers.

Afterwards, I hesitated to greet the congregation one-on-one. I still wasn't sure how they would react to my grief over the loss of a cat. After all, I was their invincible cantor. With a slight sinking feeling, I noticed Mrs. Gold approaching me. For the last few months, I'd been directing her son in his religious studies and I found the Golds to be the most demanding, least flexible family I'd ever worked with. But as she got nearer, I saw compassion in her eyes. She took me gently into her arms, saying, "The rabbi told me about your Petey. I'm so sorry. It's hard to lose a dear friend."

When she released me, we smiled at each other, and both our faces were shining with tears.

And so it continued, members of the congregation clasping my hand or embracing me, as they spoke kind words of condolence. I saw that Mark was having the same experience. This wave of comfort poured over us like warm honey as we began to feel our grief over losing Petey.

And though we had lost a loved one, we'd found something, too—the people in our congregation, a large and loving family to share our lives with. While Petey lived, he brought people together, and our Shabbos cat continued to do so—even with his passing.

~Jacqueline Shuchat-Marx
Chicken Soup for the Cat and Dog Lover's Soul

Walking with Ace

I think about you constantly, whether it's with my mind or my heart.
~Albany Bach Reid

Ace, a black-and-white shorthair cat, gave new meaning to the words loyal, steadfast and true. He came when called, sat in my husband's lap at the end of the day and slept pressed up against me at night. His dependable, even-tempered nature and gentle demeanor earned him the title My Good Ace.

Ace was stoic; he never complained when neighborhood children carried him around the house like a sack of potatoes. Those of us who could read his soulful expression and doleful eyes understood his patient tolerance. He greeted houseguests inquisitively and politely, and then retreated to his private corner, only crossing the bounds of good manners occasionally to beg for treats at the dinner table. (Turkey was his absolute favorite! Running a close second was the shrimp my adult son would indulge him in from time to time.)

Ace was an indoor cat who took every opportunity to try to sneak out whenever someone opened the door. Understanding his "call of the wild," I would sometimes sit with him on the front porch and stroke his sun-warmed fur. More often, cradled in my arms, his back against my chest, I carried him for walks around the neighborhood. He never once risked the privilege of further ventures by trying to jump out of my arms and escape. (Did I mention Ace was also very intelligent?) Whenever I looked down into his face during our walks, he blinked and purred in pure contentment, and I am absolutely certain that there was a smile playing around the corners of his mouth. He would divide his time between looking up into the trees, craning his face toward the sun and sky, or turning his head to observe the passing scene. Neighbors would sometimes call out, "Hey, how's Ace?" and I would always lift his front paw, wave and answer, "He's just fine!"

I am a runner, and these short walks were not my major form of exercise. But the walks invariably produced, if not an aerobic high, a sense of calm and well-being. Ace and I continued this routine for sixteen years. I ran in the mornings, pounding out the miles, noting those runners whose leashed dogs trotted at their heels with seriousness of purpose. And, in the golden-shadowed afternoons and balmy summer evenings, it became a ritual for me to walk and smile with my cat. We were a team, enjoying each other on a special level during these daily perambulations. I was certain no runner and his dog could ever know the intimacy of silent communication that a slow-measured pace brought. Ace and I were both in the moment, savoring the delight of our outing. As we neared the end of each walk, I'd give him a comforting squeeze and say, "Ace, it doesn't get any better than this."

Sixteen years is a very long time in the life of a cat, and, one day, I began to notice the telltale indicators of old age. On one of our walks, Ace's body, once sleek and well-muscled, showed signs of some weight loss. And then his thirst increased as his appetite decreased. It wasn't very long before our vet diagnosed Ace with kidney failure, a common ailment in cats his age. While he still responded to the carving of a freshly cooked turkey, it took him somewhat longer to get to the kitchen; gradually, his interest in food became less and less. In an attempt to stimulate his appetite, my son made trips to the fish market to entice him with succulent fresh shrimp. When Ace made only a token attempt to pick at the treat, we feared the worst.

It was a beautiful, crisp October that year. The skies were a breathtaking blue, and the colored leaves of the trees played against them like a Technicolor movie. When I carried Ace on our walks, he seemed lighter than a feather, and I could feel every bone in his body.

He needed cushioning and a little protection against the cool fall air, so I wrapped him in an old, soft baby blanket. We took our walks at noon, when the day was at its warmest. His once-strong purr had become labored. Never a complainer, Ace made little mewing sounds as he lifted his face in the breeze, trying to gather warmth from the sun.

We didn't give up our walks, not even on the day that I knew would be Ace's last. I could barely feel him cuddle in the blanket, his brave little face peering out. I knew how much he was suffering, and I told him as we began our walk that it was all right if he wanted to give up.

We continued around the block, and he tried to look up at the sky and me, but he wasn't smiling anymore. I knew it was time. As we approached home from our last walk, I stroked his head, whispered my love and said my goodbyes.

I still begin my days with a run, and I have not given up walks around the neighborhood. On the pale, new green days of spring, in the lush, heavy sweetness of summer and on the crimson-hued days of autumn, as I approach home, I look at the sky and say, "Ace, it doesn't get any better than this."

~Edie Scher
Chicken Soup for the Cat Lover's Soul

Elvis Has Left the Building

Giving up doesn't always mean you are weak;
sometimes it means that you are strong enough to let go.
~Author Unknown

He had been my best friend and companion for more than twelve years, a first-year anniversary present from my husband when I told him I wanted something soft and warm to take care of. He had been with me through several jobs, earthquakes, fires, the L.A. riots, and five or six moves to different apartments. He was my surrogate child, my baby, my pal and protector when my husband was working late. He took care of me, followed me everywhere and loved me unconditionally.

So, when the veterinary surgeon told me that my beloved cat Elvis would die within a few weeks, I was devastated. I had just become pregnant with my first child, and so badly wanted my baby to know Elvis and come to love him as much as my husband and I did.

It had happened so quickly: One week, my husband and I noticed that our usually healthy and robust black-and-white cat was rapidly losing weight. After a few more days passed, we noticed a distinct loss of energy, and we took Elvis to be examined.

Finding an abnormality in the blood, the vet referred us to a wonderful internal-medicine group for animals. There, Elvis suffered through a battery of tests, which eventually determined his fate. He had a rare form of mast-cell cancer that was untreatable. But that didn't stop him from befriending the receptionists and lab technicians, who quickly grew to love him. Whenever we would come to pick him up, we could hear them in the back yelling, "Elvis has left the building!"

As the weeks went on, the doctor taking care of Elvis left it to us to decide how to proceed. We decided to try anything we could to keep Elvis alive and give him a chance to fight. That meant spending more than five thousand dollars, and coming in two to three times a week to give Elvis blood transfusions and chemotherapy—none of which guaranteed his recovery. But we had to try.

At night, Elvis slept cuddled up in bed near us. He was so gaunt and weak that he needed our body heat to stay warm, and he would press his head against my arm as if to say, "Stay close." During the days he was home, he would lie on the couch and sleep, occasionally raising his head and giving me his trademark meow, a strange, nasal "maaaaa!"

As the baby inside me grew bigger, Elvis grew weaker, and my husband and I realized he was losing his battle with cancer. It was January, and my baby was due in March. If only Elvis could hold on a little longer—but, as the month wore on, it was obvious the chemo was not working. Elvis had lost more than half his body weight, and he could barely move. His blood levels were dangerously anemic. The doctor didn't even think he could handle another transfusion.

So, on a cold day at the end of January, my husband and I carried Elvis back to the doctor's office one final time. In what seemed like a surreal dream, we were led through the surgery area to a room in the back called "the grieving room." It was a peaceful, friendly room with a couch and curtains, designed to make a painful process a little more comfortable. We were given a half hour to say our final goodbyes. Then the doctor came in, said a prayer for Elvis, and injected a syringe into a vein.

As I felt my friend, my beloved Elvis, go limp in my arms, I held him close to my huge belly, hoping that maybe part of his spirit would go into my unborn child. It was a silly fantasy, but it kept me going long enough to leave the office without crying—until I heard one of the lab techs say sadly, "Elvis has left the building." The receptionist was crying, and, as she hugged me, I broke down in tears.

It took a few weeks before I could get through the day without weeping. Reminders of Elvis were everywhere. But, as March approached, my focus turned to my upcoming C-section. Our little boy, Max, was about to make his appearance into the world. My husband and I had picked out his name, Maxwell Gordon Jones, and, on March 19, as scheduled, he was born—big and bouncy and healthy.

During Max's first night in the hospital, he made all kinds of strange baby noises, including a very distinct nasal "maaaaa!" My husband and I gasped, staring at each other. Could it be? "Maaaaa!" We laughed as we pondered the idea that our child had somehow absorbed Elvis's spirit. And, when Max napped next to me in the bed, I melted when he pressed his head against my arm, as if to say, "Stay close."

When we filled out the birth certificate, we decided to add a little something special to Max's name: Maxwell Gordon Elvis Jones. Now, six months later, Max acts more and more like the feline brother he will never meet—loving, affectionate and cuddly—and this comforts me.

I took Max grocery shopping recently. As I stood in line, holding him in my arms, I noticed a tabloid headline and had to laugh. It read: "Elvis Lives!"

No kidding, I thought, as I squeezed my son and kissed him on the cheek.

~Marie D. Jones
Chicken Soup for the Cat Lover's Soul

More
Chicken Soup for the Soul®

...

Share with Us

We would like to know how these stories affected you and which ones were your favorite. Please write to us and let us know.

We also would like to share your stories with future readers. You may be able to help someone, and become a published author at the same time. Please send us your own stories and poems for our future books. Some of our past contributors have launched writing and speaking careers from the publication of their stories in our books!

The best way to submit your stories is through our web site, at

www.chickensoup.com

If you do not have access to the Internet, you may submit your stories by mail or by facsimile.

Chicken Soup for the Soul
P.O. Box 700
Cos Cob, CT 06807-0700
Fax 1-203-861-7194

We are all crazy about our dogs and can't read enough about them. This new book from Chicken Soup for the Soul contains the 101 best dog stories from the company's extensive library. Readers will revel in the heartwarming, amusing, inspirational, and occasionally tearful stories about our best friends and faithful companions—our dogs.

These true stories will make you appreciate your own dogs and see them with a new eye. Some of these stories describe amazing contributions made by dogs and highlight their intelligence and intuitive abilities. Many of these stories will make you laugh or cry. They will all renew your admiration for your canine companions.

978-1-935096-05-4

Check out another great book for Pet Lovers from

Our 101 BEST STORIES

Chicken Soup for the Dog Lover's Soul
0-7573-0331-5

Chicken Soup for the Pet Lover's Soul
1-55874-571-8

Chicken Soup for the Cat and Dog Lover's Soul
1-55874-710-9

Chicken Soup for the Cat Lover's Soul
0-7573-0332-3

Chicken Soup for the Horse Lover's Soul
0-7573-0098-7

Chicken Soup for the Horse Lover's Soul II
0-7573-0402-8

Chicken Soup for the Soul®

Enjoy these other fine books about our beloved pets!

About the Authors
&
Acknowledgments

Who Is
Jack Canfield?

Jack Canfield is the co-creator and editor of the Chicken Soup for the Soul series, which *Time* magazine has called "the publishing phenomenon of the decade." Jack is also the co-author of eight other bestselling books including The Success Principles™: How to Get from Where You Are to Where You Want to Be, Dare to Win, The Aladdin Factor, You've Got to Read This Book, and On Mutual Love and Admiration of Focus: How to Hit Your Business and Personal and Financial Targets with Absolute Certainty.

Jack has recently developed a telephone coaching program and an online coaching program based on his most recent book The Success Principles. He also offers a seven-day Breakthrough to Success seminar every summer, which attracts 400 people from fifteen countries around the world.

Jack is the CEO of the Canfield Training Group in Santa Barbara, California, and founder of the Foundation for Self-Esteem in Culver City, California. He has conducted intensive personal and professional development seminars on the principles of success for over a million people in twenty-three countries. Jack is a dynamic keynote speaker and he has spoken to hundreds of thousands of others at more than 1,000 corporations, universities, professional conferences and conventions, and has been seen by millions more on national television shows such as The Today Show, Fox and Friends, Inside Edition, Hard Copy, CNN's Talk Back Live, 20/20, Eye to Eye, and the NBC Nightly News and the CBS Evening News.

Jack is the recipient of many awards and honors, including three honorary doctorates and a Guinness World Records Certificate for having seven books from the Chicken Soup for the Soul series appearing on the New York Times bestseller list on May 24, 1998.

To write to Jack or for inquiries about Jack as a speaker, his coaching programs, trainings or seminars, use the following contact information:

Jack Canfield
The Canfield Companies
P.O. Box 30880 • Santa Barbara, CA 93130
phone: 805-563-2935 • fax: 805-563-2945
E-mail: info@jackcanfield.com
www.jackcanfield.com

Who Is
Mark Victor Hansen?

Mark Victor Hansen is the co-founder of Chicken Soup for the Soul, along with Jack Canfield. He is also a sought-after keynote speaker, bestselling author, and marketing maven. For more than thirty years, Mark has focused solely on helping people from all walks of life reshape their personal vision of what's possible. His powerful messages of possibility, opportunity, and action have created powerful change in thousands of organizations and millions of individuals worldwide.

Mark's credentials include a lifetime of entrepreneurial success. He is a prolific writer with many bestselling books, such as The One Minute Millionaire, Cracking the Millionaire Code, How to Make the Rest of Your Life the Best of Your Life, On Mutual Love and Admiration of Focus, The Aladdin Factor, and Dare to Win, in addition to the Chicken Soup for the Soul series. Mark has had a profound influence in the field of human potential through his library of audios, videos, and articles in the areas of big thinking, sales achievement, wealth building, publishing success, and personal and professional development.

Mark is the founder of the MEGA Seminar Series. MEGA Book Marketing University and Building Your MEGA Speaking Empire are annual conferences where Mark coaches and teaches new and aspiring authors, speakers, and experts on building lucrative publishing and speaking careers. Other MEGA events include MEGA Info-Marketing and My MEGA Life.

He has appeared on Oprah, CNN, and The Today Show. He has been quoted in Time, U.S. News & World Report, USA Today, New York Times, and Entrepreneur and has had countless radio interviews, assuring our planet's people that "You can easily create the life you deserve."

As a philanthropist and humanitarian, Mark works tirelessly for organizations such as Habitat for Humanity, American Red Cross, March of Dimes, Childhelp USA, and many others. He is the recipient of numerous awards that honor his entrepreneurial spirit, philanthropic heart, and business acumen. He is a lifetime member of the Horatio Alger Association of Distinguished Americans, an organization that honored Mark with the prestigious Horatio Alger Award for his extraordinary life achievements.

Mark Victor Hansen is an enthusiastic crusader of what's possible and is driven to make the world a better place.

Mark Victor Hansen & Associates, Inc.
P.O. Box 7665 • Newport Beach, CA 92658
phone: 949-764-2640 • fax: 949-722-6912
www.markvictorhansen.com

Who Is
Amy Newmark?

Amy Newmark was recently named publisher of Chicken Soup for the Soul, after a thirty-year career as a writer, speaker, financial analyst, and business executive in the worlds of finance and telecommunications.

Amy is a graduate of Harvard College, where she majored in Portuguese, minored in French, and traveled extensively. She is also the mother of two children in college and has two grown stepchildren.

After a long career writing books on telecommunications, voluminous financial reports, business plans, and corporate press releases, Chicken Soup for the Soul is a breath of fresh air for Amy. She has fallen in love with Chicken Soup for the Soul and its life-changing books, and found it a true pleasure to conceptualize, compile, and edit the "101 Best Stories" books for our readers.

The best way to contact Chicken Soup for the Soul is through our web site, at www.chickensoup.com. This will always get the fastest attention.

If you do not have access to the Internet, please contact us by mail or by facsimile.

Chicken Soup for the Soul
P.O. Box 700
Cos Cob, CT 06807-0700
Fax 1-203-861-7194

Thank You!

We would like to thank the entire staff of Chicken Soup for the Soul for their help on this project and the 101 Best series in general. Among our California staff, we would especially like to single out D'ette Corona, who is the heart and soul of the Chicken Soup publishing operation, and who put together the first draft of this manuscript, Barbara LoMonaco for invaluable assistance in obtaining the fabulous quotations that add depth and meaning to this book, Patty Hansen for her extra special help with the permissions for these fabulous stories and for her amazing knowledge of the Chicken Soup library, and Patti Clement for her help with permissions and other organizational matters. In our Connecticut office, we would like to thank our able editorial assistants, Valerie Howlett and Madeline Clapps, for their assistance in setting up our new offices, editing, and helping us put together the best possible books. We would also like to thank our master of design, Creative Director and book producer Brian Taylor at Pneuma Books, for his brilliant vision for our covers and interiors. Finally, none of this would be possible without the business and creative leadership of our CEO, Bill Rouhana, and our president, Bob Jacobs.

Chicken Soup *for the* Soul

www.chickensoup.com